The Utopian Vision

D0620049

The Utopian Vision

Seven Essays on
the Quincentennial of
Sir Thomas More

Edited by E.D.S. Sullivan

San Diego State University Press

Published by San Diego State University Press
San Diego, California 92182

Copyright © 1983 by
San Diego State University Press
All rights reserved

Library of Congress Cataloging in Publication Data

Sullivan, E.D.S.—editor
Title
Bibliography
Index

1. Utopias 2. Title 3. Utopias, bibliography 4. Sir Thomas More

Library of Congress No. 82-50755

Hardback ISBN 0-916304-51-5
Paperback ISBN 0-916304-52-3

Contents

Preface

The five hundredth anniversary of the birth of Sir Thomas More was certain to provoke an outpouring of appreciation for an extraordinary person regarded by many today as England's finest example of the legendary "Renaissance Man" and by some as a martyred saint. The year 1978, therefore, was marked in England and the United States and undoubtedly elsewhere throughout the intellectual world for celebration of the man and his works, whether in literature, statecraft, religion, or in all of these.

At San Diego State University, the College of Arts and Letters paid tribute to More the Christian Humanist in a series of lectures by seven members of its Faculty which were given at fortnightly intervals during the Spring Semester of that quincentennial year. The talks were intended to be popular in the sense that they would be primarily informative and would appeal to the non-specialist rather than attempt to break scholarly ground. While they were all to concern themselves with some aspect of utopia as an enduring symbol of mankind's hopes, the speakers were asked to give their lectures a practical application insofar as this was possible, so that the audience could be made aware not only of the aspirations but also the expectations of latter-day utopian writers and their followers.

The lectures proved gratifyingly successful—well attended by faculty, students, and the general public—and, in consequence, the San Diego State University Press suggested that they be gathered into a volume. For several reasons, two of the original participants were unable to take the time to revise their lectures for publication and withdrew from the effort. Fortunately, however, Professors Vanderbilt and Bartholomew were attracted to the subject and were persuaded to write essays which added scope and interest to the anthology. Meanwhile, Dr. Julio Martinez had been approached to prepare an annotated bibliography on the subject of utopianism which may be the most complete compilation of that subject to date. Although complications of various kinds delayed publication of the volume for some months after the conclusion of the quincentennial year, the essays—like the subject itself—have a pertinence and interest which is not circumscribed by time.

Given the range of possible aspects of utopianism and the fact that the individual participants were free to select their own emphases, the sequence of presentations in the original lecture series was largely arbitrary and so, to a lesser degree, is the arrangement of essays in this volume. But, as in the series, the initial article is necessarily one dealing with that quintessential utopia, the heavenly garden. E.N. Genovese discusses two myths having to do with peace and prosperity: one envisions a past golden age and the other a remote paradise. Although these traditions originally developed separately, they evolved over the centuries into the concept of the golden paradise for which divinities acted as guides. In consequence of this involvement of the gods, the religious aspects were intensified and are reflected in the sacredness attributed to the logic by which social and political utopias are conceived. Since such communities would be perfect, it follows that their inhabitants would consequently be unaffected by the grosser desires and necessities which taint the citizenry of other societies.

A measure of just such idealism is to be found in More's volume and that of Skinner since both writers exalt rationality and the inevitable happiness that attends their carefully wrought utopias. There is, nevertheless, a darker side to this "paradise." My own essay examines four of the best-known utopian and dystopian books and finds in their two seemingly opposing positions a basic similarity which centers on the necessity of work. Whether it be More's commonwealth or Huxley's monster state, everyone has an occupation. It is therefore one's function or, to use a word from the essay's title, one's "place" which defines his status in the society. The emphases regarding obligatory work in utopian and dystopian literature are in essential disagreement, but their conflict is one taken for granted by critics and is hence infrequently, if ever, explored in the analysis of their differences.

Francis Bartholomew looks at the religious and secular forces in Russia which attempted with indifferent success to bring about in this world a condition of material bliss. Paradoxically, the efforts of the various movements inadvertently prepared the way for that particularly questionable form of utopia known as Communism. By continuing to emphasize the Second Coming of Christ and the establishment of an earthly millenium, the Eastern Orthodox Church nourished the idea in the Russian masses that earthly beatitude would be realized through the apocalyptic struggle between the host of Christ and Satan. To the peasant mind, the result would be an egalitarian redistribution of Russia's agricultural lands. While the nineteenth century saw the development of secular programs aimed at achieving major improvements for the peasantry, little came of these plans, although the traditional notion of a violent cataclysm producing a village-based utopia continued to haunt most socialists until the Communist Party seized power. The Communists' utopian leanings were reflected through the widespread social experimentation between 1917 and 1928. But with the introduction of urban-industrial planning that promising period came to an end, and both the Soviet government and people abandoned the utopian dreams of the twenties in favor of more prosaic objectives.

The ill-defined and theoretical goals of much of nineteenth-century socialist thought in Russia and elsewhere were enunciated and codified by that authoritative and methodical utopian, Auguste Comte. Oscar Martí demonstrates just how detailed a philosophy Comte formulated as he marshalled scientific arguments to support utopian views. Comte's positivism contains an encyclopedic theory of science, a law of historical development, and an ethical system, all culminating in the discovery of sociology. By means of this new science, Comte hoped a new polity would be established, complete with sociologist priests and capitalist knights, in which order and progress were reconciliable and where altruism would be the motive for all actions. This promise of a perfect scientific industrial society appealed to a wide audience of social reformers in various walks of life and from a number of countries but, when confronted with intractable realities, positivism proved the unworkable dream.

In a frankly polemical approach to the question of natural economic limits, John Hardesty anticipates what some would consider a truly utopian eventuality. Unlike Adam Smith and

Karl Marx, who maintained that nature presents opportunities rather than obstacles, Professor Hardesty agrees with David Ricardo and John Stuart Mill that natural forces will gradually bring an end to growth. Consequently, he foresees the imposition of a "stationary state" economy regardless of the will or desire of people or government. Some prominent modern economists see such a restriction in dystopian terms as being inevitably totalitarian, but Hardesty holds out the possibility of a stationary state socialism that consists of a more democratic, humane, and satisfying society than humanity has yet known.

Even more utopian, and often provocative and uplifting, are the fantasies which mark some of the feminist literature examined by Patricia Huckle in her analysis of the experiences of women in the nineteenth and twentieth centuries. She juxtaposes the idealism of fiction with the rarely-attained goals of actual communities to suggest how difficult change can be in male/female relationships and expectations. The value of both the novels and the accounts of the communities lies in the social criticism they provide as well as in the development of a feminist ideology. Women still cherish the objective of sexual equality and a non-hierarchical social order, though they have realized from their experiences in these communities that traditional sex-roles tenaciously govern our behavior.

Continuing the investigation into the contemporary novel, albeit with a different emphasis, is Kermit Vanderbilt's article on Kurt Vonnegut, whom he describes as possessing "the best utopian imagination in American literature since World War Two." Vonnegut's social idealism reaches back to the utopian fiction of Bellamy and Howells, and his sense of the engaged and prophetic writer places him in the Emerson-Whitman tradition. After tracing the utopian elements through the first seven novels, Professor Vanderbilt then examines Vonnegut's journalistic pieces and public speeches in the Vietnam period. There he finds a transitional phase in Vonnegut's outlook on America's present and future as well as in Vonnegut's view of the writer not only as an enlightened alarmist but also as an "agent of change." Finally, Vanderbilt interprets the utopian themes in the recent two novels, *Slapstick* and *Jailbird*, for indications of Vonnegut's progress out of the 1970s on the road to 1984.

In what may well be the first fully annotated bibliography of major utopian literature written or translated into English, Julio Martinez has rendered a valuable service to scholars and educated lay readers alike. The first of his two sections includes general bibliographies on utopias—books and articles on utopianism in general and on utopian settlements in particular. The second part catalogues over fifty seminal utopian fictional and nonfictional works. Each of the books considered in this segment is followed by at least one critical evaluation and, in most cases, by several assessments which have appeared in monographs or in journals.

The variety in subject matter covered by the essays suggests the almost limitless scope afforded by the topic of utopianism to those interested in the study and welfare of humanity. It was More's social and moral dissatisfaction over certain conditions in the England of his time which prompted the fictional portrayal of a realm where a form of benign communism brings about individual and collective happiness and harmony. And it is the well-being of mankind which has animated thinkers through the centuries to set down their hopes and fears in imitation of More. The continuing fascination exerted by thoughts of "what could be" have given rise to that category of writing called utopianism and accounts for the esteem in which More and his principal work have been held from the sixteenth-century until this day.

When his otherwise unknown contemporary, Robert Whittinton, concluded a paragraph of praise with the felicittous and widely-recognized characterization of Sir Thomas More as "a man for all seasons," he paid an enduring tribute to the multifaceted quality of this illustrious and extraordinary person. And, while More's life and death have been chronicled in considerable detail through the centuries, it is in his most famous written work, *Utopia*, that the man's true nature is most frequently sought and from which diverse judgments of his personal traits have been derived by a bevy of scholars, members of the professions, and ordinary readers alike. There are those historians who contrast the literary advocate of freedom for all religions with the actual Lord Chancellor who ordered heretics burned at the stake. These are joined by certain theologians who point to the implied criticism of the Catholic clergy More puts into the mouth of Hythloday, but are puzzled by the heroic inconsistency of the man who will go willingly to his death rather than renounce that Church. And to the lawyers, his beheading is, on one side, defended as the regrettable but necessary consequence of disobedience of a legally valid enactment by a prominent member of the bar; yet others see his unyielding stand as laudable and striking evidence that the higher law of conscience exists. These specialists, together with sociologists, economists, political scientists, adherents of the Left and the Right, and other exponents of various philosophical and practical views find in the *Utopia* convictions they either espouse or deplore, all the while attributing them to the real Thomas More. Thus from being "a man for all seasons," a compliment which More might well have found agreeable, he and the book he intended to be at once playful and meaningful have taken on the extended implication of being "all things to all men."

Although the occasion for this volume is to commemorate the birth of Sir Thomas More, its subject matter is only incidentally concerned with the man and only one of the essays regards his *Utopia* at some length. It is the wider consideration—the subject which takes its name from More's best-known literary effort—which occupies our attention. And it is well that such should be the case since, for most people, the word "utopianism" has a popular connotation which has little to do with familiarity either with More or his book. I should not be greatly surprised—nor disturbed—if the majority of those who refer to or write about utopianism (including the contributors to this anthology) had never read the More work. Over the intervening centuries, utopianism has taken on a significance of its own which includes, but goes far beyond the condescending dictionary definition ("visionary or impractical") and, rather, suggests to those who use it a bright vision of a world where things will be far better than they are now. In almost every instance such works are ringing affirmations of the human potential and, in most cases, of material progress. Any anti-utopian qualms or doubts about the possible consequences of such a future do not seem to have affected the mass of mankind where the majority is intent upon improving its lot by the means at its disposal. Whether aware of the term "utopianism" or not, and no matter how ill conceived or defined it may be where it is known, for many the word has become synonymous with optimism and hope.

Nevertheless, for a growing number of the thoughtful, the unbounded expectations so characteristic of More's time and, later, of the nineteenth and early twentieth centuries—still operative among a wide segment of peoples everywhere—have diminished considerably. Sober observers today perceive correctly that limitations of many types, physical as well as material, are already upon us and more are in the offing. Professor Hardesty's essay in this volume considers some of the steps that may be essential to preserve dwindling natural resources, but even such a relatively innocuous regulation as the 55-mile speed-limit instituted not for increased safety but for energy conservation, or the possible reinstitution of Selective Service presage civil steps which will increasingly affect the freedom of action and choice so long generally accepted in the United States. Paradoxically, it may be that just such restrictions on human freedom and individual privilege may result in the attainment of an approximation of More's fictional ideal of optimistic egalitarianism. A lower standard of living for the West accompanied by an improvement of that of the Third World would reduce the shameful gap in the level of diet and comfort which has so long existed and replace it with a measure of the economic equality which was so much a part of More's aim in writing *Utopia*.

On the other side of the coin is More's recognition that rectifying outstanding inequities does not alter man's flawed nature. As an orthodox and devout Catholic, More feared that the evil in mankind—even in Utopians—could undermine the tranquility of the commonwealth. He therefore envisioned a state which would powerfully restrict the activities of the citizenry. In real life, too, the abridgement of freedom by conquest or political maneuver is certainly not new, although it does seem that the post-Vietnam period has seen oppression increase not only in Asia, but in Central America and in the Middle East. All such subjugation is ostensibly carried out in the cause of a restricted yet somehow better life for all except, of course, the opponents of that official "utopian" vision. It is this problematical curtailment of personal liberties which is at the root of much anti-utopian opposition—and a very real concern it is.

The essays which follow, then, are reasonably diverse, drawing as they do on religion, history, philosophy, and economics. The articles that deal with literature of necessity consider the utopian and dystopian "classics." But there is also an examination of feminist works and the novels of Vonnegut— the distinctly utopian aspects of which are overlooked more frequently than not. Thanks are due to the contributors for their patience and understanding in the long months of preparation of the volume for publication, to The San Diego State University Press for the proposal to convert the lectures into book form, and to its Director, Roger Cunniff, for the care he has taken in the production of this book.

E.D.S.S.

1

Paradise and Golden Age: Ancient Origins of the Heavenly Utopia

E. N. GENOVESE

One and one-half millennia before our common era, a scribe sat cross-legged on a reed mat in a windowless cubicle deep in a temple complex.[1] Oil lamps guttered in the dampness and shadows danced across the young scribe's forearm on which rested a smooth slab of clay. There were other scribes there, too, heads bowed to their work, attentive to the graybeard in their midst. Stiff-backed, eyes closed, the old one intoned from memory antique verses of a language for centuries unused in the daily lives of these people. His phrases were rhythmic and repetitive. His voice settled gently on his audience, as the slave beside him unconsciously matched his tempo with sweeps of a fan. In barely perceptible jerks the blunted stylus in the scribe's hand pecked and jabbed a column of minute wedged impressions down the face of the clay. Like an efficient, soundless typewriter, hand and stylus jumped to begin a new column. Soundlessly, the fan kept time in this timeless place.

Beyond the insulating antechambers, past the massive walls of the temple precinct, throngs seethed through the narrow alleys between the mud-brick dwellings of merchants and artisans. Beyond the crowded city flowed the huge, eternal river known as Buranun.[2] The sun crashed against its waters and glistened on the back of a farmer, straining as he swung a water-heavy basket to an irrigation lock. In the muggy air the bleating of goats and the incessant hum of insects thrummed in the man's ears; the noise was not unlike the old priest's melodious droning deep within the forbidden walls of the temple complex. Indeed, the priest's recitation within the temple and the peasant's numbed thoughts at the muddy canal were the same: of a cool and quiet place far off, lush and protected, where ease of living was the delight of deathless beings. The peasant's thoughts drifted away on a welcome breeze, but the scribe's stippled tablet was carefully baked and stored away in the temple archives at Nippur. It was dutifully copied and reproduced again and again, as city and century yielded to flood and sand and conqueror's torch.

Beginning with this undocumented but not improbable event, I propose to trace a confluence of traditions of the first, eternal, and ultimate utopia—paradise. The evidence will show that neither is our Judaized concept of paradise unique nor is our Christianized concept merely eschatological. In sum, we shall see how our paradise tradition arises in Mesopotamia and combines with the Indo-European cyclic golden age myth to produce a prevalent belief in heavenly reward after death, all of which forms the basis for man's centuries of utopian dreams.

But let us return to that tablet, forgotten among the unhappy ruins of an ancestral civilization. After millennia, it—or a tablet like it—would be reclaimed, and in 1915 its transcribed text would be published. But not until thirty years later would its 278 lines be fully rendered from the ancient Sumerian into a modern tongue; they began:[3]

> The land of Dilmun is pure, the land of Dilmun is clean . . .
> It is a clean place, it is a place most bright . . .
> In Dilmun the raven utters no cry,
> The kite utters not the cry of the kite,
> The lion kills not,
> The wolf kills not the lamb,
> Unknown is the kid-killing dog,

Unknown is the grain-devouring boar . . .
The sick-eyed man says not, "I am sick-eyed,"
The old woman says not, "I am old."

By virtue of its antiquity, its style, and its content, we today would classify this passage as myth, a word that in this rationalistic, technological world bears unfortunate connotations. Let us recognize in this discussion, however, that for the ancients who composed and transmitted such myths there was never any question as to the fact or fiction of the story. All myths were to them true and real simply because they had no concern to prove them false; for what good would it serve but to destroy beauty and to bring ignorance? People believed in myths, that is, they accepted their truth without evidence, simply because they wanted to. Myths were different, other, transcendent, and thus gave their hearers pleasurable escape from the harsher realities of experience. And so the peasant dreamt in the noonday heat and the scribes dutifully preserved the traditions. I confess that I began this discussion with a lesser kind of "myth" to illustrate this point: the story of the scribe and the peasant was real and true, not because it happened (for I've no evidence that it did) but because it was readily believed.

Thus I would ask that the reader accept the following definition or understanding of myth as applicable to a paradise or golden age: a story of unknown origin, revealed through tradition and dealing with extraordinary events, factual or not, which bring us in touch with the stark profundity of life and death.[4] The myth of paradise is varied: for some it is a lost existence or an immemorial golden age; for others it is a present state of happiness beyond reach; for others it is a future reward after death. But despite the variation, the paradise myth inevitably presents an extraordinary place where we might be free to do those things with which we identify happiness in this life. Thus it is with this ancient Near Eastern myth of Dilmun.

Like so many cultural traditions, the notion of paradise or golden age is shared by peoples of no obvious association. For example, Cheyenne myth embraces a once-upon-a-time age in which men lived naked and innocent amid fields of plenty; Egyptians believed in the fields of happiness which the souls of the dead would leave periodically to visit the earthly comforts of their tombs; the Hindus believe that there is a paradise here on earth, but inaccessible to men, whose destinies are in the heavens; the Greeks had a tradition of the Hyperboreans—fortunate, semi-divine beings who lived each for a thousand years far to the north beyond the wind.

From these traditions and countless others like them we may distill some basic and important motifs. First, paradise is different from man's experience inasmuch as it lacks conflict. Conflict is brought on by our seeking goals which impinge on one another; paradise, however is a state of utter fulfillment; hence goals have no meaning. Crime, evil, immorality—whatever they are in this life—lack motives in paradise, since no one is in want: there is, therefore, a literal innocence, a "not harming." Second, paradise is remote and not easily attainable. It is reached either not at all, because it no longer exists, or with the loss of all we possess, namely, this life. Third, paradise is timeless: either it exists without change from or for all eternity, or it is eternally returning. This last motif has been thoroughly analyzed by the well-known comparative religionist Mircea Eliade in numerous works but particularly in *The Myth of the Eternal Return*.[5] Eliade demonstrates that various cultures display in their myths a longing to regain a paradise or blessed age when men were as near as possible to gods or God. He calls this idealized lost or distant existence *illud tempus*, "that time." He contends that men, dissatisfied with the imperfections and pains of human events, strive to escape from the structured limitations of time to the timeless, changeless world of a paradise. This release is accomplished by means of myth, which remains the only constant thread to that existence. Eliade, like so many interpreters of myth, postulates a mono-myth from which all others derive; for him it is a lost, blessed age which inevitably will return.

Much of what I discuss below is more fully, if not repetitiously, considered by Professor Eliade, and to him I acknowledge my debt. I do not intend, however, to reargue his thesis, for I have concerns of my own: to illustrate by select, related examples how the ancients conceived of a paradise or golden age; to explain the confusion among a long-lost age, a life after death, and a return of an earthly paradise; and briefly to suggest why we of the Judaeo-Christian Western tradition resort to these ancient myths in our quests for utopias. I assume that we agree that paradise is synonymous with heavenly reward and eternal happiness with the divine creator. I contend that this notion is born of a lengthy and complex evolution that draws on two mythic sources—the Near Eastern Garden of Eden and the Indo-European returning Golden Age—and that, furthermore, although both Paradise and the Golden Age are placed in the lost past, Paradise is originally a secluded earthly place which we have transformed into heavenly eternity by giving it the cyclic retrievability of the Golden Age.

Let us return, then, to that Sumerian tablet from Mesopotamia, from which we shall trace the confused origins of our Paradise from the Jews, the early Christians, the Persians, the Greeks, the Indic Brahmans, and the Romans. We must examine the Sumerian description of Dilmun on two levels: its beauty and its unattainability. First, its obvious imagery is of unqualified, unlimited life in security through the absence of killing, age, and disease. Purely in reaction to this life of toil, peril, and decay, one marvels at such a desirable state. The bright light illuminating Dilmun means no stealth, no fear of an unforeseen end to a tenuous existence. The poet finds difficulty in relating an experience so utterly different from our own, and so he is obliged to negate a series of epithets—"kid-killing," "sick-eyed," etc.—which are to us inseparable from men, animals, and plants, for he must show that loss and end have no meaning in Dilmun. Thus, prosaically: if we lived in Dilmun, we would find that wild animals—if they were wild or if there were any at all—would not deprive us of our sustenance; or would we experience infirmity and old age when we would expect them. But on a deeper level, the purity, cleanliness, and brightness of Dilmun reflect more starkly the impossibility of reconciling our experience with that place. Clearly, the poet recognizes that the absolutely sterile and static nature of Dilmun is attractive to us only so far. Beauty depends on substance as much as order, and if the poet is to describe the comforts of eternal life, he must do it in the familiar terms of productive nature. Thus, since the only lack in Dilmun is fresh water, the sun god Utu at the command of Enki, god of fresh water, sucks up springs from the earth, and

Dilmun abounds with green and fruitful fields.

But herein lies the rub: in man's experience and understanding, generation must be balanced. And so in the garden of
Dilmun, once change is admitted, all the tensions of change
must follow. The poet continues: Ninhursag the great mother
goddess, by an intricate but toilless process, causes eight
plants to grow there but forbids them to all; Enki, however,
eats the plants and is punished with a fatal sickness, and this
causes a dilemma for our poet. Eternal life demands no change;
change precludes eternal life; thus is threatened the essential
premise upon which Dilmun is conceived. But Ninhursag, the
life-giver, is persuaded to save Enki from divine death. Enki's,
and the poet's, immediate problem is solved, but there is established a new order of things; for while eternal life is still possible, it is no longer inevitable. This change allows, then, for
the existence of a second kind of being, the "dark-headed" humans, born to serve the gods and die. Of these dark-headed
ones we read elsewhere that only the just king Ziusudra and
his wife survive the great Deluge and are admitted to the eternal life of the Sumerian gods.

We find this paradisal tradition passed along to the Sumerians' Semitic successors, the Akkadians and Babylonians, in the
Flood Tablet of their Gilgamesh Epic. To gain the secret of life
without end, the hero-king Gilgamesh seeks out his immor-
talized ancestor, Utnapishtim, who is now the just man saved
from the Deluge and dwelling in serene happiness "far away at
the mouth of the rivers" (11.195 ff.)., i.e., beyond the sea
which lies past the mountains of sunset. Because Gilgamesh
must travel beyond the borders of death, his journey is westward, to the waters of life. This one detail should seem at odds
with the other Akkado-Babylonian tradition which places Dilmun, "the land of the living," somewhere to the east "where
the sun rises." As we shall see, this contradiction, rather, inconsistency, will serve to prove our point that the primal
garden and the destination beyond death are one in the same.

As we have seen in Dilmun, water, an obvious symbol of
coursing and unlimited life, is essential to the paradisal setting.
In *Genesis* 2:8 and 10-14 the primeval place of creation and
happiness is located at the source of rivers, four of them, including the Tigris and the Euphrates. Perhaps this derives from

a far older tradition of world-quartering rivers which branch out into the cardinal directions; at any rate, the creation paradise of *Genesis* is located somewhere "to the east" in a "garden." When one recalls that the Hebrews traced their patriarchal origins to Mesopotamia and were for a time displaced to Babylonian cities, it is not difficult to understand the similarity between those Mesopotamian accounts and this in *Genesis*.[6] The very name Eden, which sounds like the Akkadian word *edinu*, "prairie," is possible evidence of this link, as is *Genesis'* mysterious '*ēd*, a spring or mist which rises from the earth as does water in Dilmun. Much like Ninhursag, Yahweh the god of the Hebrews causes plants to grow, but his are called the Tree of Life and the Tree of the Knowledge of Good and Evil. The former is a frequent motif throughout the ancient Near East and is usually associated with a serpent and a goddess of life, a fertility earth mother.[7] In the Sumerian story, Enki has his servant bring the plants to him; in *Genesis*, the companion of man brings the fruit of the forbidden Tree of Knowledge, and both man and woman are cursed, like Enki, with pain and sickness, the harbingers of death. The rib-born woman in Eden is called Eve, our corruption of Hebrew *Hawwah*, which means "living." This, too, recalls the Sumerian myth, inasmuch as Ninhursag heals Enki in the eight ailing parts of his body by creating eight healing goddesses, and Ninti, "Lady of Life," is the goddess who heals Enki's rib, for *ti* also means "rib."

The fact that Enki is restored to health and continues to dwell in eternal happiness in Dilmun points to the essential and affective difference between the Sumerian and the Hebrew paradise: Dilmun is the habitation of gods, Eden of men. A simple distinction between gods and men is that which the Greeks apply: men die; gods are undying, immortal. Eve has been warned that to eat of the Tree of Knowledge will bring death. But how can this be? For in their paradisal state, Adam and Eve are protected from the blows of time and space. Eden is, therefore, like Dilmun, not any place—utopia.[8] Once, however, Adam and Eve receive knowledge of good and evil, they symbolically come to know measure, i.e., limitation, i.e., time and space. Thus their lives become limited and they no longer belong in the Garden because they have lost their absolute and discrete mode of existence. They have experienced; thus they suffer, and by suffering they will continue receiving the limited, and limiting, knowledge for which they had no need in Paradise. Because this imperfect knowledge will drive them back to the Garden, Yahweh stations cherubim with flashing swords to prevent their reentry, lest by tasting of the Tree of Life they "live forever" (*Gen.* 3:22-24); likewise, Gilgamesh must pass the Scorpion Men who guard the way to the lands of immortality.

In order to distinguish, between the two notions of paradise, that of a long-lost age and that of an age to come, we must recognize the critical importance of the expulsion episode. Before his sin, man had no need of knowledge, since knowledge gives one contact with things not possessed, and all things in the Garden were his. But now the prize of knowledge becomes man's burden, since he is forced through all the passages of time to recall not only what happiness might have been but also what happiness *can* be. Life in this vale of tears will be measured against the paradisal past, and if life is to have meaning, man will strive to match that paradise. Failing that, he can only hope for something better beyond this life.

The term "paradise" (Greek *paradeisos*, Hebrew *pardēs*) derives from Old Persian *pairidaēza* (*Vidēvdāt* 3.18),[9] meaning "mold around," i.e., a walled area, especially a royal park or hunting ground. Today we might call it a preserve, where things are untouched and allowed to flourish. The term is used in this secular sense in the Hebrew Scriptures, but it is also used for the Garden of Eden in the Greek Septuagint version of *Genesis* 2:8. In the New Testament, however, "paradise" is used as a destination. It exists not merely in past time, but in the present and the future, although properly it is a time and place beyond what we know as time and place. The famous passage of reference is *Luke* 23:43, one of the most simple yet moving speeches in the gospels: Jesus, in his human torment on the cross, turns to the repentant thief and promises, "This day you will be with me in paradise." This startling guarantee brought forth a notion new to the Jews. For when the Old Testament was composed, the Jews had no clear idea of personal, individual immortality. They knew that Yahweh dwelt in heaven, but where the good and just went after death was problematic. After the Babylonian Captivity, the Jews were thinking in terms of a future resurrection of the dead, of a last judgment, themes probably drawn from the Zoroastrian influence of the Persians. Rabbinic tradition preserves the idea of *Gan Eden*, the Garden of Eden, where the righteous dwell after resurrection. And so, in effect there is a restoration of Adam's paradise which will be revealed and reopened to *people*, not shades or souls of the dead that dwell in the Hebrew underworld Sheol.

In a promise of punishment to the enemies of Israel, the prophet Isaiah describes an ensuing *illud tempus*; the passage (11:6-8)[10] is not only familiar, but recalls the untroubled state of Dilmun:

> And the wolf will dwell with the lamb,
> And the leopard will stretch out with the kid,
> And the calf and the young lion and the fatling together;
> And a little child will lead them . . .
> And the nurseling will amuse himself over the hole of the cobra,
> And the weaned child will stretch out his wand over the
>   viper's nest.

This idyllic scheme is marked mainly by the dissolution of natural enmities which characterize the evolution of the physical world; appropriate to this static lack of conflict is the eternal *youth* of the passage. Paradise admits of no growing old, no coming, no going.

The promise of a messianic age began with the early prophets of the Old Testament. Throughout their labored and fractured history, the Jews looked for a release from suffering, when they would receive their reward from the god with whom they kept trust. Kings and priests brought them to heights of glory, but the cycle of suffering and captivity soon renewed. The second-century B.C. *Book of Enoch*, especially Chapters 24-32, 45-71, and 90, provides clearest evidence of this expectation of an earthly kingdom with an earthly prince whose capital is Jerusalem. Although pseudepigraphic, *Enoch* seems to have been a link between the canonical prophets and the apostles. Others in desperation and anger had turned to leaders and saviors in the past and were deceived or destroyed;

nevertheless, these Jews now turned to Yeshuah, called *ham-Māshīyah*, "the Anointed "—Jesus the Christ. Doubtless, many saw in him the "Son of Man" prophesied in *Enoch*—a king who would lead his people in a messianic age in which the elect would enjoy every good thing of the earth and would each father a thousand children. But with Jesus' death any narrow political hopes were effectively lost; caught up in a religious fervor, his closest followers preached the savior's imminent return followed by a cataclysmic rectification. They would be restored to the state of happiness forfeited by Adam; and in this peaceful garden Jesus, the new Adam, would be master. In *Revelation* 2:7 we find the promise that eluded Adam: "To him who is victorious I will give the right to eat from the Tree of Life that stands *en tōi paradeisōi tou Theou*—in the garden of God."

The second coming for which these Christians looked was not far off in the vague future: they expected it within their suffering lifetime. But soon the first generation of believers passed on, then the second, and so on. The survivors began to worry about where the holy and deserving dead were going—surely, they hoped, to reward and rest. Thus the return to paradise came to be considered immediate after death. An indication of the early Christians' expectation of reunion with Christ is found in the feast of love, the *agapē*, which was not only a memorial of the devoted gathering with him at the Last Supper but an affirmation of the future gathering of all the elect. As Paul reminds, "Such things which an eye has not seen, which an ear has not heard, and which have not reached a man's heart, has God prepared for those who love him" (1 *Cor.* 2:9).

By this abstract anti-description of paradise Paul avoids the excesses that have become too familiar to us in the cliché of the Muslims' unending banquet in the garden of Allah. But while Islam's paradise is unabashedly materialistic, it is not of this world. The *jannāt 'Adn*, "gardens of Eden," below which flow four incorruptible rivers of milk and honey, and *al-Firdaws*, "Paradise," as large as the earth and heavens combined, clearly share their origins with Judaic and Persian traditions, for example: the "Eden, a garden of God," to which Ezekial compares Tyre (28:11-19), and the subterranean garden palace (*vara*) made by Yima, the first mortal to whom

Ahura Mazda taught his religion (*Vidēvdāt* 2.1-43), might well be found in the Koran. I shall not dwell on Islamic beliefs, since their influence is late and negligible; rather, I shall use Islam as a clear link with those Persian traditions to which I have briefly alluded.

In the seventh and sixth centuries B.C., Medes and Persians became the first Indo-Europeans to become established in Mesopotamia. They brought with them versions of gods and myths which find strong parallels in the Indic *Vedas*, in Homer, in the Icelandic *Eddas*, and so forth.[11] But they also spawned the religion of Zoroaster (Zarathushtra), which postulated a world alternately controlled by personal forces of good and evil. Despite basic conflicts between Zoroastrianism and Indo-European mythology, there is one identical aspect of great importance: the repetitive cycle of good to evil. The Zoroastrian cosmos begins with a creative period of light and truth, during which Yima builds his garden, but these eventually yield to darkness and the lie. The same obtains for the Indo-European ur-myth of the first creation, the Golden Age; for this, too, yields to successively worse ages, culminating in a world destruction. The Persian effect of this theme on Christianity is apparent, and the theme is explicit and complete in the mythic literature of India and of Northern Europe, but strangely our best-known sources, the Greek epic poets, neglect this universal destruction and seem content to reminisce like Babylonians about the lost age of grace and point to a place where the dead may recapture some measure of that happiness.

This imitation of the Golden Age is the Elysian Fields, also called the Islands of the Blest, located somewhere to the west near the great world-encompassing river called Ocean. Only in later Greek and Latin authors was Elysium situated below the earth in Hades' realm. Like the Mesopotamians who located Dilmun somewhere beyond their lands, perhaps on the east shore of the Persian Gulf, the Greeks tried to make their Elysium a remote but reachable place. Pausanias (3.19.11-13) tells of a certain Leonymus who supposedly sailed to White Island near the mouth of the Danube on the Black Sea, where he met Achilles, Helen, and others living a life of eternal happiness.[12] The first promise of reward in the Islands of the Blest was made by the prophetic sea god Proteus to Menelaus in Homer's *Odyssey* (4.561-568):[13]

> But it is not ordained for you, Zeus-fostered Menelaus,
> To die and find your lot in horse-pasturing Argos,
> But to the Elysian plain and the bounds of earth
> Will the immortals escort you, where blond Rhadamanthys is,
> Just where life is easiest for men;
> There is no snow, for there is neither wintry weather nor
>   ever rain,
> But always gusts of shrill-blowing Westwind
> Does Ocean send up to refresh men . . .

The Indo-European origins of this description are fairly confirmed by a similar description of the Celtic Avalon, a warm place to the west where King Arthur has retired, *à la* Menelaus.[14] True to the tradition, Hesiod, another Greek, assures us a century or so after Homer that the great heroes now dwell (*Works and Days* 169-173):[15]

> . . . at the ends of the earth.
> And indeed they dwell with carefree hearts
> In the Islands of the Blest near deep-swirling Ocean.
> Well-off heroes for whom honey-sweet fruit
> Blossoming thrice yearly the grain-giving fields do yield.

But unlike the Christians who ultimately join with their god and savior, these Greeks, adds Hesiod, dwell "far from the deathless gods, and Cronus rules over them." The Greek paradise, then, is glorious and beautiful, but it is not Olympus. Indeed, the once-tyrannical Cronus, now released from the bonds laid on him by his son Zeus, is generally associated with a Greek *illud tempus*. Hesiod recalls that time in the course of creative evolution (*Works and Days* 109-120):

> Golden was the face of mortal men that was very first
> The deathless gods made who have Olympian homes.
> These were of Cronus' time, when he ruled heaven;
> Just as gods they lived with carefree hearts
> Far apart from both toils and woes; nor was vile
> Old age among them, but always sound in hands and feet

They made merry at feasts, removed from every evil;
And they died as though overcome with sleep; and all
　　good things
Were theirs; and the grain-giving fields yielded fruit
On their own, abundant and ungrudging; and willingly
And peacefully they went about their business with many
　　good things,
Rich in flocks, dear to the blessed gods.

When this primeval generation was covered over by the earth, they became pure spirits, Hesiod tells us, very much like guardian saints offering rewards to the just and watching against the commission of evil deeds. After these golden men the gods made a second generation of silver and therefore of lesser worth. After hundred-year foolish childhoods these people would wrong one another, spurn the gods, and shortly die. Angrily, Zeus replaced them with a bronze race, terrible and strong, but harsh and violent. They saved Zeus the trouble by destroying one another and were followed by the epic heroes who found their reward in the Isles of the Blest. After them yet another race was formed—of iron—and it is our own, "and men never rest from labor and sorrow by day and from perishing by night; and the gods shall lay sore trouble upon them. But still, even these shall have some good mingled with their evils" (176-179). I need not enumerate the many familiar paradise motifs, but it is well to note the theme that this life is a punishment from the gods, who continue to live apart from us mortals. Hesiod warns that Zeus will destroy this race, too, and that there will be signs of our utter degeneracy: newborn infants will come to have gray hair at their temples; men will envy, dishonor, and harm brothers, friends, children, parents.

Lest I seem to wander from our happier theme, I must point out again that the Indo-European golden age arises from a cyclic myth involving a return to happiness after a course of utter degeneration, and such accounts seem to have been popular among the ancient Greeks. Plato, who wrought his own utopia in a monumental work called the *Republic*, relates in the *Politicus* (269c-273e) a view that the universe at one point reverses on itself and things digress as in the completing orbit of a circle. The myth of the cycle of ages, of which the Golden

Age is a contributing motif, finds correspondence in the Indic *Atharva-Veda*[16] (10.8.39-40) by which the universe is created and destroyed periodically. The refinement of the myth appears in Brahmanic literature (of the same era as Homer and Isaiah) and it follows a complex, mathematical scheme involving a cycle of three hundred eleven trillion, forty billion (311,040,000,000,000) years, in which many universes are blinked in and out of existence by Brahma. Our own universe's 4,320,000 years are divided into four *yugas* or "ages," the first and longest of which is the *Kritayuga*, when men are of pure caste and are just and good. The fourth and shortest age, the *Kāliyuga*, started on February 17, 3102 B.C. and will end 427,000 years hence with a *pralaya*, "dissolution," before a new cycle begins. After one thousand cycles or universes there will be a *mahāpralaya* or "huge dissolution."[17]

The total Indo-European theme of cosmic cataclysm followed by regeneration, while preserved elsewhere, is, as we have seen, lost in the Greek Hesiod's myth. It is obvious that he takes the quadripartite structure, injecting the Age of Heroes because his audience would certainly want to know where Achilles and the rest fit in, but rejecting the hopeful notion of regeneration because he is set on moralizing over his own degenerate age.[18] Hesiod also neglects the numbers (to a Greek anything past fifty was big, and for amounts past counting a myriad, or ten thousand, sufficed). Likewise, Rabbinic circles, while pointing to the return of *illud tempus*, nevertheless avoided precision in the midst of non-Indo-European tradition that had the history of the world divided into seven millennia. The Persians have both traditions: on the one hand, the four ages of gold, silver, steel, and a mixture of iron; on the other, a cosmic tree governed by metals of each of the planets—gold, silver, bronze, copper, tin, steel, and a mixture of iron.

It is a reasonable supposition that the four ages derive from the four solar seasons, for just as the season's days shorten toward winter, so too do the lifetimes of human beings shorten as the ages degenerate into cold, gray, heavy iron. Furthermore, the positions of the planets are supposed to mark the passage of time on the greatest scale, for when all seven are in conjunction,[19] what the Chaldeans called a Great Year will have been completed and the universe will suffer an eschatological ecpyrosis—the ultimate conflagration. But since fire is known to cleanse, in the *Zend-Avesta* we read that the cosmic burn-out will produce "a new world, free from old age, decomposition, and corruption, living eternally, increasing eternally, when the dead shall rise, when immortality shall come to the living, when the world shall be perfectly renewed" (*Yashts* 19.14.89).[20] Thus the Icelandic myth of Ragnarök, popularized in German as *die Götterdämmerung*, "the dimming of the gods," would see also a universal ecpyrosis, from which survives only the World Tree, protecting within its bark "Life" and his helpmate, all of which reminds us of the non-Indo-European account in *Genesis*.

Like any genuine myth, this cycle of ages lacks evidence of origin and for that very reason has tempted much scholarly conjecture. The nineteenth-century theory which held a celestial origin for all myths has been rightly challenged and disposed of. But there remains good reason to recognize the plausibility of part of the theory which deals with the return of the Golden Age. And for our purposes, the Greco-Roman treatment of it draws our attention to the return of a paradisal age to earth, not to heaven. I speak of the so-called Precession of Equinoxes, caused by a wobble of the rotating earth. Thus over the millennia the star pointed to by the Big Dipper will not always be over the pole, since the heavens revolve imperceptibly over a 26,000-year period, causing the constellation which governs the horizon at sunrise on the first day of spring to be always moving, giving way to another constellation roughly every 2,200 years, from Aries to Pisces and now to Aquarius. This phenomenon was recorded for the Western world by the Greek Hipparchus in the second century B.C.; it is likely, however, that the Precession was observed by Akkado-Babylonians at least two millennia before Hipparchus.[21] It is also likely, therefore, that mythic thinking not only in Mesopotamia but also in India and parts of Europe was influenced by the Precession. Whatever the causes, the myth reaches down into the third century B.C., when the Greek poet-astronomer Aratus speaks of the ancient time when the Maiden Justice left the earth (*Phaenomena* 101 ff.):

> . . . Of old she was an earth-dweller,
> And she used to meet men face to face. . . .
> And they called her Justice. . . .
> Not yet then did they know of sorry strife
> Nor blameful decisions nor uproarious confusion,
> And just so they lived . . .
> . . . And by herself, mistress of peoples,
> Justice, giver of just things, supplied all numbers of
>   things.
> She was there so as long as earth still nurtured the
>   golden generation.
> But with the silver age seldom and no longer wholly ready
> Did she mingle, yearning for the ways of peoples of old.
> But nonetheless she remained during the silver generation;
> But from the echoing hills at evening she came
> Alone, nor did she deal with anyone with gentle words. . . .

The Maiden rebuked them and promised wars and woes,

> And just so she spoke and sought the hills and left
> All the peoples gazing towards her still.

After the silver generation died, it was succeeded by the bronze generation, who were the first to forge weapons and eat beef. At this, Justice abandoned the earth altogether and took up residence in the heavens. It is certainly plausible that Aratus refers here to the yielding of Virgo to Leo in the Precession as she leaves the horizon for thousands of years.

The myth of the passing and expected return to the earth of the Golden Age of Justice continued to survive, and two centuries after Aratus, the Roman Vergil published a collection of poems called the *Eclogues*,[22] the fourth of which referred to the return of Virgo the Starry Maiden (4-10):

> The last age of the song of Cumae has now come;
> The great order of ages begins all over.
> Now also the Maiden returns; the reign of Saturn returns;
> Now a new progeny descend from high heaven.
> Now you, pure Diana, look kindly on the child being born,
> Under whom first the iron race shall cease,
> And a golden one rise up all over the world; your brother
>   Apollo now reigns.

Vergil is singing of the Tenth Age prophesied in the sacred books of the Cumaean Sibyl—the end of Hesiod's age of iron and the renewal of the cycle with a glorious age of gold. The world will receive from the skies the Maiden of Justice, and a just race will rule the earth. Vergil asks the goddess of childbirth to smile on the birth of a child which will usher in this age, ruled by the glorious and shining god of reason and the arts. Scholars debate the child's identity; many people throughout the Christian era were certain the poet prophesied the coming of Christ, the Messianic Age; and so Vergil, along with the just and wise Socrates, achieved unofficial sainthood.[23] It is more likely, however, that Vergil is speaking metaphorically of the new empire springing to life under the guidance of the adopted son of the slain Julius Ceasar.

The *Eclogues* are pastorals, taking as their setting and theme the carefree, natural, and especially peaceful life of shepherds. In that vein Vergil promises (18-25) that for the "child" the earth will pour forth

> . . . with no tilling, as its first pretty gifts,
> Ivy wandering everywhere about with foxglove . . .
> And the beanplant mingled with smiling acanthus.
> Goats will themselves bring home udders swollen
> With milk, and the herds will not fear mighty lions.
> Your cradle itself will pour forth harmless flowers.
> The snake, too, will die, and the deceitful poison herb
> Will die; Assyrian nard will grow everywhere.

It is easy enough to sense the kinship of spirit between this passage and that of *Isaiah* 11:6-8, discussed above: the child, the beast and the flock, even the snake. This tradition, it would seem, was strong in the Mediterranean world; furthermore, the ties with the paradisal Near East are found in Vergil's reference to an exotic Assyrian plant become commonplace in the returning Golden Age. This new age, Vergil continues, will be more than tranquil survival; amid ease and beauteous luxury it will see glorious achievement. A new wave of heroes will emerge and build a civilization that will mingle with the gods, just as once in Italy, the "Western Land,"[24] men of the former Golden Age flourished under the reign of the "abundant" Saturn, the Italian equivalent of the Greek Cronus. The transition of the Age of Iron to the Age of Gold without an ecpyrosis, is contrary to the Stoics' notion that the unending recurrence of identical worlds must be effected by universal conflagration. In Vergil's prophecy, Stoicism is displaced by its strongest rival of that era, Neo-Pythagoreanism, which held that the renewal of the world cycle is through metacosmosis, a non-violent world-change. But Vergil's Neo-Pythagorean optimism was not easily born of the turbulent history of Rome, over whom Stoicism and its formal and general aspects seems to have hovered. Ruled by fate and resigned to fatalism, the Romans could easily feel that the twelve birds which appeared for Romulus at the founding of Rome meant a mystical duration of the city.[25] But when Rome still prospered after 120 years, they set and would reset their sights on other multiples of twelve. Now, at the time of Vergil's writing, having survived the evils of civil wars, Rome was on the brink of the *Pax Romana*. Had mankind through the frustrations of fallen empires and wasted ages finally achieved the pinnacle of its destined achievement? Had a paradisal golden age returned at last to the very land in which it was first enjoyed?

The answer, rather, the half-answer lies in an incomplete, anonymous poem, after the manner of Vergil's *Eclogues*, dating from the earlier part of Nero's reign.[26] A shepherd complains to his companion that he finds himself anxious and troubled:

> . . . Worries disturb my joys:
> Worry pursues my feasting; it rises all the more when I
>   am in my cups,
> And grave anxiety delights in swooping down on my
>   happiness.
> You may hardly think it, but satiety vexes my joys.

The shepherd then enumerates the peaceful joys with which he is sated in this "golden reign," and the words of prophetic Vergil find echoes:

> The days of Saturn have returned with the Starry Maiden,
> And ages have returned safely to the olden ways. . . .
> Tigers chew at reins, lions endure the harsh yoke:
> Pure Diana, look kindly; your brother Apollo now reigns.

But here ends the fragment, and we are left to guess why our shepherd finds the Golden Age a huge bore. This Golden Age, however, wore on—through tyranny and license, through conquest and dissolution—until three centuries later on the 24th of August, when a Visigothic army under Alaric spilled into the city of Rome. It required of them barely three days to plunder. By our reckoning the year was 410; by the Romans' it was 1163 from the founding of the city—twelve centuries, obedient to the twelve birds of Romulus.

More tenaciously, perhaps more fanatically, than any other civilization the Romans strove to match historical events with mythic traditions. The mythopoeic age had long since vanished, but the promise of the myths was nurtured and adapted to a political situation, if not to political purposes. The myth-born Golden Age of Imperial Rome was a luxury which eluded the Jewish prophets and zealots who yearned for a messianic age. The Jews' imagery was probably influenced by Persian traditions of a *saushyant*, "savior." The Romans certainly assumed many similar Asiatic Greek traditions: the virtual religion of the Imperial legions was of Persian Mithras who periodically sacrifices the cosmic bull to bring justice and bounty. In the end, however, their golden paradise on earth and in history proved either a grand illusion or a reality beyond control. It was easy, then, for a man such as Augustine, who had known the delusions of seeking his own personal earthly paradise, to argue that the state of happiness was to be found in a heavenly city built from the ruins of an earthly one. Augustine looked not for the return of paradise to us but for our return to it through our denial of the earth and this life.

A great paradox of myths is that they endure simply because they change. There is no real or true version of a myth, since properly there are no versions of any myth, for every myth is real and true in itself, existing wholly in its telling and the hearing at that moment. The myths of paradises, saviors, and golden ages appear and disappear like so many seasonal flowers, alike but each with its own life affecting the person and the moment. But civilizations tend to memorialize these myths by pressing them into broad mythic traditions which in turn become cultural doctrines. Utopias—improbable possibilities—are little more than new mythologizations which draw upon these traditions in reaction to the political or social *status quo*. For this reason utopias tend to be nostalgic of a pre-historical freedom. The myth of the primal paradise is, ra-tionalistically, a utopia—a wished-for no-place—which has two functions: to distinguish the gross inadequacies of the present and to suggest how they came to be. Because, however, that paradise is now lost to us, we cannot expect of it what we ex-pect of other utopias: the possibility of possessing it.

But there is limited satisfaction derived from recalling this lost paradise, for after the momentary reverie we are faced with the frustrating reality of our existence and imminent demise. To make sense of our existence philosophies are de-vised; to make sense of our demise, religions. The will to be convinced that paradise is once again attainable produces the myth of a golden age. Whether that age comes in this life or after it, depends on the religious, political, or philosophical orientation of the culture. The common Christian concept of heaven, Dante's *Paradiso* or Augustine's *Civitas Dei*, is vir-tually a conflation of three traditions: 1) the Jews' borrowing of Sumerian Dilmun, 2) an assurance of paradisal return as in the cyclic motif of the Indo-European Golden Age, and 3) the Greeks' Elysian resting place for the righteous dead.[27] The union of these three traditions effectively removes any of their inherent distinctions of past, present, and future. Like many myths and all mysteries, paradise cannot be understood by di-rect logic. We know it by what it is not: it is not here, and to say that paradise recurs and is cyclic is merely our imperfect rec-ognition that it exists only insofar as our little life interrupts it; in itself it is whole and seamless, an eternal, timeless now.

Utopias, then, are incomplete paradises devised to meet needs totally in terms of this life. By comparison with the Edens, the *Paradisi*, and the Blessed Isles, utopias are forth-rightly temporal and literally mundane intellectualizations. But like all these eternal "no-places," utopias reflect and to an ex-tent answer man's basic need to escape the vicissitudes of this life and to rest secure in the soothing light of a wiser and just world.

2

Place in No Place: Examples of the Ordered Society in Literature

E. D. S. SULLIVAN

The fascination of the utopian idea for the imagination of Western intellectuals over the centuries is one of the intriguing aspects of literary history. Theologians, philosophers, historians, sociologists, and psychologists are among those who have planned or sought a new and better society—one in which life is uncomplicated, more equitable, and where an ideal moral, social, and political climate is to be found. With such traditionally inflated expectations, it is not too surprising to find the adjective "utopian" is defined as a "visionary or impractical thought or theory."[1]

The literary "utopians" prominent in the English-speaking world begin, of course, with Sir Thomas More, whose essay in 1516 gave the distinctive name to the genre. But the general ideal was continued with Sir Francis Bacon's *The New Atlantis* in 1627, on through Edward Bellamy and William Morris in the late 1800s and H. G. Wells in 1905, to B. F. Skinner's *Walden Two*, published in 1945. Even such seemingly contrary movements as eighteenth-century neoclassicism and nineteenth-century romanticism find a connection with sixteenth-century humanism. For the neoclassicist the emphasis on reason, the assertion of the dignity of man, and the concept that political institutions exist for the human good would have been applauded by the social satirist, Swift, just as they were by More before him and Skinner after him. The nineteenth-century romantics, too, found the utopian idea every bit as congenial, although there was an important shift in emphasis. Instead of the goods of utopia being attained through the medium of a benevolently controlled society as in earlier models, the romantics characteristically stressed individualism and liberty within a community based upon rural and agricultural life where man's potential for perfectability could be realized. This primitivism, with its admiration for the simple virtues of simple people, is associated with the idea of "the noble savage" and, while different in degree from the literary manifestations of utopia, resembles them in the belief that physical labor is both desirable and good.

But whether humanism, neoclassicism, romanticism, or twentieth-century materialism—all the utopian examples of society's aspirations for what could or should be are predicated on a concept of order which derives from function: the performance of certain work; the knowing and doing of one's job. Initially, such societal order stemmed from an assent to the rational idea that everyone should perform useful labor contributing to the general good as in More's and Bacon's formulations. But the full impact of the Industrial Revolution made for a division in viewpoint between the economic and the literary utopians of the nineteenth century. Although the former group was troubled by the plight of the exploited industrial workers, their hope was for a future of endless production and progress resulting from technology (rather as in Bacon's *The New Atlantis*) with all doing the work for which they were best qualified and in which, consequently, they were happiest. But the semiegalitarian aspect of earlier, largely unmechanized utopian schemes was abandoned in the face of the requirement for increasingly diverse worker and managerial skills. Their literary counterparts, on the other hand, though they shared the age's enthusiasm for individualism and self-fulfillment, nevertheless had a vision of the ideal society which was not essentially different from More's. The principal dissimilarity was that harmonious interdependence would come not by imposition of rules and regulations (no matter how logical and benign), but of itself when men put behind them the artificial strictures of society to operate in accord with the intrinsic nobility of their natures. One imagines that just such an idealization was seen as governing the never-to-be-realized Pantisocracy of Coleridge and Southey on the banks of the Susquehanna.

The modern application of the idea of order through function owes something to all of these approaches. The intellectual recognition that essential (even disagreeable) tasks must be performed for individual and collective well-being is joined to the romantics' emphasis on individualism and self-interest by making the particular work to be performed a free choice. Indeed, freedom to choose is an important factor in all utopian programs although voluntary acceptance of duties might arise from such different motivations as high-minded rationality, natural altruism, or enlightened personal considerations.

Nevertheless, whatever the underlying reasons, the utopian aim of "happiness" envisaged labor as a necessary good though not an end in itself. Leisure as devoted to cultural and intellectual pursuits might be more prized and ample time provided for it, but everyone worked a set period: six hours a day for More's Utopians and the equivalent of four hours by the inhabitants of Walden Two. It is precisely this obligation to perform specific duties which was the basis for the essential order—and therefore harmony—of the utopian community. And it is this aspect which the dystopian writers have seized upon to create their mindless, human beehives where individuals are the cogs of a monolithic machine—selectively bred or mentally programmed for particular jobs in the service of an all-powerful State. Let us examine, therefore, the idea of function or "place" in the "no place" of "utopia" by considering with varying emphases four of the best-known literary examples in English. Two of them are classics of the type: More's *Utopia* and Skinner's *Walden Two*. The former because, though not the first of the genre, it is the model for subsequent utopian writings; the latter because *Walden Two* is the clearest expression of the utopian concept in modern terms. The remaining two books provide an interesting counterpoint to More and Skinner because they represent the most noted dystopian novels: Huxley's *Brave New World* and Orwell's *Nineteen Eighty-Four*. These works do not lend themselves to point-by-point comparison and contrast with prototypical utopian thought. They are chosen, as suggested above, because they demonstrate in an interestingly paradoxical way how fundamental agreement and disagreement in both utopian and anti-utopian literature center upon the logical role of function as the main factor in social order. The utopians see assigned or assumed work as logical and imperative for the attainment of the common good; the dystopians perceive it as the logical source from which tyranny and dehumanization will inevitably flow.

More's *Utopia* was published in 1516 and has its roots in Plato's *Republic* but also in Lucian of Samsota, the second-century Greek satirist of manners and morals. The concerns of these two authors—shared by More—together with the interest in ancient thought characteristic of the English humanist trend then in its infancy, all determined him to make a statement which would invite scrutiny of the present state of the country and direct attention to what, instead, it should be. It was written in Latin, the international language of the day, and brought its author virtually instant fame throughout the Continent so that it was said that—apart from the king and, possibly, Cardinal Wolsey—he was the best-known Englishman outside of England. Indeed, the work went through five editions in four years, although it was not translated into English until thirty-five years following the initial publication and sixteen years after More's beheading by order of Henry VIII.

Like all such literature, More's book is intended to be a comment on the world as it exists at that particular time. *Utopia*, therefore, is a condemnation of the abuses in European institutions of the late fifteenth and early sixteenth centuries.[2] Chief among the causes for these abuses was the inordinate appetite for riches, most particularly in the wanton acquisition of property which enabled a few to live in luxury and idleness at the expense of many. In *Utopia* matters were much better ordered. There, one finds an almost classless society where the products of the household, the farmer, and the artisan are deposited in warehouses from which every head of family selects what is needed without any sort of payment. Property is held in common and, to keep people from becoming attached to things, houses are changed by lot every two years. The Utopians trade their surplus goods abroad for those materials they lack and although they also receive payment in gold and silver these riches are so little regarded that they are used to fashion chamber pots and fetters for criminals and slaves.[3] As is clear, this egalitarian social system where there is common ownership of the means of production and subsistence is practically a textbook definition of communism, and More is indebted to Plato's *Republic* for the idea.

Yet, as Surtz has pointed out, nothing illustrates better "the independent and original use made of classical models by the best spirits of the Renaissance"[4] than a glance at the differences between the principles applied in Platonic and Utopian communism with regard to the state and the individual. Whereas the common life is led only by the soldiers and guardians in the *Republic* who are also exempt from manual labor, all the Utopians share in the goods produced and all, except 500 scholars per city, work as farmers or craftsmen. Government in the *Republic* is aristocratic, but in *Utopia* it is by comparison democratic and essentially casteless. Of the two approaches, More's appears to be the more attractive and it is his concept of communism which has been echoed by the various devisers of utopias down to and including B. F. Skinner.

But More's book title is a pun on the Greek *ou topia* (no place) and *eu topia* (good place) and because the book is called *Utopia* or "No Place," it might be conjectured that only in Heaven (the "Good Place") could individuals be expected to apply so enthusiastically and disinterestedly the fundamentals of communism. While More holds out the vision of a community founded upon individual benevolence and industry, he nevertheless had the Aristotelian reservations about the effects of communism:[5] with no prospect of personal gain, the impetus to work would largely disappear, and without work the abundance necessary for the good life would not materialize. As mentioned earlier, the utopian goal is individual and collective happiness; its attainment is dependent on order, which is to say regulation, so that one person's happiness does not become the occasion of another's sadness. Although there are considerable limitations of freedom imposed on—and willingly accepted by—the Utopians, there are remarkably few rules specified in the book which pertain to labor apart from the important statement, "Of the day's twenty-four hours, the Utopians devote only six to work."[6] No punishment is noted for failing to observe that hourly work period although, in the discussion of travel within Utopia, there is the requirement, once he has reached his destination, that the traveller "gets no food until he has completed a morning's or an afternoon's stint of work"[7] presumably in the fields or in a fellow artisan's shop.

The seemingly intrinsic good of physical labor is a hallmark of utopias. In More's commonwealth every man and woman without exception does farm work for two years. Besides this agricultural experience, everyone has a particular trade of his own: the women perform the lighter crafts such as linen-making and wool-working while the men are assigned to heavier work. Sons ordinarily follow their father's craft but, again with happiness as the utopian goal, if one is attracted to another occupation, he is transferred by adoption to a family practicing that trade.[8] Therefore, for the majority of the populace, their "place," in the sense of their contribution to the functioning of the state, is that of farm worker/artisan. Nevertheless, there is a hierachy of sorts which reflects the uncomplicated and essentially democratic government of Utopia. Each of the fifty-four cities of Utopia has a prince who is elected for life from among four nominees selected and voted for by a group of 200 officials called syphogrants who themselves are elected for a year. Over each group of ten syphogrants there is another official called a tranibor and these twenty individuals form the nucleus of a senate which meets with the prince at least every other day to discuss affairs of state. They, too, are elected for a term of a year but are usually reelected. Insofar as there is an aristocracy or elite, it is in the group of scholars. In each city no more than 500 men and women are officially and permanently exempted from manual work. Almost half of this number are the syphogrants who, to set an example, don't take advantage of the privilege; the remainder are those who devote themselves to study and it is from this group that the ambassadors, priests, tranibors, and even the prince are selected. Yet if any of the scholars fail to live up to expectations they can be returned to the ranks of workmen,

just as craftsmen who diligently cultivate the intellectual life in
their leisure time can be raised to the eminence of scholar.

Other than the prince, the tranibors (and other scholars),
and the syphogrants, all of whom are elected or selected, the
remainder are all workers, though again divided into three un-
equal groups. There are the heads of households—the oldest
parent—who are responsible for between ten and sixteen
adults made up of unmarried daughters and male children and
their wives, if any. These members of families and their minor
children make up the second group which comprises the mass
of the population of Utopia. Finally, there are the slaves who
perform all the truly disagreeable work, including the slaughter of animals. More's use of the Latin word *servus* may not be
the equivalent of chattel slavery, but those so designated are
clearly the lowest of the workers and the utopian ideal of happiness is considered, if at all, only incidentally as their due.
They are comprised of war prisoners, those condemned to
death in other lands but purchased by the Utopians, those described as "hardworking penniless drudges from other nations
who voluntarily choose to become slaves" in order to live in
Utopia and, most interesting in view of More's failure to spec-
ify punishments for infractions of the apparently numerous
rules which assure "order," there are "former citizens, en-
slaved for some heinous offense."⁹

Thus, place in "No Place" consists of an elected or selected oligarchy of officials and scholars while the remainder
of the citizens function as farmer/artisans and, finally, a slave
class. All, however, accomplish assigned duties in accordance
with a benevolent but rigid regimen of rules and regulations
which are intended to make for an ordered, hence "happy,"
society. More was holding up for emulation a commonwealth
based upon Platonic reason. Not only did he not intend it as an
ideal state—an unattainable goal—but, indeed, he was pointing
out that, by combining reason with divine revelation, the
Christian nations of Europe should not only be able to attain to
Utopian excellence, but surpass it. Nevertheless, there was a
price to be paid. Given the realities of observed human nature,
the desirable state enjoyed by the Utopians was possible only
by placing the individual in the position in which he would be
most effective and productive and, therefore, happy. Nowhere

in his *Utopia* does More envisage the happy drone, much less
what is to be done with him. Everyone is to have a clearly defined and productive place in "No Place"—a job which is to be
willingly and joyously performed because the result will be individual and collective happiness and harmony precisely because of the order imposed.

It is interesting and instructive to observe that, with the
exception of the slaves and, to an extent, the scholars, the program and hierarchy of Skinner's *Walden Two* are strikingly
similar to that of *Utopia*. But there are also important
differences. Like the Utopians, community members do only
meaningful labor during their average four-hour workday and,
while hard labor is not avoided, the necessary but uncreative
and uninteresting work is done as much as possible by machines. The governmental structure is different from that of the
Utopians because it reflects the more complex technological
aspect of Walden Two, but in essence the various ranks are not
too dissimilar. In place of the prince elected for life, there are
the six Planners who make policy and have certain judicial
functions and who serve for not more than ten years after
which they then return to the category of Worker. Under them,
and similar to the Utopian tranibors, are an indefinite number
of Managers—the specialists who head the divisions and services making up Walden Two. These are neither elected nor do
they have a term of office, but instead they are selected by the
Planners following training in their specialties and after having
performed in intermediate positions which roughly corre-
spond to the role of the syphogrants of Utopia. Nearest to Utopia's scholars are the very few scientists. But, because no pure
science is officially authorized, their function is directed
toward such inquiry and research as will have direct benefit to
the community, such as animal breeding and infant behavior.
All the rest of the members are Workers who devote the approximately four hours of their day to tasks of their own
choosing.

It is in this last respect that Walden Two more closely realizes the utopian ideal of voluntary and productive employ-
ment. In Utopia, the assumption was that once one had freely
chosen a particular job and was proficient in it, he would be
happy and productive indefinitely. In Walden Two, the actual

stint of work outweighs the resultant level of productivity. Except, presumably, in the most technically skilled jobs, a Worker can sign up for any work and in consequence efficiency may suffer. As Walden Two's founder and apologist, Frazier, concedes: "It's an extravagance. . . . In another generation we shall do better; our educational system will see to that."[10] This work flexibility is encouraged by a system of credits which rewards labor in relation to the characteristics of the job. An accumulation of 1200 labor credits a year is required of each member at Walden Two although how these are amassed is up to the individual; they can be crammed into six months of eight-hour days or spread over the whole year at approximately four hours per day. But time on the job is not the criterion. Rather, it is the ease or difficulty or the attractiveness or unattractiveness of the task which determines the credit ratio per hour's work. Hence the sewer man receives about one and one-half credits for each hour on the job and therefore need work only slightly more than two hours each day. Other, more agreeable, tasks will require five or more hours daily to total the 1200 demanded each year. The hourly labor credit values are reviewed by the Planners from time to time and are adjusted according to need. Thus, where all work is made equally desirable either by its nature or its labor credit rewards, freedom of choice is preserved, personal happiness achieved, and collective productivity effectuated.

One's place in "No Place," therefore, is an essential element in the successful operation of the community—whether in one of the cities of Utopia or in Walden Two. Most of the citizens are Workers, as we have seen, but again collective happiness is assured by adherence to an accepted order. There is a governmental structure to plan and coordinate the activities of the society and to deal with such communication with the outside world as is necessary or desirable. Moreover, central control is not limited to one's work but extends to personal relationships as well. Utopia is more lenient in this regard than is Walden Two and this relative moderation probably stems from More's concept of the family as a basic social unit. Nevertheless, even in Utopia there is a form of population control: families are kept to between ten and sixteen adult members, and if the group exceeds this number the excess is moved to a family which is fewer in number. Equally, when the city totals 6000 households, any additional families are moved to other Utopian cities or to the neighboring mainland. Marriage, too, is limited by age: women must be at least eighteen and men twenty-two years old.

In Walden Two there is rather more regulation of personal lives, but it is exercised more subtly because of a philosophic difference that Sir Thomas More might have admired because of its rationality but deplored because of its attentuation (and eventual destruction) of the family relationship. In Walden Two one might marry at the age of fifteen or sixteen, but children of the union are raised and cared for from infancy until thirteen years of age in nurseries and schools provided and staffed by the community. At thirteen the children move into the adult building where they live in pairs according to sex until they marry. In effect, Walden Two replaces the family not only as an economic unit but as social and psychological support as well. This development is the beginning of the "Behavioral Engineering" which has attracted so much attention to the theories of Professor Skinner. As described in *Walden Two*, this social control is all-pervasive and is aimed at providing a managed environment which will produce happy and healthy members of the Walden community. These will be individuals who by personality, temperament, and motivation follow the Walden code strictly yet feel free because they want to do what is best for themselves and, incidentally, for the community.

Unlike Utopia where controls are accepted because of an intellectual perception of the need for an ordered life based upon observance of rules and regulations, the inhabitants of Walden Two are in effect scientifically "designed" to conform to a desirable pattern. Thus, babies and children are gradually introduced to measured frustrations in order to build tolerance for coping with obstacles in later life while feelings of superiority or inferiority are obliterated for the sake of general happiness because the personal triumph of one implies the personal failure of another. In line with this idea, there are no titles: medical doctors are addressed as "Mr." and parents are called by their first names; all of the administrators from the Planners on down do some manual labor every day so that no cultural prejudices arise that one type of work is better than another. In short, where the Utopians do right because they are preeminently *rational*, the members of Walden are *conditioned* to do what is right. They are almost always doing what they want to do, but the Planners see to it that they will *want* to do what is best for themselves and the community. In a curiously paradoxical sense they are predestined to be "free."

This sense of freedom may be in part spurious, but it is vital to that most important element of all utopias—happiness. Whether they live in Utopia or in Walden Two, all the needs of the inhabitants are provided: their food, clothing, education, health care. No wonder the Utopians could make chamber pots of gold; the only need for money was to provide them with those few essential items which their island lacked. "Iron is far superior" to either silver or gold because "men could not live without iron . . . any more than without fire or water,"[11] as Hythloday observes in the course of his discussion on so-called precious things. The same attitude toward money is taken in Walden. It is something with which to pay taxes, utility bills, to buy tractors, etc. Aside from the Planners no one handles it and, more important, no one thinks about it. But just as the accumulation of riches is no joy, neither does happiness derive from some romantic concept of a return to the earth. Primitivism is not a part of either Utopia or Walden Two. The manual labor enjoined upon most or all of the community is in line with esteem for the simple but satisfying life, but all the Utopians have a good grounding in literature and can study all branches of learning while, in Walden Two, there are lectures, concerts, and drama by the inhabitants, by records, or by radio.

Understandably, the question as to labor-saving devices does not arise in More's sixteenth-century *Utopia*, but it is a significant part of Skinner's twentieth-century *Walden Two*. In line with the goal of happiness, all the most arduous or disagreeable work that can be performed by machine is so done. The constantly changing work credit scheme ensures that unattractive work, which is not yet capable of being done by machine, will be made desirable in view of the reduced hours needed to reach one's quota. Hence, happiness is assured because not only is the unpleasant work freely chosen, but it is rewarded in direct proportion to its difficulty or its distasteful nature.

Next to happiness, the other imperative for utopian literature is rationality—more important to More, perhaps, than to Skinner, though of major importance to both. *Utopia* was an amiable condemnation of the Christian nations of the sixteenth century, particularly England. Purposely, More "restricts his humanistic vision by the self-imposed limits and capabilities" of reason unaided by revelation. His purpose is to demonstrate that "conditions in Christian Europe are worse, not better, than those in pagan Utopia"[12] and thus to shock Christians into a recognition that they, "fortified by revelation and grace" plus natural reason, could and should remedy contemporary evils and surpass the Utopians in "high morality, intellectual culture, and benevolent government."[13]

This emphasis on reason and nature must be kept well in mind in a reading of *Utopia* because, when some of the reasoned procedures of Utopia may impress us as being absurd or extreme, More is warning us that it all happens in *ou topia* or "No Place." As C. S. Lewis notes, "It is doubtful whether More would have regarded euthanasia for incurables and assassination of hostile princes as things contained in the Law of Nature."[14] Yet both of these are advocated. The incurably ill are counseled by pagan priests and public officials to take "a potion which puts them painlessly to sleep"[15] though, should the patient refuse, no further pressure is applied and there is no diminution of care. The same logic is applied with respect to rulers who plot aggression against the Utopians. By offering large bounties for the lives of these princes, the Utopians sow suspicion and distrust in the ranks of the enemy and avoid or limit warfare. As Hythloday says: "Everywhere else in the world, this process of bidding for and buying the life of an enemy is condemned as the cruel villainy of a degenerate mind; but the Utopians consider it good policy, both wise and merciful. . . . It enables them, by the sacrifice of a few guilty men, to spare the lives of many innocent persons who might have died in battle, some on their side, some on the enemy's."[16] Such a defense is worthy of Machiavelli who, though a contemporary (*The Prince* was published in Italy in 1516, the same year as *Utopia*), was unknown to More at that time. In any event, More would have opposed everything that Machiavelli represented and would have regarded his work as illustrating exactly what can come of reason when it refuses to be guided by Christian revelation. As it is, More listens without demur to these and similarly repugnant practices recounted by Hythloday, who has lived among the Utopians, and brings the book to a close by saying of his fictional informant, "Though he is a man of unquestioned learning, and highly experienced in the ways of the world, I cannot agree with everything he said. Yet I confess there are many things in the Commonwealth of Utopia which I wish our own country would imitate—though I don't really expect it will." [17]

In *Walden Two* reason is also important but, as previously noted, not to the same degree as in *Utopia*. Frazier, our guide through the community, tells his listeners that "Experimentation . . . not reason" is the basis of Walden Two. [18] However, Frazier has just been indicating that the aim of behavioral technology is to determine the psychological characteristics of human behavior and determine how these can be modified and how other suitable ones can be produced. And, once behavioral engineering has "created" the desired type of person, his course of action seems to be—and, indeed, is—rational. As has previously been noted, having been motivated by his training, the community member wants to do what he has been conditioned to do and thereby feels not only that he is acting of his own volition, but that he is acting in the only rational fashion.

Whether in Utopia or Walden Two, the manner of life and the conduct of human relationships are closely, if not obviously, controlled. And not a little of the disciplined harmony resulting from such governance can be ascribed to the voluntary acceptance by its members of obligatory work. Everyone has a place in this ordered society and functions seemingly without question or protest. It is seen as a sensible arrangement because the collective good is thereby served and, because the work appears to be freely chosen, the individual is happy in performing it. Yet control in the name of happiness and rationality is precisely the aspect of utopian thought which has been seized upon by anti-utopian writers. So frequently one reads of dystopian literature as portraying ideally hideous societies or as visions of the present world gone wrong. Although not incorrect, these definitions miss the point. The anti-utopians have seen that the controlled society—no matter how benevolent originally—can be twisted and manipulated for thoroughly irrational and, ultimately, completely unhappy ends.

Both utopian and dystopian books are a response to their times. More wrote his genial reproof to sixteenth-century Christian Europe; Aldous Huxley's *Brave New World* is a 1932 protest against the impersonality of the assembly-line mentality and the encouragement to consumerism. And, by a coincidence, the years 1945 and 1948 saw the writing of two quite dissimilar books: Skinner's *Walden Two* and Orwell's *Nineteen Eighty-Four*. Both of these last are reflections of the state of the respective countries of their authors in the immediate post-World War II period. In his 1976 essay, "Walden Two Revisited,"[19] which prefaced the most recent printing of his famous novel, Skinner recaptures and expands upon some of the ideas which led him to write *Walden Two* in 1945. The war had ended, with all of its regimentation, vastly expanded industrial production, and enormous consumption of energy and resources. Skinner's thoughts turned to a dream of simpler life based upon smallness, community, and conservation as well as his plan for the development of the individual (called Behavioral Engineering in the book). Orwell's *Nineteen Eighty-Four* reproduces the London of 1948 with its shortages, drabness, and grey uniformity. Most disquieting of all for him was the continued enforcement of certain of the war-necessitated restrictions. In these personal restraints he saw governmental inclinations to social control—a possibility which he feared could become a reality given the disheartening stability of the dictatorships of the Franco Right and the Stalin Left with which Orwell was so disenchantedly familiar.

As literature, no great claim can be made for any of the overtly utopian or dystopian novels in English. Of them all, perhaps More's *Utopia* is the most uniformly readable if one recognizes the deliberately ambiguous position More adopts for effectively concealing his own opinions: sometimes using Hythloday to put forward his point of view, sometimes advancing it in his own person as a participant in the dialogue.

Nevertheless, he handles the exchange of views in an easy and natural manner and, except for those who insist upon seeing the work as a polemic or blueprint for the future, the easy good nature and occasional irony of his speculations on the society of pagan Utopia vis-à-vis Christian Europe warrant the enduring interest and importance his book has enjoyed over the centuries.

The same cannot be said about the other three volumes. Almost by definition, utopian literature is didactic and contentious and therefore is written to make a fairly undisguised point. Characterization is consequently minimal and conflict is either nonexistent, as in the true utopian novel, or crudely obtrusive in the dystopian work. *Walden Two* follows the lead of Plato's *Republic* and More's *Utopia* by being mostly dialogue, with Frazier setting forth the principles of Walden to a skeptical Professor Castle and an eventually converted Burris. There are subordinate plots involving two young couples, one of which stays and lives happily ever after, the other drawn back to the world preferring its superficialities to the simplicities of Walden, but these are the merest concession to the novelistic format. The real essence of the book is in the often heated dialogue between Frazier and Castle. There, the pros and cons of the ordered society are argued out and Skinner manages to set forth a workable design of a community which now is being acted upon by enthusiasts of his theories in several parts of the United States.

The two anti-utopian novels make a greater effort to develop a story line and Huxley, perhaps, takes his more seriously. Orwell, on the other hand, seems weary of the plot and, toward the end of the book, throws off all pretense that the grubby little romance between Winston and Julia is central to the work and, in a didactic and thoroughly unsubtle manner, simply reproduces two chapters of the infamous and banned book of his fictional spokesman, the hated renegade, Emmanuel Goldstein. It is the most economical and direct means of advancing Orwell's philosophical point without the clutter of plot. Following the capture of Winston by the Thought Police, Orwell again virtually abandons the story. He devotes the final third of his book to the dialogue between Winston and O'Brien in the course of which, after months of brainwashing and torture, Winston is brought of his own accord to make his final submission to absolutism.

Nineteen Eighty-Four is a forceful indictment of power and a warning against a police state where the past is continuously being rewritten to accommodate the present and where "Newspeak," the official language, is employed to limit intellectual concerns and eliminate independent thought. But it is also an anti-war tract. As has been noted, Orwell had experienced in war-time Britain the shortages and rationing of even essential items of food and clothing, the curtailment of traditional liberties and freedom of speech—all accepted in the spirit of "getting on with the War" or "winning through to Victory." He perceives that just such an appeal to survival (rather than to patriotism) can serve to unify the people, explain the shortages, and justify the regimentation while the Inner Party hierarchy consolidates its power and increases the control over a society that has no privacy and where unorthodoxy is punishable by death. Hence the perpetual war of Oceania against either one of its rivals and the importance of Goldstein, a former leader now proclaimed traitor and defiler of the Party's purity, who serves as a focal point for citizen hatred. Goldstein's daily appearance on television is an overlooked minor triumph for Orwell's major point. Goldstein's denunciation of the Party and its doctrines are valid but, presented as they are during the Two Minute Hate period, the rank and file of Party members hear the truth but reject it without examination because of its source.

Although there is no evidence that Orwell was familiar with Skinner's behavioral engineering theory, the picture of truth being hooted down during the Two Minute Hate is a somber reminder of the grave consequences of mental conditioning which is at the core of Orwell's work. Another telling warning which is left ambiguous but is highly suggestive is Goldstein himself. When O'Brien, the Inner Party member who has trapped Winston, reveals that he had written part of the Goldstein book, the reader cannot help but wonder if the hated Goldstein himself, far from being a renegade and traitor, is not still a secret Party functionary whose duty it is to keep the truth before the people. In consequence, the validity of Goldstein's accusations cannot be pondered without conscious disloyalty and, more probably, his indictments of the system will not be seriously entertained because of the source from which they emanate. In any event, the constant state of hatred engendered and encouraged by the Party, whether against a nation or an individual, is profoundly useful. It distracts Party members from questioning why, though set production quotas are always officially announced as having been exceeded, the quality of life never improves, and it also serves by focusing mental energies into mindless denunciation which might otherwise be channeled into speculative thought. To sustain this beleaguered atmosphere, the Party must manufacture enemies where they don't already exist.

Compared to the grimness of *Nineteen Eighty-Four*, Huxley's *Brave New World*, oddly enough, seems almost lighthearted—an extravagant fancy which is not diminished by the device of setting the story in the seventh century A.F. (after [Henry] Ford) and punctuating the narrative with such schoolboyish allusions as "Ford's in his flivver, all's right with the world." Nevertheless, from the standpoint of a controlled society and the apportionment of functions, Huxley outdoes Orwell and anticipates Skinner. *Nineteen Eighty-Four* had essentially only three levels in its hierarchy: Inner Party members or the governing power structure; the Party members themselves who fill all of the remaining Party posts, and the Proles, or proletariat, who seem to live without very much reference either to the Party or its members. Huxley's world state, on the other hand, owes its social stability to a scientific caste system. Human beings, graded from highest intellectuals to lowest manual workers, hatched from incubators and brought up in communal nurseries, learn by methodical conditioning to accept their social destiny. Although Huxley's book was written thirteen years before *Walden Two*, here is Skinner's behavioral engineering carried to its grotesque extreme. Once again the hero is an unorthodox young man dissatisfied with conditions who has his discontent clarified for him when he visits an Indian reservation in New Mexico and returns to London with one of its members, referred to as the Savage. Huxley uses the Savage in somewhat the same way, though for a different reason, that Orwell employed Goldstein: to be a spokesman for a better, happier, more rational life—the classic utopian goals. Although the Savage is at first fascinated by the new world, he is at last repelled by the system and, in a confrontation with the World Controller, Mustapha Mond, inveighs against the crushing of individual liberties for the purpose of achieving a scientifically harmonious society.

As will have been noticed, the dystopian authors have relatively little to say regarding the function of individuals in their controlled societies, and with good reason. They have perceived the essential vulnerability of true utopianism and have exploited it. More's Utopia succeeds only because it is peopled by high-minded altruists; Walden functions solely because its members have been conditioned to do good. The anti-utopians have seen correctly that the order which keeps Utopia and Walden operating, together with the general indifference as to who exercises authority so long as basic needs are provided for, combine to suggest that—in unscrupulous hands—there is a very small step that separates Skinner's from Huxley's vision of the future. With the dystopian emphasis on total control of intellect and action, where mindless conformity is the substitute for utopian happiness, it is not surprising that concerns about function and variation in contribution are obliterated. "Place" is effectively reduced to the two categories of Controllers and Controlled. And, implicit in the anti-utopians' predilection for the untrammeled freedom of the Proles and the Savages who somehow manage to survive, there is the conviction that, as society becomes increasingly complex and highly organized, individual liberties will be subordinated in favor of regimentation.

Grim as the dystopian vision may be, it can hold up to inspection the salient disadvantages of utopias. Writing in 1702 about Bacon's *The New Atlantis*, the Abbé Raguet correctly complained of the boredom seemingly inevitable in a utopia. And even in the 1000-member community of Walden Two there is a sense of blandness. In a group where competition is outlawed, as in Walden Two, there can be no heroes and talent can go unrewarded. Despite the abundant free time and a bulletin board crammed with notices of various educational and cultural activities, Walden comes through as a curiously unintellectual society composed of happy mediocrities. The reader feels that Castle's spirited opposition to Frazier's defense of the philosophy and the behavioral engineering of Walden Two is the first sustained intellectual exercise Frazier has encountered in most of the ten years since the foundation of the community and regrets that it is not the gadfly Castle who elects to return to Walden, but the already half-convinced Burris.

It is instructive that it is a novel by an actual participant in a utopian experiment that touches on just such a limited life of the mind as well as other aspects of existence in a fellowship conducted along idealistic lines. Nathaniel Hawthorne has written satirically and ironically of his stay of several months at the mid-nineteenth-century experimental community at Brook Farm, called Blithedale in the book. Unlike the four works just examined whose authors could readily adjust the varying degrees of good and evil in their imagined communities without the necessity of incurring the consequent reality, Hawthorne had known—and rejected—the American version of Charles Fourier's social philosophy of small self-sustaining groups. While the setting of *The Blithedale Romance* is important in order to account for the concentration of the liberal intellectuals who inhabit this transcendentalist utopia, the author is concerned only incidentally with presenting an evaluation of the success or failure of such philantropic experiments. Yet the novel has both utopian and dystopian aspects. There we find the pastoral background, the physical labor, and the egalitarianism. But there is also the monomaniacal leader, an insistence on a single view of the project, and an intellectual rebel in Zenobia, the novel's heroine. The narrator, an effete dilettante by the name of Coverdale, is clearly the author's *persona*, and his opinions and actions reflect Hawthorne's participation in the Brook Farm movement. This experiential knowledge gives substance to his fictional conclusion that living in a real-life utopia can be a very trying experience indeed.

Function—or place—in this Massachusetts-style utopia/dystopia is, in its own fashion, a confirmation in actuality of the indifferent quality of the so-called intellectual life that one senses in Walden Two. In Blithedale, the shrewd Yankee farmer, chosen for his expertise to guide the erstwhile urban utopians in their new agricultural life, does not gain culture or knowledge through association with his displaced "betters."

On the other hand, Coverdale laments the fact that, instead of fulfilled expectations of spiritual exhilaration, the hard labor leaves him mentally sluggish.[20] In short, there is a general homogenization; not through Skinneresque behavorial engineering (though that would hasten the process in subsequent generations), but in a downward intellectual leveling which would bring a wry nod of recognition from Orwell.

The objectives of the traditional utopias—rationality and happiness—were certainly basic to the Blithedale philosophy. Yet, even here, Hawthorne's tongue-in-cheek attitude is apparent. His tragicomic heroine, Zenobia, is a study of an intellectual who has lived her life in accord with one or another literary or political idea and who, accordingly, is attracted to the high-minded concept of a utopian community.[21] The reality of the life—for her as for Coverdale—theoretically reasonable though it may be, does not provide the happiness foreseen. It would seem to be Hawthorne's implied judgment that not only does happiness not necessarily follow from rationality, but that it might actually be inhibited by it.

How different from Thomas More's belief that virtually automatic good might be expected when those two qualities are present and aided by Christian faith and revelation—though More would undoubtedly attribute Brook Farm's eventual failure to the disproportionately small emphasis on religious practice as a complement to the community's abundant social fervor. Nevertheless, whether happiness and rationality are present or absent in either real or fictional utopia/dystopias, the basis of the philosophy which seeks to ensure them is one of imposed order. C. S. Lewis has pointed out that "It is not love of liberty that makes men write Utopias"[22] of either kind. An ideally ordered society is possible only through the curtailment of freedom, both personal and collective. In such a society one will have a defined place and will fulfill a specific function.

But the warning regarding control is clear and implicit in either literature or life. The semipastoral, egalitarian proposal to bring plenty and contentment to one and all may, as portrayed by the humane and benevolent Thomas More, seem light-years away from, say, a modern-day China whose relative agricultural sufficiency has been attained only at the cost of a ruthless reordering of the lives of its people. But the under-lying method is the same, because whatever is good or bad in either the fictional Utopia or the all-too-real China comes about through a control which is exercised through law and employ-ment regardless of whether those means are benign or oppressive.

3

Illusions of Endless Affluence

JOHN J. HARDESTY

The utopia I would like to discuss is often referred to as the American Dream, but this American Dream is an anti-human, self-defeating, ecologically impossible utopia which is fast becoming a nightmare.

The genus *homo* evolved to *homo sapiens*, and continued to develop largely as a result of being a conscious social animal that shared food and knowledge about the surrounding environment in order to survive.[1] Today we want to deny those social bonds and get as far away from other members of the species as we can. We want ranch-style suburban homes with as much land around them as possible, surrounded by a five-foot redwood fence, with at least two American foul-breathing, gas-eating dragons in the driveway waiting to meet our every transportation whim—however frivolous—in isolated, glass-and-steel-encased splendor. We can go to church, the bank, a movie, or out to eat without encountering another human face-to-face. Privatistic consumption patterns encourage every nuclear family to have its own color TV, stereo system, water heater, washer, dryer, air-conditioner, and fully equipped kitchen. Even in education we are using more television and computers so that teachers and students do not have to deal directly with each other.

Such a way of life alienates us from our social human essence. It is also self-defeating, and impossible in the long run, because it moves against the very process of human evolution that made us what we are and because it violates crucial laws and limitations found in nature. It is for just such reasons that we must call the American Dream a utopia. It is utopian precisely because *it is a dream*; it is a socio-economic condition that can actually exist only for a tiny minority on earth, and even for them the dream must quickly fade. Now I should make clear that I don't attribute this selfish, shortsighted way of life to an inherently corrupt human nature. Indeed, current behavior is a response to the requirements and exigencies of a private enterprise economy, an economy which must produce and reproduce the American Dream on the installment plan in order to maintain and increase the flow of sales and profits.

On the other hand, for those leftists who would maintain that the working class is *coerced* into reluctant acceptance of this utopia, I can only point out that never have so many given in so readily to so few. Yet even those, or perhaps especially those, who have not shared as fully in the American Dream often support it enthusiastically. Of course, forty or fifty billion dollars of corporate advertising expenditures do play a significant role in promoting the American Dream mentality. The one-dimensional image of what constitutes the "good life" is more subtly conveyed by the media (especially television) and by clergymen, politicians, teachers, social workers, employers, and union leaders. Even more profoundly, in an economy founded upon market allocation of goods and services, outputs and inputs, it seems inevitable that people will come to recognize their social interconnections only through the commodities which are constantly supplied and demanded. Life becomes a process of buying and selling; and in our own conceptions of ourselves and others, human attributes take on a commodity-like meaning. For example, a pleasant smile becomes worth a certain sum of money in the labor market. Many years ago Karl Marx called this phenomenon "commodity fetishism."

But there is a small and growing recognition of trouble in paradise, of a possible monkey wrench in the engines of superabundance. It does seem, unfortunately, that this awareness is increasing, and will continue to increase, only because nature itself is forceably tearing the blinders from our eyes. As a result of current difficulties, some people are beginning to recognize that energy from any source will be limited and costly and that the earth's ecosystems, including climate and weather systems, are in delicate states of equilibrium which will probably be adversely affected by continued human intervention. All we can hope for—and work toward—is a rate of growth of popular awareness and action which is more rapid than actual ecosystem intervention and breakdown.

The point on which I would like to focus is that today in the United States we have not only an illusion of endless affluence, but in the history of economic thought there have been endless illusions of superaffluence. This kind of thinking began in the Enlightenment and proceeded to influence all major economists from Adam Smith to the present. I am referring, of course, to the utopian notion of the desirability of never-ending economic growth and technical progress, and of the ability of a rational humanity to overcome any obstacles to such "progress."

This is not to say that various impediments to economic growth have not been recognized by economic thinkers. In general, two kinds of obstacles have been discussed: social and natural. Exemplary thinkers falling into the first category includes Adam Smith and Karl Marx, and the latter T. R. Malthus, David Ricardo, and J. S. Mill. The writings of these men occurred in the century from the 1770s to the 1870s. It is to our detriment that the succeeding century, from the 1870s to the present, has lacked such creative and daring economists.

Marx and Smith shared the view that a vast amount of economic progress was possible within the framework of a capitalist economy but also agreed that the same economic relationships which originally promoted economic growth would someday bring it to a halt. For Adam Smith, economic growth would some far-off day become difficult because of the dual effects of expanding competition: first, increasing numbers of capitalists trying to sell growing volumes of commodities in limited markets would bid down prices while, second, these same capitalists would bid up wages by attempting to recruit enough workers to increase production. Caught in the closing vise of rising wage costs and declining prices, profits would fall to zero, net investment would cease, and so would economic growth. Smith called this resultant state of affairs the "stationary state".[2] It had arisen as a result of forces entirely endogenous to the society. Nature had played no role.

Marx concurred in seeing a passive role for nature. Nature would serve humankind more and more fully as human knowledge and productive powers developed. Marx thought of nature as the "inorganic body of man." This image appears again and again throughout Marx's works. In the 1844 *Manuscripts* he wrote:

> Physically man lives only on these products of nature, whether they appear in the form of food, heating, clothes, a dwelling, etc. The universality of man appears in practice precisely in the universality which makes all nature his *inorganic* body. . . . Man *lives* on nature . . . nature is his *body*, with which he must remain in continuous interchange if he is not to die (emphasis added).[3]

The *Grundrisse*, written some thirteen years after the *Manuscripts*, contains the same phrase, the earth as the individual's "inorganic body,"[4] and again, in *Capital*'s Volume I, ten years later Marx writes:

> Thus Nature becomes one of the organs of his activity, one that he annexes to his own bodily organs, adding stature to himself in spite of the Bible.[5]

The first point the metaphor confronts is the overall degree of interrelationship between humanity and nature. If we think of nature and humankind as circles, there are four possible relationships between the two. The most extreme is that they are entirely independent of each other. Neoclassical economic theory has generally operated as if this were so. Thus, ecosystems are considered irrelevant to economic activity; finite resources are termed a Malthusian fantasy and pollution becomes of real concern only when it impinges on one's personal health or convenience. This characterization also fits a significant number of Marxist intellectuals today, although

Marx and Engels are not themselves guilty of such ultra-anthropocentrism. Most important, the economic relations of capitalism operate on just this basis, as if there were no interconnection between nature and human activity beyond nature's presumed capacity to provide infinite portions of material resources to expand the Gross National Product.

A less extreme position is to permit an area of limited overlap between the circles of nature and human society. The more quick-footed of neoclassical economists fall into this camp. They have recently begun to see, as a result of public outcry and available research grants, that there exist substantial "external diseconomies" in some production processes and that the most significant of these reflect an interaction between nature and economic activity; for example, that the sulphur dioxide pouring out of electric power plants does not just "go away" but that it has a detrimental effect on human health. For their limited appreciation of natural processes they have equally limited solutions which, astoundingly, they view as virtual panaceas. The most frequently mentioned panacea is the imposition of a tax (or price) on pollution.

The third and fourth logically possible nature/humanity relationships both involve concentric circles, lying one within the other. Either nature is a part of humanity or humanity is a part of nature, depending upon which forms the outer circle. Both arrangements state correctly that nature and human society exist as mutually interacting opposites united in a solitary world. However, as in any dialectical relationship, we can determine which aspect is the principal one. This writer takes the position that natural and physical sciences demonstrate nature, the nonhuman universe, to be the ultimately dominant force which conditions and severely limits the scope of human activity. Marx, on the other hand, clearly took the opposing view, and it is reflected in his choice of an image of nature as the inorganic body of humanity rather than humankind as a part of the organic body of nature. As Maurice Dobb has indicated, the Marxian dialectic begins with nature and with humanity initially integrated therein. But because the human distinction is that we are conscious beings, we struggle with, against, and rise above nature, transforming it to our own purposes in the course of history.[6]

Marx's body image also makes it clear that nature exists to serve humanity as a body serves a person; that it has no independent existence but is subject to the control of human reason and consciousness; that it is to be mastered as in learning to walk. It also implies that nature cannot be a "thing-in-itself," that it is as knowable as a body, and that it is unlikely to stand in rigid opposition to the whole self. The "inorganic" modifier reminds one that Marx sees nature as an object, essentially dead, and it also suggests that nature is a source of raw materials as well as a tool used in production, in the form, for example, of agricultural land. Finally, the exploitation and alienation of capitalism is vividly portrayed by this image as the separation of working people from a part of their own bodies.

Given this concept of nature, the only forces left to stop growth would be the contradictions inherent within the capitalist economy. For one thing, the capitalist economy was seen as prone to increasingly severe crises of overproduction: the paradox of too many commodities and too many needy people with too little money to spend. Marx believed that, within this context, the business firms would become fewer and larger; the rich, fewer and wealthier; and the working class larger and more oppressed—until finally the laborers would revolt and bring about a socialist transformation.

Marx also agreed with Adam Smith that the rate of profit would tend to fall and become a barrier to economic growth in the long run. This state would occur because capitalists would be forced by competition to replace living labor with machines. But because only living labor produces surplus value, profit for the system as a whole would fall as a percentage of total investment. However, unlike Smith who seemed to think a long-term, stationary-state capitalism would result, Marx knew that no-growth capitalism was a contradiction in terms. Stagnant capitalism is capitalism at the end of the line. It would be replaced by a new system of economic relations based on common ownership of the factories, banks, natural resources, and means of distribution and transportation: socialism.

Marx argued that in a rationally-ordered socialist economy, with the aid of unlimited technical progress, economic growth could proceed forever, providing both superabundance and increased leisure for all. He thought it one of capitalism's most progressive features that more and more machines were used in production. Of course, within capitalist institutions this had to mean increased unemployment, but for socialism it would mean high levels of production and a much shorter working day. Marx's future society would be highly automated with people functioning in production as tenders of machines.[7] It is consistent with his view that while society could decide to stop growth, nature would not force this eventuality. Such is Marx's impossible utopia.

It is no accident that Marx's left-hand man, Friedrich Engels, explicitly rejected the second law of thermodynamics, also called the law of increasing entropy. This law holds that *all* energy used is ultimately degraded into waste heat. We now know that another century or two of continuous energy growth will raise world temperatures sufficiently to severely disrupt weather patterns, causing havoc with world agricultural production. Engels based his rejection of the second law on flimsy philosophic and scientific ground: because, on a cosmological scale, the second law predicts an end, it must therefore imply a beginning, and thus a Creator. Many modern cosmologists maintain, contrary to Engels, that the end of his particular universe, with its associated laws of nature, may well be followed by the beginning of another universe which evolves according to its own, perhaps different, laws. That our particular universe ends or had a beginning implies nothing regarding ultimate ends or beginnings.

Malthus and Ricardo did not see any irreconcilable contradictions within capitalism *per se*, but they did perceive certain difficulties in society's interactions with nature. Malthus first took an interest in the question when his conservative sensibilities were outraged by the optimistic visions of the eighteenth-century utopian philosophers Condorcet and William Godwin in which they foresaw a future of human perfection and ultimate happiness. Malthus believed that this faith of the Enlightenment in the ascendency of human reason failed to answer a very basic question: how is a continuously growing population to be fed? He began with the puzzling observation that while a fertile woman was capable of giving birth to, say, three daughters during her childbearing years, thereby presumably tripling the population every generation, actual population growth was observed to be quite low. The answer to this apparent paradox was found to lie in the restricted ability of nature to provide additional food. Agricultural production could be increased but only rather slowly compared to the potential geometric rate of population growth; and, although technological improvements could speed up production, in Malthus's view their contribution was neither continuous nor unlimited. Therefore, it followed logically that certain restraints were constantly acting on population to keep it in balance by means of a limited food supply. Malthus found these checks in war, starvation, disease, "bad nursing of children," and in such "vices" as adultery, prostitution, and sexual abstinence within marriage as well as in "improper arts" such as abortion or "unnatural" practices like birth control. The only check on population which received the Malthusian stamp of approval was "moral restraint" by which he meant refraining from both marriage and sex outside marriage.[8]

But Malthus was not referring to some population holocaust to come, as many think, nor even to a stationary-state economy. In his mechanical interpretation of the world, there could be no historical evolution, only constantly repeated oscillations. Within his model, both quantitative economic growth and capitalism could go on forever in spite of the continuously acting obstacles to population growth. His error, of course, was in failing to see that economic development, improved distribution of income, increased literacy, old-age economic security programs, and more equal treatment of women would lower birth rates dramatically. What remains of value in Malthus, besides a hint of diminishing returns, or limits to the powers of the earth, is an astonishingly accurate conception of the modern food/population dilemma. One does not need Malthus's specific population law to see that a continuously growing population (for whatever reasons) would require "the power of production in the earth to be absolutely unlimited."[9] It seemed inconceivable to Malthus that subsistence could "be increased every twenty-five years by a quantity equal to what the whole world at present produces."[10]

In arguing that food shortages would eventually be experienced even in such an immensely fertile land as the United States, Malthus uncovered an excellent conceptual framework not only for the food/population dilemma but for many ecological considerations:

> Where there are few people and a great quantity of fertile land, the power of the earth to afford a yearly increase of food may be compared to a great reservoir of water, supplied by a moderate stream. The faster the population increases, the more help will be got to draw off the water and consequently an increasing quantity will be taken every year. But the sooner, undoubtedly, will the reservoir be exhausted and the streams only remain. When acre has been added to acre, till all the fertile land is occupied, the yearly increase of food will depend on the amelioration of the land already in possession; and even this moderate stream will be gradually diminishing.[11]

The reservoir analogy can be extended in other directions; for example, fossil fuel reserves which are drawn down as economies grow. Soon, having used up this "geologic capital," we will be forced to live on the "stream" of energy income from the sun (solar energy).

The most important contribution of Malthus's discussion of the difficulties of increasing food production was the idea it gave to his brilliant contemporary, David Ricardo. Diminishing returns to the earth, not only to agricultural production but also to mining, would dramatically push up prices of such commodities. Consequently, unless higher wages were paid, the workers would not be able to buy sufficient food and coal to live and, as they died off, the supply of labor would be restricted and wages forced upward—thus leaving the surviving work force with the higher money wages necessary to cover the essentials of life. This meant that all capitalists not producing commodities related to the earth and therefore not subject to diminishing returns would find wage costs rising while prices of their products remained constant. Clearly, their profits would fall. But neither would agricultural and mining capitalists maintain (or increase) their profits because landowners would naturally charge higher rents for use of their land in order to reap the gains from rising prices for themselves.

The upshot is that diminishing returns to the earth eventually result in a falling profit rate and, by halting investment in new plants and equipment, they create a stationary-state economy. Like Adam Smith, Ricardo thought this extremity to be far in the future and not very desirable—but it was quite compatible with capitalism. J. S. Mill, who essentially agreed with Ricardo's analysis, was the first to point out that the stationary economy could well represent a higher form of social existence: one based on justice, equality, and human growth rather than on profit, inequality, and productive growth. Mill lamented the loss of solitude resulting from population growth. He went on to say:

> Nor is there much satisfaction in contemplating the world with nothing left to the spontaneous activity of nature; with every rood of land brought into cultivation . . .; every flowery waste or natural pasture ploughed up, all quadrupeds or birds which are not domesticated for man's use exterminated as his rivals for food, every hedgerow or superfluous tree rooted out. . . . If the earth must lose that great portion of its pleasantness which it owes to things that the unlimited increase of wealth and population would extirpate from it, for the mere purpose of enabling it to support a larger, but not a better or happier population, I sincerely hope, for the sake of posterity, that they will be content to be stationary long before necessity compels them to it.[12]

Echoing Smith and Marx, and rejecting Ricardian notions of limits, the dominant trend in current economic thought is profoundly optimistic. Neoclassical economists see the crisis of the ecosphere as a fairly uninteresting theoretical matter involving certain costs called "externalities" which are not reflected in the market or private decision making, but instead are inflicted on the public as pollution. They see the solution as a simple matter of "internalizing" the externalities; that is, identifying and acting on such reprehensible conditions by imposing financial penalties on those responsible. With such a system of pollution taxes, it is held, any adverse effect on the economy arising from environmental considerations could be handled with judgment and discrimination. Ecologists usually do not give such a notion of "environmental fine tuning" the dignity of a response. Popular as severe taxation of polluters would be, ecologists know better than anyone that the scientific ability to predict the future ecological impact and dollar costs of every product and technology does not exist. As for resource and energy limitations, economists of the right, left, and center agree that somehow technology will allow expansion to continue indefinitely. The lessons of the second law of thermodynamics, which holds that nothing in the universe is unending, have not yet been learned.

The Marxists share with Marx the confidence that the only problems are with capitalism itself. If technology is creating environmental problems, then it is due to the profit motive of corporations and the unplanned character of the market. The energy crisis is thought to be a fraud, something contrived by the multi-nationals who are withholding oil and gas supplies to increase their profits, to achieve price deregulation, to win tax credits and stave off tax reforms, and to get their way with new pipelines, refineries, liquid natural gas terminals, and environmental controls. Detrimental technologies like nuclear power are sometimes supposed by orthodox Marxists to be problems only under capitalism, as though they could be incorporated safely into a rational socialist economy. Economic growth would actually accelerate under socialism. The widely respected Belgian Marxist economist, Ernest Mandel, maintains that once rid of the unemployment and unplanned anarchy of capitalist economies, Western Europe and the United States could grow twice as fast as during the postwar experience.[13] This growth orientation of twentieth-century Marxists is buttressed by the fact that socialist-like transformations have as yet occurred only in underdeveloped Third World countries, countries which everyone would admit are much in need of economic growth. Yet an age-old—but still important—debate among Marxists centers on whether socialism can really exist under conditions of severe underdevelopment. Ironically, it seems easier to achieve a major social transformation in underdeveloped, neo-colonized countries but much harder, perhaps, to make that transformation truly socialist. Nevertheless, it is a frequent practice of the Left to confuse conditions in the overdeveloped capitalist countries with those in the Third World.

One of the greatest of mainstream economists, John Maynard Keynes, shared with Marx a vision of a better future built upon a foundation of vast material abundance. In Keynes's words:

I see us free, thererore, to return to some of the more sure and certain principles of religion and traditional virtue—that avarice is a vice, that the exaction of usury is a misdemeanour, and the love of money is detestable, that those walk most truly in the paths of virtue and sane wisdom who take least thought for the morrow. We shall once more value ends above means and prefer the good to the useful. We shall honor those who can teach us how to pluck the hour and the day virtuously and well, the delightful people who are capable of taking direct enjoyment in things, the lilies of the field who toil not, neither do they spin.[14]

However, the immediate realization of this vision is not for us, said Keynes, using an argument similar to Stalin's position on the need for continuing sacrifice by Soviet workers:

But beware! The time for all this is not yet. For at least another hundred years we must pretend to ourselves and to everyone that fair is foul and foul is fair; for foul is useful and fair is not. Avarice and usury and precaution must be our gods for a little longer still. For only they can lead us out of the tunnel of economic necessity into daylight.[15]

Fortunately or unfortunately, this utopia of superabundance will never be—whether capitalist or communist. And it is the ecologists and geophysicists who are arguing this case—certainly not the economists. The great increase in economic production that *has* occurred in the forty years since Keynes wrote was realized only by mortgaging the future of humanity. The energy necessary to produce the rapid increase in the Gross National Product since World War II was provided by readily accessible—and therefore cheap—stocks of irreplaceable petroleum and natural gas. These domestic supplies have been largely exhausted,[16] and for what? The American Dream! What will be our reputation among the generations who come after us? And what of the environmental costs of such economic growth and energy waste? Increasingly, serious scientists are speaking of possible near-term inadvertent alterations in climate and weather patterns.

With the consecutively devastating winters of 1976-77, 1977-78, and 1978-79, one begins to wonder if the earth is entering a new ice age; perhaps we are contributing to it with airborne particulate pollution or offsetting it with waste heat and a human-induced "greenhouse effect." There are no good answers to either question, but, most sobering, there is mounting evidence that human economic activity is reaching an order of magnitude comparable to natural processes and is thus capable of altering delicate balances of destabilizing natural cycles. According to one study:

> Human input of oil to the oceans exceeds natural seepage by perhaps twentyfold. Human activities have increased the atmospheric content of carbon dioxide by ten percent since the turn of the century. Roughly five percent of the energy captured by photosynthesis on earth now flows through agricultural ecosystems supporting the metabolic consumption of humans and their domestic animals. The flows of many metals and chemicals through industrial society exceed the natural flows of these materials through the biosphere. Heat released by human activities in urban regions of thousands of square miles is equivalent to five percent or more of the incident of solar energy falling upon those regions. Such figures do not prove that disaster is upon us, but they are cause for concern. In terms of the scale of disruption mankind in the second half of the twentieth century is for the first time operating on a level at which global balances could hinge on its mistakes. Human knowledge of the threshholds by no means matches the human capacity for rushing toward them.[17]

In other words, Ricardo was right, and dramatically so. He was correct in ways he could never have dreamed. There *are* diminishing returns to human domination of the earth which may go far beyond the economic. But the economic effects themselves are likely to prove powerful enough. We can expect more and more output to be channeled into unproductive sectors of the economy which merely attempt to offset the damage done by growing production itself: into pollution control, general health care, and occupational health and safety.

When I term this expenditure "unproductive," I mean that it does not increase growth or profits for the economy as a whole. Neither do additional expenditures of money and resources for acquiring more expensive sources of energy such as geothermal, solar, or nuclear, nor is it productive to increase spending for deeper oil and gas wells or for liquifying gas or gasifying coal. As Ricardo stated, the effect will be to reduce the funds available for other uses; profits will decline, investment funds for expansion will diminish, and growth will slow. Nor will industry alone be affected. We are already seeing government agencies economize through a reduction in social services.

The "era of limits" politics will become the order of the day. The only question will be, who is to suffer the cuts: business or labor? consumers or producers? rich or poor? the United States and other developed nations or the Third World? Everyone will come to accept economic planning as a means to increase economic efficiency; but that statement suggests another question: by and for whom? Will we continue to have socialism for the rich and free enterprise for the poor? The answer is probably in the affirmative. In all likelihood there will probably be tremendous pressure to increase subsidies going to business for energy and for environmental protection.

But in my estimation Marx was also correct. A capitalist economy characterized by a low and falling rate of profit is in real trouble. No-growth capitalism, in effect, is no capitalism. This fact is so for both macroeconomic and microeconomic reasons. On the macro level, when economic growth stops, so too does the growth of employment. Today, the economy must increase about 4 percent each year in order to prevent unemployment from rising. In other words, in the capitalist macroeconomy one must run to stand still. On the micro level, capitalist firms exist for the sole purpose of maximizing profits which, once made, are reinvested so as to increase output and to make more profit. In a no-growth/little-profit future economy, individual companies could grow and increase profits only to the extent that other firms shrink and lose money. The capitalist class as a whole reaps very small profits for which there are few profitable investment outlets. Even luxury consumption would likely be difficult because the government might have to confine production to necessities in a stationary-state economy.

The American Dream has fueled the consumer fires which have helped to keep the economic treadmill turning. In the Ricardian world we are now entering, the American Dream is becoming a policy maker's nightmare in yet another sense. The bloated suburban, automobile-based, individualistic consumption standard is becoming too expensive for an economy that must raise ever more funds for environmental controls and energy investments. Nuclear power, as noted earlier, may be profitable to the firms involved, but its enormous capital costs place a great deal of strain on money markets. It is in this context that we can explain the move to increased apartment living, condominiums, fast-food "dining," laundromats, and mass transit. They are economically more efficient ways of providing a semblance of the American Dream to young people not yet weaned of its lure.

So what is the solution? It would seem that, unlike Smith, Malthus, or Ricardo, Marx was right when he maintained that socialism alone could solve the problems engendered during the capitalist period of history. His socialism envisaged a completely new, fully democratic society which was to be based on production for human needs rather than on profits, thereby replacing the marketplace with popularly-determined decentralized planning. But, unlike Marx and most Marxists today, I think it is clear that the new society must be based on the stationary-state economy. We must learn to live with nature rather than conquer it; we must take as little and return as much as we can and still remain tolerably comfortable; we must accept more of what nature offers and in the form in which it is provided instead of trying constantly to bend natural things to our will. Such a stationary-state socialist society will be frugal but it need not be primitive and unhappy. On the contrary, much as Keynes imagined, it will reopen paths to the pursuit of simple pleasures which have been lost for the majority of people since the advent of capitalism.

Keynes's lilies of the field metaphor is actually quite inapplicable because work will be necessary in such a society, but it will be meaningful labor which encourages individual growth and expresses the cooperative social bonds between people. Moreover, the work will be of a kind which does not alienate the worker, freely chosen, thus representing democracy extended to the economic sector. There will also be much more leisure time because production will be minimized rather than maximized. The logic of the stationary state is that once an agreed-upon level of material well-being is established, all effort should be directed to maintaining that scale with a minimal measure of actual economic production; for example, by making sure that what is produced lasts just as long as possible, requires the least amount of energy to operate, and is capable of being shared among the greatest number of people. Time spent outside production would not only be devoted to lily-like simple pleasures but also to study of the great human questions: why are we here? where did we come from? what is our fate as a species as well as that of the universe? what are the building blocks of matter? Science has made some great strides toward elucidating these mysteries; but think of what will be possible when, instead of being the preserve of a tiny minority of professionals, these questions become the daily sustenance of an entire human species, highly educated and curious and, moreover, with the time to devote to such pursuits.

The stationary-state reasoning is frequently criticized for implying that the largest segment of humanity, the world's poor, would be frozen at their present intolerably low standards of living. It implies no such thing. The stationary-state concept stresses first and foremost the necessity of distributive justice. When the economic pie is no longer growing, the way it is sliced becomes the paramount concern. This is another reason why only socialism with its stress on equal distribution of income is compatible with a stationary economy. The necessity of distributive justice is international as well as national, and in today's growing world economy, the underdeveloped countries fall farther and farther behind the overdeveloped ones. In the stationary state, the previously overdeveloped countries would stop growing and reduce to a minimum their already disproportionate share of nonrenewable energy and materials. This step would leave considerable opportunity for previously underdeveloped countries to raise standards of living and narrow the disparity. Equally significant, with the multinational corporations removed from their economies, they

would be free to take meaningful advantage of such an opportunity.

It may seem that I am proposing another utopia, as unre-
alizable as the American Dream and, indeed, perhaps I am. But
there is a difference: the American Dream—that illusion of
endless affluence—is on the decline. It has no enduring
viability because it violates recognized laws of nature and it is
that characeristic which makes it truly utopian.[18] The stationary
state, on the other hand, will become a reality precisely because of those same natural laws; that is to say, the plundering
of the earth will come to an end, one way or another, inten-
tionally or perhaps catastrophically. But will the end of economic growth mark the end of the human species? Or the
beginning of a new barbarism? Or the creation of a democratic,
human, stationary-state socialism? I think these are the
choices. If the last of these alternatives is to be realizable instead of utopian, two influences are required: (1) that the inherent structural forces I have outlined push us in that direction, and (2) that people join together and actively exercise
their free will to bring about an intentional stationary state.

Perhaps it all comes down to a matter of faith. Not faith in
an abstract God or in some kind of personal salvation, but faith
in our kind: that we will exercise our will, our social consciousness, and our sense of human solidarity in order to avoid
becoming a short-lived, unique species which perished because it destroyed the ecological niche which gave it a place in
the universe.

4

The Russian Utopia

FRANK M. BARTHOLOMEW

'I believe in Russia. I believe in the Greek Orthodox
Church. I-I believe in the body of Christ—I believe that the
second coming will take place in Russia—I believe—' Shatov
murmured in a frenzy.
'But in God? In God?'
'I-I shall believe in God.'

—F.M. Dostoevsky, *The Devils*.

Western man has long been captivated by utopian
ideas. Ancient cultures contained myths about the
existence at the dawn of history of a perfect society
where all men's needs were satisfied without struggle, suffering, or property worries. Yet it was Christianity that provided
Europeans with the popular belief that social perfection would
again be reestablished here on earth through divine intervention. These notions are most fully stated in the Book of Revelation's prophecy that Jesus Christ would soon descend from the
heavens to lead an apocalyptic struggle against the forces of
the Antichrist, with the result the establishment of His personal
dominion on earth for a thousand years. At the close of this
millennium the Antichrist would renew his attack on the
forces of good, only to suffer a second, fatal defeat. God himself
would then appear to conduct a Final Judgment of all men who
had ever lived. Those who passed divine scrutiny would be

allowed to live in eternal bliss on earth with God, who would do away with all human suffering: "And God shall wipe away all tears from their eyes; and there shall be no more death, neither sorrow nor crying, neither shall there be any more pain; for the former things are passed away."[1]

Greek missionaries spread these expectations of a theocratic utopia among the Russian people centuries after they had ceased to be prominent in the West. The historical consequences of this conversion proved to be profound and far-reaching. First, utopian thought was never elitist in that country: the masses themselves became accustomed to expect the glorious reordering of life in Eastern Europe as part of a global transfiguration. In time, biblical pronouncements were confused with earthly desire in the peasant imagination, and the millennium was equated with mass freedom and land redistribution. Nineteenth-century socialists eventually rejected the concept of theocracy, while incorporating peasant aspirations into their secular plans. Thus religious millennium became socialist utopia: man would create a perfect society, not God. Indeed, the popular sources of the socialist call for revolution largely explain why only left-wing parties gathered any mass following during the revolutionary events of 1917-18.

A second result of this biblical legacy was that the Russian masses were accustomed to think of violent upheaval as a precondition for realizing social well-being. Revelation had spoken of enemies "slain by the sword," people "cast alive into a lake of fire," and "fowls filled with flesh"; while the Russian peasantry gave substance to these predictions in repeated uprisings against the landowning nobility, who were accused of serving the Antichrist.[2] In this way, the peasant imagination transformed apocalypse into class struggle, just as it had transformed the millennium into land seizure. Eventually, modern revolutionaries were greatly aided by this mass readiness to use force to realize social goals.

Finally, the religious background of the revolutionary urge to realize a Russian utopia also influenced the mentality of later radicals. Russian activists were more likely to seem like religious zealots of past centuries than contemporary Europeans. Almost all scholars of the revolutionary movement agree on this point. As British scholar Hugh Seton-Watson has stated the matter: "It has often been pointed out that when young Russians lost their religious faith, they seldom became rationalist sceptics, as was usual among their contemporaries in north-western Europe, but carried into their atheist beliefs and their doctrines of social revolution a religious fervor, and in many cases a personal saintliness, which recall to western minds the age of medieval heresies or the religious wars."[3] The millenarian tradition encouraged these men to conceive of a future society in absolutistic terms. They were not seeking less suffering, less hunger, less injustice, or less cruelty, but *none at all*. Since the loftiness of that vision remained unchanged from medieval times, so did the intensity of the quest. It was "religion in the reverse," to use Vladimir Wiedlé's apt phrase: "And the terrorists it formed were often ascetical and pure-minded, saints of the black halo and blood-stained dagger."[4]

Yet if the frantic search for a millennial utopia through apocalyptic violence remained surprisingly unchanged over the centuries, Russian history has supplied many more examples of the latter than the former. This tragic fact explains why apocalypticism has outlived utopian yearning in the Soviet Union. Today, Russians seem to have quite prosaic expectations regarding the future: they expect to see neither the divine government promised by Revelation, nor the stateless utopia predicted by Karl Marx. But the fear of impending crisis persists unabated among Soviet dissidents; and visitors to eastern Europe regularly note popular apprehensions of nuclear holocaust, invasions by Asian hordes, or a new German *Drang nach Osten*. Of course, these fears are scarcely unrealistic. Life has never been easy for the Russian people, and now the entire world seems to be moving towards multiple catastrophes. Only Russians no longer exercise a monopoly over gloomy presentments; nor are they unique in their doubts concerning the possibility of religious or secular millenniums following a modern apocalypse.

Those expectations of the Second Coming first seem to have reached the common people during the age of Mongol domination, 1240-1480. It was then that the Russian masses began their perennial search for signs of the Antichrist, whose brief reign was supposed to precede those solemn events predicted by Revelation. Any unpopular ruler, foreign or domestic, was likely to be considered Satan in disguise, touching off a wave of frantic preparations for the Second Advent. Peasants abandoned their crops in the field, slaughtered their animals, and built coffins in which to rest in anticipation of the end of the world. The fact that Jesus failed to appear never dampened apocalyptic hopes. Christ's absence was usually ascribed to miscalculation and new computations were undertaken. Especially important in the millenarian numerology was the number, 666, which the Book of Revelation had called the mark of the beast, that is, the Antichrist. Woe to the ruler in whose reign sixes played a prominent role, like Alexis Mikhailovich, who was reigning in 1666, since he was likely to be accused of being the Antichrist and to encounter widespread difficulties as a result of this allegation![5]

The theological background of these attitudes is not difficult to reconstruct, although certain items are subject to controversy. The Roman Catholic Church had begun to discourage millenarian fervor in the third and fourth centuries in favor of the promise of individual resurrection immediately following death. Subsequently, heavenly salvation replaced world transfiguration in the western hierarchy of goals,[6] but the Eastern Church never followed this theological reorientation. So the expectation of the Second Coming was still strong among those Greek churchmen who introduced Eastern Orthodoxy into Russia at the close of the tenth century and who continued to dominate the Russian episcopacy until the Mongol armies of Batu Khan brought eccesiastical change in their wake. Not only did control of the Russian Church then pass to native clergy due to shattered ties with Constantinople, but the church structure also spread to the rural hinterlands for the first time, thereby bringing about the belated Christianization of the popular masses.[7] One of the results of that conversion was a mass preoccupation with the Second Coming.

It is possible that apocalyptic religion was more in keeping with the pagan traditions of the Russion people than the sacramental rites of Greek Orthodoxy, which were more oriented towards personal salvation. Though not much has survived from that pre-Christian heritage, scholars generally agree that a pervasive animism existed. The pagan was surrounded by supernatural forces, such as sacred trees, magical rocks, miracle-working springs, wood spirits, and water nymphs, most of which were apparently benevolent, as might be expected among an agrarian people.[8] Given this familiarity with a world where divine beings lived among men, it is likely that early converts were attracted to those religious texts that told of Christ's return to earth, especially since the Second Coming promised a social perfection that pagan deities had never provided.

The idea of a *Holy Russia* would seem to reflect this same pagan inclination to deify this world. Early in the Christian era, Russians began to conceive of their country as coterminous with true Christendom. Russian rulers were routinely canonized, whether they displayed any visible religiosity or not, simply because their political position made them defenders of the Christian heartland.[9] Since this practice was not common to the Byzantine Empire from which Russia received its religion, it would seem to reflect native tradition rather than foreign influences. A convenient explanation for this phenomenon can again be found in that same pagan disposition to view the surrounding world as the mystical abode of divine spirits.

This feeling of uniqueness was reinforced by the Turkish conquest of Constantinople in 1453. Russians believed that the Second Rome, Byzantium, had been destroyed by God because of its efforts to reconcile itself with the western church, and they were soon talking about their own country as the Third Rome, the Eternal Rome, which would last until the end of the world. Russian princes proceeded to adapt the Roman emblem, the imperial title of Tsar, Byzantine court pageantry, and even to relate their lineage to a mythical brother of Augustus Caesar![10] Yet, in doing so, the Russian court tended to stress the saintliness and durability of the present order at the expense of a notion of imminent transformation through the Second Coming, thereby weakening the latter tradition in official circles.

The Church Schism of 1666-67 had a similar impact on the millenarian movement. Patriarch Nikon and his assistants wanted to bring Russian religious texts, ritual and liturgy into line with Greek practices, which seemed especially appropriate at a time when Russian rulers were beginning to regard themselves as the defenders of all Orthodox Christians. The problem was that many Russians felt that foreigners should be imitating them, not vice versa, because Russia had higher claims to holiness. Those that bolted the church over this question became known as *raskolniki*, and they tended to take much of the millenarian fervor along with them. The official church subsequently placed less stress on the Second Coming and millenarian promise, while the schismatics became obsessed with the matter, viewing the church reformers and their government protectors as instruments of the Antichrist who had now taken control of the world just prior to the reappearance of Christ as prophesied in the Book of Revelation.[11]

The raskoliniki were not just a marginal group of religious fanatics. The group grew in numbers, rather than diminishing, and its members helped spawn other millenarian sects, until perhaps twenty million Russians were found on the side of non-conformity at the close of the nineteenth century.[12] Latter-day dissent took many forms, such as milk-drinking during fasts, spirit-wrestling, and castration. But the common element, insofar as one existed, was the belief that Christ would soon return to earth to live among his people in peace, harmony, and contentment.[13] The political situation was certainly volatile with so many Russians awaiting the Second Coming with suspicions that the present ruler was the Antichrist.

The Russian government first received news of the lawless activities of a renegade cossack, Stenka Razin, while the Church Council of 1666-67 was passing that monumental legislation which drove the raskolniki into rebellion. Razin managed to elude the Tsar's forces for the next three years, during which time he became a popular hero among the Volga masses thanks to his generosity and swagger. Then Razin's tactics suddenly changed in 1670 when he summoned the masses to seize their freedom, take the land, destroy the nobility and establish self-government. The response was immediate and far-reaching. Vast areas of Russia soon flared into open revolt. And a religious fever gripped the masses during all this vandalism and murder, as the following description of Razin's entry into Astrakhan clearly shows:

> An apocalyptic frenzy had seized the city, whose inhabitants looked for signs which, according to the prophetic tradi-

tion, would herald the approach of the millennium. Men reported a strange shaking of the earth beneath their feet, and it was said that the night before Razin's coming an eerie ringing of bells sounded from the Cathedral of the Blessed Virgin. To a superstitious people these omens betokened imminent redemption![14]

Razin began his revolt in the name of the ruling monarch, Alexis, whose life was supposedly being threatened by the aristocracy because of his sympathy for the common people. Alexis's forceful denunciation of the rebellion apparently forced Razin to abandon this tactic and to claim that he had the People's Tsar in his camp. Adherents were required to take an oath of allegiance to the pretender, who was alleged to be Tsar Alexis's son, the report of whose recent death the rebels represented as having been false. The People's Tsar, in turn, dutifully counselled his subjects to persevere in their noble struggle. So great was the reaction to this summons that tens of thousands of rebels had to be shot, quartered, decapitated, hung, impaled and mutilated before the government could restore order.

The Razin revolt contained the recurrent ideology of peasant uprisings in Russia. The existing ruler, or a legitimate claimant, attempts to defend the common people against the aristocracy who react by attempting to assassinate the people's defender. The plot proves unsuccessful and the People's Tsar goes into hiding while the aristocracy announce his death from natural causes. Eventually, the popular hero returns to lead the people against the common enemy, the landed nobility and government officials, whose defeat will guarantee freedom, land, and self-government under a Christ-like sovereign![15]

The peasant ideology was an obvious reworking of the legend of Christ's Second Coming: the agents of evil unsuccessfully try to kill the Savior who returns to vanquish his enemies and establish a reign of justice on earth. It was a claim that allowed the cossack leadership of these rebellions to sanctify their cause and prepare for the legitimate transfer of power. Yet it was also designed to exploit existing religious attitudes. The lower classes readily confused a popular rebellion with the apocalypse. The end of the world seemed imminent; the millennium at hand. Soon the peasant would enjoy freedom from serfdom, abundant land, self-government and social justice. Such was the nature of the peasant's perfect society; such was his millennium. It was a pastoral utopia that mixed earthly desire with biblical prophecy. The fact that schismatics played an increasingly visible role in these disturbances suggests that they also understood the millenarian significance of these peasant disturbances.

The nineteenth century saw the rise of secular inquiries into the nature of social perfection in Russia. The evolution of this new speculation is usually divided into three phases prior to the rise of Russian Marxism: the Decembrist movement, 1816-25; the first-generation socialists of the 1840's; and the second-generation socialists of the 1860's and 1870's. While each phase roughly corresponds to the contemporary thought of the west—or the Enlightenment, romanticism, and post-romantic materialism respectively—each also bears the peculiar mark of those millenarian-peasant ideas already examined. The Decembrists were clearly transitional in this respect, with western constitutionalism overshadowing indigenous elements. But later radicals returned to the notion that a violent struggle between the forces of good and evil would produce a new social order of peace and freedom. Apocalypse was transformed into revolution; and millennium became utopia, without the essential nature of the rural dream being altered.

The Decembrists were a group of fairly prominent young nobles who unsuccessfully attempted to transform Russia into a constitutional state by means of a military *putsch* in 1825. They were committed to those familiar ideas of life, liberty and the pursuit of happiness that eighteenth-century thinkers had popularized on both sides of the Atlantic. Unfortunately, this unanimity rapidly disappeared when the Decembrists began to consider specific goals and tactics. The northern branch leaned towards an American model, including thirteen states, constitutional liberties, a lower house with delegates allotted by population, and an upper house with members apportioned by state for six-year terms. Since the program also involved making the Russian Emperor a salaried official without bloodshed, emancipating the peasantry without offense to either serf or master, and developing the Russian economy without strain or stress, even this modest plan can be called utopian, at least, in the secondary sense of the word: glorious but farfetched.[16]

The southern branch favored a program that demanded more comprehensive change. Its author, Paul Pestel, conceived of a semi-communistic utopia twenty years before that term entered the Russia vocabulary. Roughly half of the land in Russia was to remain public property after Pestel's proposed emancipation of the peasantry in order to guarantee a livelihood to the common people, even if they were not successful in competing in the marketplace. Pestel's project contained other remarks that reflected a precocious concern for the evils of urbanization, the threat of concentrated wealth and the Jewish question. This final interest was probably as political as it was cultural, because Pestel believed that ethnic differences created instability within a state. After the Jews and Poles were given the chance to establish their political independence, the other minorities were to be forcibly assimilated so that Russia would contain only one religion, one language, and one law.[17]

If the southerners were closer than the northerners to later generations of radicals in their wish for a thoroughgoing reorganization of society, they were also closer to the earlier peasant tradition. The basic unit of social life was to remain the village, since cities were regarded as evil places. The peasant was to obtain much of that land for which he had struggled for generations; while popular intolerance of minorities, especially Jews, was to be institutionalized by complete Russification of the country. But it should be noted that neither wing of the Decembrists was particularly sympathetic towards peasant rebellion. Both southerners and northerners were much too genteel to accept the notion of mass violence that was so central to rural tradition.

Textbooks usually focus upon a small number of men when they discuss the radical utopias of the eighteen-forties: Vissarion Belinsky, Michael Bakunin, Alexander Herzen, the Petrashevsky Circle, and the Slavophiles. Except for the final group, most of these men called themselves socialists, by which they meant, among other things, that they rejected laissez-faire economics, rule by the rich, and extremes of wealth and poverty. This label also signified that they believed that a comprehensive reorganization of society was necessary if all were to enjoy material well-being, emotional security and political expression. Finally, all seem to have been influenced by the village millennium which had dominated the peasant imagination for so long.

The Slavophiles were a small group of prominent thinkers from those same Romantic Forties who helped turn the attention of contemporary radicals to the virtues of the Russian Village. They distrusted officials, the nobility, cities, Jews and the West, and they wished to ruralize their society by making the local parish the basic unit of social life. But they were not exactly liberals, because they were opposed to constitutions as being foreign to Russian tradition; and they were not socialists, since they rejected schemes calling for a redistribution of wealth. Yet they were definitely utopians, because they thought that social perfection could be attained in a rural setting where men lived in social equality, religious brotherhood, and shared well-being. In this ambience, the Slavophiles imagined that Christian love would solve all problems of economic injustice.[18]

Belinsky, Bakunin, Herzen, and Petrashevsky, unlike the Slavophiles, were militant atheists who ridiculed such thinking. But, with the possible exception of Belinsky who died early in life, all were directly indebted to the Slavophiles for their ideas about the rural structure of a utopian society. Bakunin and Herzen share the honor of having devised the Populist doctrine, which dominated the socialist movement for generations prior to 1917. The Populists maintained that the Russian peasant was a socialist by instinct, since the village, not the individual, generally controlled agricultural lands which were periodically redistributed among families in accordance with their changing size. Thanks to this tradition, it was argued, the task of introducing socialism in Russia would be much simpler than in the West. If the government and its supporting nobility were overthrown—and this was a job for which the peasant was well-trained—Russia would dissolve into its constituent villages where socialist cooperation was an established way of life. "A free association of free associations" was the slogan that Populists employed to describe their anarchist utopia, which was a collectivist version of the world that peasant rebels had sought for untold generations.[19]

Though the ties between the Populists and the Petrashevsky Circle are real and important, they had generally been ignored by scholars. Michael Petrashevsky played host to a group of talented young men who met each Friday to discuss plans for social reform until the government terminated their speculations with wholesale arrests. Petrashevsky and many of his guests desired a society composed of rural communities much like those sought by Populist and Slavophile ideologues. It is true that the internal structure of those model settlements was generally taken from the thought of Charles Fourier, a rather eccentric French socialist, who looked forward to a new age of free love, domesticated tigers, and lemon-flavored oceans. But the Petrashevists never talked about those humorous theories of the French master. For them, the Fourierist phalanstery was essentially a place where men were well-fed, well-clothed and comfortably housed; where all were handsomely rewarded for the work, talent and capital that they contributed to the common cause; and where members were placed in occupations that were suited to their personal needs. Finally, all of this was to be realized in villages containing no more than two thousand people who enjoyed self-government.[20]

An interesting aspect of Russian thought during the eighteen-forties is that, as the hopes of social theorists began to approximate more closely the aspirations of the peasant masses, so did their expectations of apocalyptic upheaval. It is not surprising that Ivan Aksakov, a Slavophile, would see a shattering confrontation approaching between Russia and the West, since he and his associates believed that Western Civilization represented the antithesis of Christian brotherhood, spirituality, and goodness which found their purest expression in Russia.[21] But it does seem somewhat incongruous that left-wing atheists would employ biblical imagery to describe the social revolution they saw hovering before the Russian Empire. For example, Herzen noted:

This will be neither judgement nor vengeance, but a cataclysm, a revolution. This lava, these barbarians, this new world, these Nazarenes, advancing to end the senile and impotent, and to clean the way for the fresh and the new, is closer than you think. You see, it is they who are dying from hunger, from cold, murmuring overhead and underneath, in the attics and cellars, at the moment that we, *au premier*, drinking champagne, discuss socialism.[22]

Bakunin expressed this same mood in one of his most famous statements on revolution:

. . . even in Russia the dark storm clouds are gathering! The air is heavy with storms!

And therefore we call to our blinded brothers: Repent! Repent! The Kingdom of God is coming nigh.

Let us put our trust in the eternal spirit which destroys and annihilates only because it is the unsearchable and eternally creative source of all life. The passion for destruction is also a creative passion.[23]

But it was Michael Petrashevsky who conjured up the most faithful apocalyptic images. In his most substantial propaganda effort, the *Pocket Dictionary of Foreign Words*, the Russian Fourierist buried an ideological message deeply inside an entry entitled "Oratorio" in an effort to escape the watchful eye of the censor. The word of love and freedom, so the article affirms, had been proclaimed long ago in the Roman province of Judea. It was then that man renounced all thought of mine and yours; it was then that a simple parable showed that each human has an equal right to nature's treasures. But Christ's temerity did not go unpunished; and his death was accompanied by ominous signs that can only be recaptured in music. At this juncture, Petrashevsky begins quoting St. Matthew on the Second Coming, which he observes is a theme well-suited for oratorio:

For as the lightning cometh out of the east, and shineth even unto the west; so shall also the coming of the Son of Man be.

For wheresoever the carcass is, there will the eagles be gathered together.

Immediately after the tribulation of those days shall the sun be darkened and the moon shall not give her light, and the stars shall fall from heaven, and the powers of the heavens shall be shaken.

And then shall appear the sign of the Son of Man in heaven: and then shall all the tribes of the earth mourn, and they shall see the Son of Man coming in the clouds of heaven with power and great glory.

And he shall send his angels with a great sound of a trumpet, and they shall gather together his elect from the four winds, from one end of heaven to the other.[24]

Alexander Balasoglo was one of the regular participants in Petrashevsky's weekly discussions of political and social questions. An archivist at the Ministry of Foreign Affairs, he never achieved the great fame of such members of the group as F. Dostoevsky, N. Danilevsky and M. Saltykov-Shchedrin. But he did leave a most stirring description of the Russian apocalypse to haunt the minds of the Petrashevists. The world, according to Balasoglo, was in a state of moral turpitude: no one cared about morality or religion; humans distrusted one another; and man put his faith only in money. The fateful hour of collapse was at hand: "Wars will break out, orators will incite people to butcher, to destroy taverns, to rape women, to dismember nobles and officials; foreigners will be torn to pieces."[25] At the same time, the Empire's minorities will establish their independence at the cost of great bloodshed. Not only will the Poles, Ukrainians and Caucasian peoples claim their independence, but the Asian groups will rise to attack Russia. Nor will the troubles end there: "And then, when throughout Russia will wander bands of new Razins and Pugachevs, who will make themselves generals, the English will seize under cover both the American colonies and Kamchatka, grab the Amur, and spill over into Russia the entire mob of Eastern Asia."[26]

It is not difficult to guess why the utopian compositions of radical socialists were filled with the apocalyptic refrains of popular culture. All these men had been raised in a belief-value system that stressed that an apocalyptic struggle would precede the Christian millennium. Since they retained their yearning for social perfection on earth, even when they came to doubt the prophecies of the Bible, it was quite natural that they would continue to expect the new world to undergo a baptism of fire. Likewise, the rural setting of the Russian utopia accorded not only with peasant tradition, but also with demographic realities in a country where 80 to 90 percent of all Russians lived in villages. It was essentially just a matter of applying familiar attitudes and images to new inquiries into the nature of social perfection.

Both Balasoglo and Petrashevsky were arrested during the political reaction that followed the European revolutions of 1848-49. In Russia, the repression continued with changing intensity until the Emancipation of 1861, when the peasantry was set free with a land settlement which left neither them nor their sympathizers satisfied. The intellectual discontent that was elicited by peasant reforms began a new chapter in the history of Russian radicalism. Angry young men ceased simply talking about the use of force and the possibility of mobilizing the masses, and they began to carry guns, throw bombs, and agitate among workers and peasants for revolutionary action. The tone of the new era was set forth by an anonymous proclamation that appeared in 1862, entitled *Young Russia*, in which the author described what would happen if the government offered opposition to the forces of revolution: ". . . with full faith in ourselves and our strength, in the people's sympathy with us, in the glorious future of Russia, to whose lot it has fallen to be the first country to achieve the glorious work of socialism, we will utter a single cry: 'To the axe!' "[27]

Earlier ideologists had generally come from well-to-do families, as did Bakunin and Herzen, or from professional backgrounds, as in the case of Belinsky and Petrashevsky. By contrast, the newcomers were socially more diverse, frequently coming from the working-class, peasantry, and church community. This change in recruitment clearly had an impact on the socialist movement. Not only does it help to explain why revolutionary tactics became more violent, but also why demands for social justice became more uncompromising. The earlier generation of radicals now seemed too moderate, too willing to waste time in talk, and too ready for compromise. Chernyshevsky, a priest's son who became the most renowned revolutionary of his generation, called Herzen a bore after their only meeting in London; while another priest's son turned radical, Dobroliubov, told Ivan Turgenev the very same thing when they met at the home of a mutual friend.[28] Herzen captured in turn the reaction of his peers to these younger dissidents when he characterized them as the "bilious ones."[29] Only Bakunin seemed capable of bridging the gap between the two groups, no doubt because of his personal fame, years in prison and irrepressible love for revolution.

Yet such differences were more apparent than real. It is true that many of the older generaton, including Herzen, were now more willing to accept gradual change, while many more of the younger men were involved in armed conspiracy. But the village utopia sought by the men of the forties was still the principal goal of radicals during the sixties and seventies when Populism dominated left-wing politics. Likewise, the vision of an apocalypse remained strong, though now it was not expressed in such biblical terms. For example, Chernyshevsky wrote about the peasantry:

> . . . dominated by primitive prejudices and by blind hatred for anything different from their own barbaric habits, they do not distinguish between the members of a class who wear different clothes and will spare neither our science, nor our poetry, nor our arts; they will destroy our civilization.[30]

While elsewhere he noted: "We shall soon have a revolution, and if it happens, I'll certainly take part in it."[31]

Sergei Nechaev, a working-class youth who was illiterate until the age of sixteen, expressed the same expectation of violent destruction with a troubling intensity:

> At the close of the ninth anniversary of its newly conceived slavery, in 1870, on the jubilee of Razin and Pugachev, this well-conceived hatred will burst forth upon the aristocracy, wallowing in corruption and baseness. Let live the hangman, ravager, and tormentor of our people, who dares to call himself its liberator—let him live until that time, that minute, when a popular storm erupts, when the common people tortured by him, awakening from a long, fitful sleep, solemnly pronounces its sentence upon him, when the free peasant, breaking the bonds of slavery, immediately smashes his head with its hated crown on the day of the people's reprisal.[32]

And a letter to Alexander III from his father's assassins, the People's Will, shows just how irresistible these young men considered the revolutionary tide:

> It is impossible to exterminate all the people or to do away with discontent by enforcing repression; indeed, this will only make it grow. And it is this that makes new elements rise from the people in ever increasing numbers to take the place of those who have been killed; and it is this that gives life to ever more energetic and violent passions.[33]

It was not only the socialist-left that had presentiments of a massive disturbance in the immediate future. Fyodor Dostoevsky provides an excellent illustration of a conservative with similar visions. Even as a young writer flirting with leftist ideas, Dostoevsky had an agonized perception of contemporary France at his trial for political crimes: "The very basic principles of society are threatening to crumble and to draw their nation into the fall.[34] Years of prison, exile, financial need, and personal tragedy only strengthened the novelist's ideological apprehensions, though his imagery was now religious, emotional, and messianic. The West seemed riddled with rationalism, disbelief, and immorality. Only Russia had preserved its Christian faith intact, thanks to the Orthodox Church and peasant devotion. But Russian goodness could not win the respect of its western neighbors, since the slavic model served as a disquieting reminder of their own evil. Indeed, the resultant hostility made war between Russia and the West inevitable. It would be a war to end all wars; it would inaugurate an age of spiritual reconciliation: "But the most essential and important part of this final and fateful struggle will be, from the one side, that it will resolve the millennial question of Roman Catholicism and that, by the will of Providence, in its place will arise Eastern Orthodoxy."[35]

Dostoevsky died not long before Alexander was assassinated on March 13, 1881. The new emperor, Alexander III, introduced a stringent regime of political repression that stifled the revolutionary cause for more than a decade. Indeed, the socialist movement did not revive until the reign of his heir, Nicholas II, when social and political discontent combined with the frustration of military defeat to produce two revolutions. Both these uprisings were accompanied by massive waves of peasant violence which embodied that traditional blend of wordly goals and religious ecstasy:

> For the peasants and for many workers the prototype of the new society remained a decentralized pastoral paradise in which they might live in peace and contentment with full economic and political freedom organized from below. Fired by simple slogans, the laboring classes aimed at a direct plebeian democracy through laboring councils and communes akin to the Cossack *krugs* of the past. Their frame of mind, moreover, remained passionately apocalyptic. They showed the same millennial drive, the same yearning for redemption, for a drastic renovation of society, as before.[36]

Though the first of these disturbances, the Revolution of 1905, was effectively suppressed by the government's forces, the second, the Revolution of 1917, proved irresistible. At last, the peasantry had accomplished the general expropriation of the landed nobility for which it had struggled so long.

If the peasant's mood and practical goals remained unchanged, he no longer turned to a rival tsar to articulate his needs, since political parties were competing for that function. Of course, the Populists were still in the field. Only now they perferred the name Socialist Revolutionaries, and they adopted a new program of two-staged revolution. The first stage, the bourgeois revolution, was to provide the civil liberties necessary to organize the peasant for a second, the socialist revolution, which would produce a slightly modernized version of the old Populist utopia.[37]

The appeal of this renovated Populism eventually proved overwhelming when the common people were given the chance to express themselves in elections for a constituent assembly that met in January, 1918: the Socialist Revolutionaries captured 410 of the 707 seats.[38] But by then the Bolsheviks[39] were in firm control of the government, the leading cities, and what remained of the military, and they were not disposed to relinquish it. So the constituent assembly was dissolved, with the Socialist Revolutionaries drifting into the anti-Bolshevik faction in the ensuing civil war. The Bolshevik victory, consequently, brought about the demise of the Socialist Revolutionaries along with all forms of organized opposition. Or, as a contemporary joke stated the matter, there were many parties in the Soviet Union: one in power; the others in jail.

The Bolsheviks had their own special ideas about the utopian world of the future, although they would have never employed that adjective to describe their long-range goals. The new society was to be industrialized, urbanized, and proletarianized. The factory worker, not the peasant, would be the principal agent for introducing this new order under the guidance of its vanguard, the Communist Party. And there was the familiar expectation of a perfect society where men contributed according to their abilities and were rewarded according to their needs; where work ceased to be repressive; where external government was replaced by self-administration; and where the full development of each became the precondition for the full development of all.

These ideas triggered a spectacular burst of creative energy during the first decade of Bolshevik rule, when communist visionaries received the opportunity to implement their ideals. Teachers dispensed with classroom formalities, conventional grading, and rote assignments. Movie directors brilliantly portrayed the heroic achievements of collectivities rather than individuals; social themes were explored in the concert hall, live theater, and ballet. Marriage was demythologized into an unpretentious civil act; divorce simplified so that either party could immediately terminate a union. Abortion was legalized, adultery decriminalized, and prostitution treated as a social problem rather a criminal act. Even unions were allowed to influence factory policies, to negotiate contracts, and to strike. It was a time of Marxist experimentation, creativity and hope.[40]

The only difficulty was that the revolution was supposed to occur in an industrially advanced country, like the United States, where capitalism had largely completed the economic base of the new order before socialism came along to apply the final cosmetics. By prematurely seizing power, the Bolsheviks were left with the unattractive task of industrializing Russia, which included withholding income from the workers for reinvestment, redirecting farm surpluses towards industrial uses, and training an agrarian labor force to perform industrial occupations. Therefore, when Joseph Stalin initiated his program of rapid industrialization in 1928, the Soviet Union began to seem surprisingly like the capitalist system that Marx had so vividly described in the Communist Manifesto:

> Masses of laborers, crowded into the factory, are organized like soldiers. As privates of the industrial army they are placed under the command of a perfect hierarchy of officers and sergeants. Not only are they the slaves of the bourgeois class, and the bourgeois state, they are daily and hourly enslaved by the machine, by the over-looker, and, above all, by the individual bourgeois manufacturer himself.[41]

Forced industrialization had a devastating effect on the social experiments of the early revolution. Traditional methods were reintroduced into the Soviet classroom. Marriage was again glamorized with lavish ceremonies, fancy dress and wedding rings; divorce became difficult and expensive to obtain. Abortion was outlawed except for limited medical reasons; people were encouraged to have large families; and Stalin was regularly shown with his mother and children. Art, literature and the stage were placed under strict surveillance in an effort to discourage works that did not further the regime's political and social goals. Trade unions lost the independence which they had enjoyed in the twenties. Political control became universal; mass arrests the norm. Indeed, many of the creative spirits of the twenties fell victim to the totalitarian system that Stalin introduced in the wake of industrial planning. Of course, the social picture was not entirely bleak. The Soviet worker possessed many benefits that western labor had not enjoyed at a similar stage of industrial growth: free medical treatment, subsidized housing, generous holidays, pensions, educational stipends, and the constant reassurance that the laboring masses were society's elite.[42] Yet, conversely, the political pressure placed upon the Soviet worker to fulfill those early five-year plans often seems staggering to the western mind.

The traditional peasantry had no permanent place in the new utopian order which the Marxists were striving to create. It was either to be absorbed into the industrial working class or become a proletariat of the field. The collectivization of agriculture was one of the first steps that the Soviet government took towards realizing these goals. Earlier, the peasant had fulfilled a portion of his perennial dream with the mass land seizure of 1917. The Bolsheviks had been forced to sanction that seizure in their quest for power. But Soviet leaders subsequently felt compelled to abandon that policy of compromise because peasant expropriations had led to a rise in the number of subsistence farms, a consequent reduction in the portion of each harvest reaching the market, and agricultural deliveries that fluctuated with price levels. To the peasant, collectivization meant government seizure of his land, implements, animals and inventories; to the government, it signified a steady flow of farm produce to rapidly industrializing cities at state-dictated prices. Sometimes the peasant fought government troops in an effort to preserve his land; other times, he destroyed his animals, tools and crops, rather than have the Soviet state seize them. But resistence proved fruitless, whatever the technique. Probably five to ten million peasants perished during the collectivization, either from fighting or from related famine. Farm statistics give some idea of the breadth of the tragedy: Russia had lost roughly one-half of its horses, over 40 percent of its cattle, and nearly two-thirds of its sheep and goats.[43]

Nevertheless, collectivization was achieved by the late-thirties. Farm products were delivered to Soviet cities, industrial output trebled and the Soviet Union moved ahead of all other European nations in the production of machines, trucks, and tractors. All that the peasant had left of his traditional dream was a garden plot which the government had conceded under pressure during those hectic years. Though small, usually from one-third to one acre in size, it gave the peasant family a place to grow crops, raise animals, and feel rooted. Even today, while declining in importance, those tiny plots still produce one-quarter of all the produce reaching the Soviet market.

If the peasant utopia fared badly, the Marxist utopia has run into trouble as well. Soviet citizens may live as long as Americans, read more books, and produce more coal, cement, iron ore and petroleum, but the state still shows no signs of withering away, work has not become joyful, and people are hardly rewarded according to their needs.[44] Utopian expectations have suffered *pari passu*. Today, the Soviet Union is an industrial society where men's hopes are just as prosaic as in most other industrial societies: television sets, appliances, furniture, more floor space, pleasant vacations, and, possibly, an automobile in the not too distant future. Of course, the politicians still pay lip service to the communist future at party congresses, but the popular mood is reflected in those abundant Soviet jokes that ridicule the notion of a future communist utopia. Or, as a fictitious Leningrader remarked to an equally fictitious American tourist who had invited him to the United States to watch for the crisis in capitalism: "I would rather stay here and watch for the advent of communism: even if the pay is not as good, at least the work is permanent."[45]

What happened to the Russian apocalypse after utopia faded away instead of the state? Well, the apocalyptic mood remained strong, especially in anti-utopian circles. The most imaginative work produced by a dissident writer, *We*, appeared very soon after the Russian Revolution. In this novel, Eugene Zamiatin described a futuristic society that was a marvel of scientific achievement with its space rockets, urban air travel, petroleum foods and transparent buildings. Yet the most noteworthy feature of this ultra-modern world was the substitution of *we* for *I*: "United into a single body with millions of hands, at the very same second designated by the Tables, we carry spoons to our mouths; at the same second we all go out to work, go to the auditorium, to the halls for the Taylor exercises, and to bed."[46] Somehow, though, man's imagination balked at this sacrifice of human freedom for the sake of material well-being; and the resultant dissatisfaction gave rise to a revolutionary movement designed to overthrow utopia, which Dostoevsky had long before anticipated in his *Letters from the Underworld*. The final scenes of the novel depict a world in chaos, with the anti-utopian forces pressing for the overthrow of regimented modernism, and the government frantically trying to destroy by mass radiological treatments that portion of the brain that gives rise to human fancy. It was an "apocalyptic hour," as Zamiatin's hero, D-503, acutely sensed:

> I do not remember how I got into one of the public rest-rooms in a station of the Underground Railway. Above, every-thing was perishing; the greatest civilization, the most rational in human history, was crumbling, but here, by some irony, everything remained as before, beautiful. The walls shone; water murmured cozily; and like the water, the unseen, trans-parent music . . . . Only think of it! All this is doomed; all this will be covered with grass someday; only myths will remain . . . .[47]

It seems likely that *We* inspired George Orwell's classic, *1984*. If so, another Soviet critic, Andrei Amalrik, has helped to balance the ledger by entitling his neo-apocalyptic tract, *Will the Soviet Union Survive Until 1984*. Amalrik's book contends that "the relentless logic of revolution" is propelling the Red Chinese towards a war with the Red Russians that will give those dissatisfied with Soviet domination the opportunity to break away from political bondage.[48] Thus, the satellite-states of Eastern Europe will be able to establish their independence, while the Soviet Union will burst asunder as a result of its so-called minorities, whose combined total actually makes them a majority, spurning Russian control. And all this turmoil will be accompanied by the familiar agony of the Last Days: "Power will pass into the hands of extremist elements and groups, and the country will begin to disintegrate into anarchy, violence, and intense national hatred."[49] It is true that Amalrik reluc-tantly admits that other alternatives are possible. But, whatever happens, the Soviet writer is convinced, like Balasoglo more than a century earlier, that the end of the Russian empire is at hand:

> I have no doubt that this great Eastern Slav empire, created by Germans, Byzantines, and Mongols, has entered the last de-cades of its existence. Just as the adoption of Christianity postponed the fall of the Roman Empire, but did not prevent its inevitable end, so Marxist doctrine has delayed the breakup of the Russian empire—the Third Rome—but does not possess the power to prevent it.[50]

A more familiar dissident, Alexander Solzhenitsyn, seems to be squarely in the apocalyptic tradition as well. In fact, the novelist's Harvard speech not only reeked of apocalypticism, but was also filled with other notions that dominated the later thought of his intellectual mentor, Fyodor Dostoevsky. For example, both men argued that the western world is decaying from excessive individualism, materialism, and legalism. Both writers also maintained that Russia is producing people who are morally superior to westerners. And, though Solzhenitsyn vilifies the Soviet Union because of its communist government, he sees the same titanic struggle developing between the forces of good and evil that obsessed Dostoevsky a century earlier:

> But the fight for our planet, physical and spiritual, a fight of cosmic proportions, is not a vague matter of the future; it has already started. The forces of Evil have begun their offensive—you can feel their pressure—and yet your screens and publications are full of prescribed smiles and raised glasses. What is the joy about?[51]

Despite these dire forebodings, the Soviet Union shows every sign of surviving beyond 1984; and so does Russian apocalypticism. From prehistoric invasions until twentieth-century events that may have taken as many as fifty million lives, Russian history has been filled with a degree of suffering seldom seen in the western world: foreign attacks, political strife, social oppression, peasant violence, epidemics, bad harvests every third year, and a life expectancy that was still only thirty-two years at the start of the present century. Is it really surprising that such experiences have produced a pessimism which is more deeply engrained than utopian hope? And, since modern society produces its own special brand of mental anguish in the process of reducing physical need, western observers can expect to hear a lot more of the Russian apocalypse.

5

Auguste Comte and the Positivist Utopia

OSCAR R. MARTÍ

During the 19th century, Europe saw a proliferation of utopian movements, such as Saintsimonism, Fourierism and Marxism. Their aim was to solve the problems created by rapid social and economic changes brought about by industrialization. One of the most interesting of these movements was positivism. Originally French, it spread from Russia to Latin America and attracted people as different as George Eliot, Samuel Gompers and John Stuart Mill to cite a few. Its founder, Auguste Comte, was a man of encyclopedic knowledge who believed that without the proper scientific study, there could be no lasting social reform. This study presupposed a science of society, which he called "sociology." He proceeded to formulate its precepts and methods, and to give the guidelines for social reorganization in accordance with sociological laws, as well as provide a detailed picture of the society that would inevitably follow. *

Comtian positivism is a conglomerate of philosophical views about ethics, religion and society united by a well defined vision of science and a faith in its power to change human affairs for the better. In this paper I will discuss the underlying assumptions of Comte's utopian positivism, outline the structure of the positive polity, discuss the efforts of its supporters to carry out such reform, and give some reasons for its decline. I will finally argue that this social reform approach is vitiated by fallacies that doom it, and similar movements, to failure. An understanding of these errors will enable us to see some of the merits and important contributions of the doctrine.

Auguste Comte was born in Montpellier, France, in 1798.[1] He studied at the prestigious École Politechnique from where he was expelled for ideals contrary to the Restoration. In 1817 he became secretary to the popular utopian socialist Henri, Comte de Saint-Simon, and worked under him until 1824 when, because of doctrinal differences and personality conflicts, they quarreled and severed relations. A mental breakdown followed in 1826, which interrupted Comte's public lectures on positivist philosophy, but he recuperated two years later and continued to carry out his monumental plan for scientific and social reorganization. Economic difficulties forced him to eke out a living by part-time tutoring in mathematics, even to live through the charity of friends and disciples. Marital problems leading to divorce, the inability to obtain an academic post, a stormy relationship with and the premature death of Clothilde de Vaux in 1846, the alienation of friends and family, the lack of recognition, all took their toll. Exhausted from intellectual labor, wretched and embittered, Comte died in Paris in 1857.

In spite of misfortunes, Comte wrote two major philosophical works, the six volume *Cours de philosophie positive*, (1830-42), and the four volume *Système de politique positive*, (1851-54).[2] In the *Cours*, Comte presents us with a programmatic reconstruction of science along positivist lines, which he considers the necessary scientific groundwork preliminary to any social reform. In the *Système*, he details the kind of society that would result from the applications of positive science. Fundamental to these works is the belief that the science of society, as Comte conceives it, is the best instrument for achieving social order and progress and, ultimately, the best society.[3]

The main epistemological assumptions of positivism are the empiricist claim that all knowledge comes from experience, and Kant's observation that this experience is phenomenal—the way things appear to us.[4] We acquire knowledge by observing the phenomena, making inductive generalizations or laws about their resemblance and succession, and incorporating these regularities into the body of knowledge available at that time. It is called positive knowledge because it is always open to verification, and because it is relative to the observer and to the stage of scientific development. Thus, we cannot have any positive knowledge of things in themselves, of their nature, or of their mode of operation apart from what is given in experience. The result of positive knowledge is positive science, whose task is to discover phenomenal facts and laws, to explain them by subsumption under more general laws, and to predict future facts by using these laws.

Part of the positivist program is to regard societies as natural phenomena whose structures and development can be explained by scientific laws? Comte believed that he was the first to formulate such laws and, borrowing an analogy from physics, called them the laws of social statics and social dynamics.[6] The laws of social statics can be discovered by studying those features common to different social aggregates—a sort of comparative politics and sociology. In Comte's system, these laws turn out to be generalizations about the individual, the family and society, such as the principle of division of labor, or that of the subordination of women to men and the young to the old—principles that account for the existence of order and solidarity in society. The law of dynamics can be discovered by studying those changes in the individual which are responsible for social change and are well confirmed by history. It states that "from the nature of the human intellect, each branch of knowledge, in its development, is necessarily obliged to pass through three different theoretical states: the theological or fictitious state; the metaphysical or abstract state; and, lastly, the scientific or positive state."[7] This law embodies the pattern of development of the human mind and of societies, and is what we mean by progress. Comte called it the Law of the Three Stages and, because of its importance within the system, it deserves close scrutiny.

The first stage of the development of human knowledge, the theological or mythical, involves the adoption of explanations that attribute lifelike qualities to natural phenomena—for instance, explaining thunder as the anger of the gods. Here, the imagination takes precedence even over observation. The typical kinds of governments that arise from this state of the mind or of civilization are theocracies or military monarchies that justify their sovereignty by appeal to Divine Authority. According to Comte, the historical period extending from ancient Egypt or Homeric Greece to the Reformation corresponds to this level of development.

Inconsistencies, inability to account for the facts or to make predictions in terms of myths, force the mind to progress to the next stage, the metaphysical. The kinds of explanations given here make use of abstractions and of self-evident principles invented by the mind and, again, immune to verification—thunder is now "caused" by stormy clouds, and Nature replaces the gods. For Comte, the metaphysical stage extends from the Middle Ages to the French Revolution but, since social change is slow, there is an overlap with the theological stage. This is a period of transition, of destruction of the old before the new arrives. Its corresponding forms of government are of the legalistic kind—for instance, democracy— which justify their rule by appeal to such metaphysical principles as universal equality or the rights of man. But difficulties again force the mind to advance to the next, the positive stage.

At this, the last stage of development, explanations are given in terms of observations and generalizations. Here, our desire for speculation is totally subordinated to experience and we finally achieve positive knowledge. Mathematical relations among phenomena now become the main explanatory concepts. Thunder, to keep to our original example, is explained by the equations of acoustics, of statistical mechanics, of molecular physics, where "cause" and "anger of the gods" have no place. If questions arise as to the nature of what lies behind these experiences, beyond the phenomenal, they are quickly dismissed as questions we have no power to understand. Industrial societies are the kind of government characteristic of this stage, the final historical development predicted by the law. Knowledge of the laws that govern social change and structure would certainly speed up the process, but in any event the outcome is inevitable.[8]

If the Law of the Three Stages is discovered in the historical development of cultures and governments, it also acts as a yardstick for measuring progress, or evolution, in an individual. "Now, each of us is aware, if he looks back upon his own history, that he was a theologian in childhood, a metaphysician in his youth, and a natural philosopher in his manhood. All men who are up to their age can verify this for themselves."[9] Because of the intimate connection between science and the kinds of explanation given, we can also use this law to measure scientific progress. Astronomy, for instance, went from the myth that the heavens were the soft underbelly of a goddess, to casual explanations, or to self-evident principles that things look for their proper place in nature. Now these have been supplanted by explanations which, like the law of gravity, express mathematical relations among phenomena but posit no ultimate principle or, for that matter, even seek to explain the fundamental nature of gravity.[10]

Science is a historical process in which the form as well as the content changes. But the Law of the Three Stages is not just a sociological law or a historical analysis; it also corresponds to a natural distinction. This assertion is confirmed by the historical order by which the sciences became positive. First came those whose subject matter was more general, and on which the development of the more particular sciences depended: mathematics, astronomy, physics, chemistry, physiology and now, the social science of sociology. This hierarchy is also a natural classification, since the hierarchically superior sciences are necessary for understanding the lower ones. Thus, chemistry is necessary for understanding physiology, astronomy for physics, and mathematics for all. And, since each science has its own proper laws, the unity of science is only one of method. So much for First Principles, self-evident truths from which all knowledge could be derived, or any other metaphysical nonsense![11]

The last science to become positive is sociology. Comte announces its arrival in the 47th lesson of the *Cours*. It took longer to become a science because of its dependence on the development of the hierarchically superior sciences. Its function is to investigate the phenomenal laws that describe society by tracing patterns of development in history and by comparing the structures of different societies at a given time. In this way, the scientist can understand societies and improve them. Thus, the sociologist's task is dual: first to discover the best social system where order and progress can be achieved, then to set up such a system. His is a problem not just of knowledge, but of practice: "Science d'où prévoyance; prévoyance d'où action."[12]

For a detailed picture of Comte's positive polity we must turn to the *Système*. In the Introductory Remarks he tells us: "Positivism consists essentially of a Philosophy and a Polity. These can never be dissevered; the former being the basis, and the latter the end, of one comprehensive system, in which our intellectual faculties and our social sympathies are brought into close correlation with each other."[13] Note that he does not call it "utopia" but "positive polity" or "sociocracy." For Comte, utopias have an idealistic character that fails to convince anyone, while a sociocracy is a fact of life discoverable by sociology—a forthcoming reality.[14]

The positive polity is a social hierarchy, with a scientist-priest class at the top, followed by an employer class that consists of bankers or "capitalist knights," merchants, manufacturers and so on, followed by the proletariat, in decreasing degree of skill.[15] Women stand outside the hierarchy in a class of their own. As in Plato's *Republic*, social mobility is dictated by a person's abilities. Given that the use of wealth is subject to the moral pressure of public opinion and that state-controlled education is universal, every citizen has the opportunity to rise to the top of the hierarchy.[16] This social mobility, Comte thought, would insure a society free from class struggle.

Every class in the sociocracy has a function. The scientist-priests are the spiritual directors. Because of their training and education as sociologists, they are able to foresee the alternatives open to the society and can predict the best course of action. Their decisions are announced as fixed and stable laws, and the capitalist knights or managers implement these "suggestions" by redistributing capital to the manufacturers, merchants, etc., while ensuring that women are relieved of work and that intellectual labor is properly remunerated.[17] The outcome would be new jobs, the needed goods, or the desirable social goals, enabling every industrious citizen to have the means to develop his own domestic life.[18] The function of women is mainly spiritual: to form public opinion, to give children the proper moral training at home, to ameliorate men's harsh character with their feminine graces.[19] All for the common good.

Unlike the philosopher-kings of the *Republic*, the scientist-priests of the *Système* have no power, not even legislative. Theirs is a moral authority that comes from a universal recognition of merit.[20] They preach, teach, conduct rituals and advise—a combination think-tank and Catholic priesthood. At the other extreme of the social scale, the power of the proletariat is a negative one—that of rejecting contracts by strikes.[21] The power to carry out the decisions of the scientist-priests falls on the capitalist knights. The principle invoked is that of efficiency: an industry with a centralized authority works better than one without it.[22] But in a society where wealth is controlled and investment decisions are determined by sociological laws rather than by self-interested responses to market conditions, to call these knights "capitalists" is a misnomer. They are more like a managerial class than the nineteenth century capitalists of Adam Smith.

If the power of the capitalist knights is an administrative one, what is to prevent them from hoarding wealth and becoming true capitalists, as Marx would argue? Comte's answer is that to counteract such selfish motives, a new feeling had to be instilled in the citizenry: altruism, or working for the sake of others.[23] The problem is that altruism and egoism are at opposite ends of the emotional spectrum. How can a natural feeling, egoism, be transmuted into an unnatural one? "The solution is to be found in another biological principle, namely, that function and organs are developed by constant exercise," that is, by repetition and constant reinforcement.[24] Its training ground would be domestic life, the province of women. The first steps come early in life along with filial love and reverence for one's ancestors, and would provide a sense of continuity. Brotherly love is the next feeling to be encouraged, which establishes a solidarity with the present generation. As one matures and associations become voluntary, conjugal love is to be developed, creating a respect for women. Finally, parental love would create an emotional link between the self and the future generations. This way the individual becomes attached to others and becomes accustomed to the feeling of subordination to humanity.

Altruism is one of the forces that keeps society together, but human nature being what it is, there is a need for external compulsion to back this feeling or motive and to maintain social cohesion. Comte found these forces in public opinion and in organized religion. Public opinion, arising out of mutual cooperation among individuals and directed by the scientist-priests, is the main weapon of women and the working classes. Through it, these classes can express their disapproval of single individuals, such as the capitalist knights, and prevent any abuse of their power. It works both because of the universal fear of condemnation by society, and because of a desire for approval strongly developed among the wealthy classes.[25]

The strongest force which allows for this public opinion to develop is organized religion. The Religion of Humanity, as Comte called it, is the culmination of the positivist reorganization of society. It represents the merger of the intellectual and emotional aspects of man. Comte meticulously worked out its doctrine, ritual and regulation. Instead of the conventional God, we now have the Great Being—the whole of mankind: past, present and future—the Great Mother, representing the planet Earth, and a Great Mystery or doctrinal body cast in ritual form. To administer the Great Worship, the office of High Priest of Mankind is instituted. Under him there is a whole hierarchy of scientist-priests. They are to manage the rituals, advise the community on moral matters, and carry on other "supreme duties.[26] To maintain the proper spirit, the citizenry is urged to keep a "cerebral hygiene" that consists of reading and re-reading a definite set of positivist "classics."[27] There is, furthermore, an elaborate worship made up of celebrations guided by a reformed calendar. Part of the worship consists of a recommitment to the positivist canons and prayers to positivist "saints," men who by their actions and intellectual capacities could provide a model for all.[28] Thus, by force of repetition and ritual, the positive life would soon become a matter of habit.

> The worship is the best expression of this state of complete synthesis the state in which all our knowledge, scientific and practical, finds its condensation in morals. The grand object of religion being to teach us to live for others, it must consist essentially in regulating the direct cultivation of our sympathetic instincts. In fact, such would be its sole function were it not that our physical wants necessitate the addition both of the doctrine and the regime, so by man's own exertions to give an altruistic character to the natural egoism of his incessant activity.[29]

Comte believed that the positive polity was inevitable, that a peaceful revolution was going to happen and would bring about the sociocracy. He made himself High Priest and sat down to wait. It never happened. There were other, more active efforts. Sympathizers, followers and disciples of Comte's reform program organized themselves into conferences and congresses, tried to carry out social and educational changes, founded temples of humanity, made alliances with other radical movements—particularly in England and France—and even went down the political road, by vote or revolution.[30] Who were these people and what did they find attractive in the doctrine?

Identifying someone as a positivist is not easy, for the movement developed a dynamics of its own in about two dozen countries where it took roots. Positivism in Mexico, for instance, is very different from its English counterpart.[31] Without doing much violence to the subject, we can distinguish three main groups: the sympathizers, the followers and the disciples. We could characterize the larger group, the sympathizers, as those who perceived some value in Comte's views about philosophy, science, sociology, etc. Among them are philosophers like John Stuart Mill, Emile Littré, Roberto Ardigo; writers like Leslie Stephen or Anatole France; scientists like Ernst Mach and Wilhelm Ostwald; Joseph Henry Allen and O. B. Frothingham, the American Unitarians; the historian H. T. Buckle and the sociologists Lester Ward and Emile Durkheim, to cite the better known. We could include among the followers those who, while adopting most of Comte's scientific, historic, political or ethical views, still refrained from taking an active part in the Worship of Mankind. They were social activists who believed that moral regeneration through the positive science was the only road to a better society. To this group belong Frederic Harrison, Edward Spencer Beesly, George Eliot, H. E. Lewes, Gabino Barreda, Benjamin Constant Bothelho de Magalhães and, perhaps, even Samuel Gompers. The third group, the disciples, was the orthodox branch of positivism which took Comte's religious views as fundamental. We can include here Richard Congrave, Henry Edger, H. Bridges, Pierre Laffitte, Emile Corra, Miguel Lemos, Jorge and Juan Enrique Lagarrigue.[32]

To state that these groups were composed of middle class liberals is misleading for, while the movement was composed of many middle class liberals, it still encompassed a larger spectrum: workers and aristocrats, radicals and women, patricians and immigrants—even some anarchists.[33] It would be more accurate to state that positivism was composed of a variety of people who were attracted by some aspect or other of the doctrine: its scientific claims (Mill), its philosophical method (Littré), its research into social problems (Durkheim), its solution to these problems (Barreda), its radical political line (Beesly), its religious concern (Congrave), and so on. In this sense positivism served a different function for different people and no general categorization is adequate.

Guided by the belief that knowledge should lead to action, positivists gave public lectures on the sciences and on positive philosophy. They were following the master's footsteps, since Comte himself had conducted several such courses for the public in 1816, 1829, 1850—primarily aimed at the French working class, but collecting a distinguished audience of intellectuals.[34] This was the model for the lectures at Newton Hall, or Pierre Laffitte's lectures starting in 1869, and the various Ethical Culture conferences in England and the United States.[35] The idea was that the establishment of a positivist utopia required an intellectual conversion. Thus, these lectures would educate the general public in the sciences which, in turn, would convert them to positivism. If they failed, at least they contributed to the movement for popular education of women and workers.

A number of sympathizers from both sides of the Atlantic contributed to the endowment of libraries and centers of learning so the general public could have access to scientific positive knowledge. We have, for instance, the Centre Positiviste Pour l'Instruction Populaire in Paris, directed by Emile Corra; Newton Hall, in London; and several small lending libraries.[36] But of more interest are the religious activities of both the followers and the disciples. So as better to spread the gospel, they founded positivist societies or churches around the world—in England, France, Italy, Russia, Sweden, Brazil, Chile, the United States.[37] Every church had its high priest, bureaucracy, liturgy and library. It held lectures and social functions, even performed marriages. Most have disappeared, but still active are the Temple of Humanity in Brazil and, in Paris, the Maison Auguste Comte.[38]

In the United States, the works of the disciples and followers are not well known. Even the sympathizers were few. Neither the first disciple in America, Henry Edger, nor the Russian emigré William Frey, were successful in founding positivist communes: Edger's attempt was within the anarchist village of Modern Times, Long Island, which functioned between 1853 and 1878; Frey's was founded about 1870 in Cedar Vale, Kansas.[39] We should not, however, underrate positivist influence on American social or religious thought. For instance, the Unitarian movement, from the 1850s on, owes a great deal of its social outlook to Comte, particularly through sympathizers like O. B. Frothingham, Noah Porter and others.[40]

Comtian positivism is a reform movement, the kind usually associated with the political left. Its members demanded major social and political changes. They claimed that their method was scientific, and that they opposed anarchy, but very often they took a hard radical line, even advocating revolution. It might be objected that historically their efforts were sometimes too meek—particularly in France where, after Comte's death and under Laffitte's leadership, positivists concentrated their efforts on public lectures rather than politics.[41] However, there were other occasions when they acted like true radicals; for example, their union activism. Why the labor movement? First, because Comte believed that an organized public opinion, directed by positivists, would eventually lead to the desired social reorganization. In this sense, the labor movement was the most likely vehicle. Second, Comte perceived the working classes as the best source of progressive ideas.[42] Their role would be that of humanizers of the capitalists.

In England, the best known positivist labor activists were Frederic Harrison and Edward Spencer Beesly.[43] Both Beesly and Harrison were Oxford graduates and disciples of Richard Congrave, the main English advocate of religious positivism.[44] They could not, however, agree to follow Congrave in establishing such a religion and, eventually, broke with him.[45] Beesly became a professor of history at University Hall, London, and Harrison, a well known lawyer. Both became defenders of labor—of the right to strike by the London Building Trades Union, in 1862, and before the Royal Commission that investigated union crimes, in 1867. On this and other occasions they distinguished themselves as friends of labor, and labor leaders repeatedly came to them for advice on difficulties.[46]

In the United States, there is also evidence of positivist influence on the labor movement. C. G. David's *Positivist Primer* exorts its members to join the labor struggle.[47] Critics and commentators of the movement speak of positivist involvement in radical causes, some in an ominous tone.[48] More concretely, the St. Louis Humanist Labor Group took an active part in the foundation of the A.F.L., and was involved in its Third Annual Convention of 1888.[49] Similar activities are noted about the Society of Humanists of New York and the Brooklyn Positivist League.[50]

Positivists also became involved in broader political problems, for instance, in England, where Beesly and Harrison wanted to make of the labor movement a political force. Beesly, in particular, considered the aims of the trade unions as narrow and argued for a broader base. He believed that they should organize into a "Labor Party"—which was to materialize forty years later—one opposed to the Liberal and the Conservative Parties. This "Labor Party's" platform would include such issues as fair wages, self-government for Ireland, resistance to imperialism in South Africa and India, opposition to the opium policies in China and so on.[51] Beesly also put pressure on the London Trades Council to make alliances with progressive and working class movements abroad. His active participation helped bring about the 1864 International Working Men's Association. These actions labelled him and other active positivists and Marxists as dangerous radicals.[52] This very militancy caused a break between middle-of-the-road unionists and the positivist movement, particularly when Beesly exposed the internal corruption of liberals and labor union leaders in power—the people who would later on become the mainstay of the Labor Party itself.[53]

To appreciate a more active politicizing of the positivist movement, we must focus on South America where, in many cases, it was a major force behind social and political changes. Here, an added feature of positivism as a religion was that it provided an alternative to Catholicism or to skepticism, and as a political theory, that it gave hope for the future through proper application of sociological and scientific methods.[54] In Brazil, the revolution against the emperor, Dom Pedro II, the setting of the constitution, the educational system, even the Republican motto "Ordem e Progresso," bear the imprint of positivist influence.[55] Its leadership included Benjamin Constant and Miguel Lemos, the latter the leader of the religious faction. They hoped for the instauration of a Brazilian positivist polity—a scientific-industrial republic, free from theology and militarism.[56] And, although sympathizers, followers, and disciples were unable to set up a sociocracy in Brazil, they did succeed in Rio Grande do Sul, the only time in history that Comte's political ideas played a major part in the setting up of a state's constitution.[57]

In Chile also, Comte's ideas found both the strict interpretation of the disciples and a wide base of support among the sympathizers. Led by the Lagarrigue brothers, Jorge and Juan Enrique, the disciples defended the truth of the *Système* in letters, speeches, and pamphlets. Like Miguel Lemos, they argued that the true positivist could not participate in a government other than the sociocracy.[58] Thus, their labor became one of propagating the doctrine, not of political involvement. Again, like Lemos, Jorge Lagarrigue became acquainted with Comte's works in the 1870's.[59] He then went to Paris where he met

Laffitte, by then the leader of the French positivist church, Lemos and Gabino Barreda of Mexico. Once under the tutelage of Laffitte, Jorge Lagarrigue became a disciple and began the propagation of positivism at home. After Jorge Lagarrigue's death, Juan Enrique became the chief apostle of Chile.[60] A persuasive writer, Juan Enrique argued for peace, national and international, for the rights of the proletariat to strike, and for the duty of the priesthood of humanity to mediate between the workers and the patricians.[61] He also gave a sympathetic account of socialism, but objected to their demand for common ownership, and reiterated Comte's view that parliamentary government, since it rested on metaphysical foundations, was bankrupt.[62] Here, he clashed with Chilean sympathizers like Valentin Letelier. Letelier had become acquainted with Comte at the same time as the Lagarrigue brothers. He agreed with the positivist program for the social science—even the ability of political science, as he called it—to discover the best values for a society. However, because of liberal commitments, he could not accept the religion or the absolutism of the *Système*.[63] This difference came to a head during the 1891 conflict between a conservatively-backed executive and a liberal congress. Letelier sided with the congress while Lagarrigue argued for a dictatorship of the executive on the grounds that it would be another step toward the sociocracy.[64]

It should be noted that the greatest political activity came from the followers, not the disciples. This is particularly true of Mexico. Here, however, we find almost no disciples.[65] Thus, Mexican positivism is less religious than either its Chilean or its Brazilian counterpart. In 1867, President Benito Juárez called on Gabino Barreda, a student and a follower of Comte, to start a series of educational reforms. The main idea was to create an educated class that, with the help of positive science, could lead the country out of economic stagnation and political chaos and set it on the road to modernization and industrialization. Positivism was seen as a doctrine that could hold the nation together in the face of anarchy. Thus, the stress on order and progress.[66]

Gabino Barreda became acquainted with Auguste Comte while studying medicine in Paris.[67] Like Beesly, he was a follower who believed that political activism, not religious diffusion, was the better alternative. But unlike Beesly he was willing to participate in a non-positivist government, if only to bring about some form of the sociocracy. Barreda believed that Mexico had just undergone a political revolution and was now ready for an intellectual one.[68] This meant the abandonment of Catholicism and liberalism as remnants of the theological and the metaphysical stages, and the setting up of a new order akin to the positive polity.[69] Faithful to Comte, Barreda also believed that a moral regeneration was needed to accomplish the desired political changes—a regeneration that only positivism was capable of inspiring.[70] His educational reforms bore fruit quickly and, a decade later, a new class of intellectuals emerged which was trained along positivist lines. Unfortunately for positivism these men—Justo Sierra, Porfirio Parra, Francisco Bulnes, for instance—would themselves abandon Comte and move toward Spencer's evolutionism to become the vanguard of the "científico" party and take an active part in the political life of Mexico from 1892 to 1910.[71]

In spite of efforts to the contrary, Comte, his disciples and followers were unable to create a positive polity or instaurate the Religion of Humanity. Many reasons can be given. One is that elements of intransigence—not to be confused with conservativism—permeated the movement. For instance, during the turbulent days of the 1848 Paris revolutions, the newly formed Positivist Society took a number of steps to help set up a provisional government.[72] At first Comte agreed, but then became inflexible and refused to deal with the Left, particularly the communists. His position was that these revolutionaries were disrupters of order, purveyors of immorality and detainers of progress.[73] He asserted that positivism was superior to communism and that it was they who had to come around to his way of thinking.[74] This stand crippled any negotiations and angered a potential group of supporters and allies.

Another reason for failure was the controversial nature of the political and religious utopianism even while Comte was alive. Aside from personal reasons, this utopianism was one of the main factors that had alienated John Stuart Mill and Emile Littré.[75] Both defended the scientific rationalism of the *Cours*, but blamed the utopian and religious implications of the *Système* on Comte's mental aberrations. They felt that if positivism was to be consistent it should be divorced from politics, least of all advocate a religion. Actually, nothing made the doctrine more unpalatable to the majority of socially committed intellectuals than this sociocratic stand. Mill called it "the completest system of spiritual and temporal despotism, which ever yet emanated from the human brain, unless possibly that of Ignatius Loyola."[76] Karl Marx called it "positivist rot" and T. H. Huxley, "Catholicism minus Christianity."[77]

The positive polity and the Religion of Humanity did not always go hand in hand for many. Quite the contrary, it became a source of controversy. In the 1870s, Pierre Laffitte's leadership came under attack from correligionists who felt that the Positivist Society was not active enough. Laffitte defended the orthodox position that positivists, basing themselves on moral authority, should not aspire to political leadership.[78] In England, Congrave also took an orthodox religious position against the social activism of Beesly and Harrison. A serious rift developed in 1877-78, with the latter moving out of the Chapel Street congregation and into Newton Hall. Similar rifts occurred elsewhere: in Brazil between Lemus and Constant, and in Chile between Lagarrigue and Letelier.[79] The lines were drawn between the disciples who considered positivism a religion and the followers who saw it as a gospel of social reform.

This sectarian spirit spread to the rank and file of the disciples, and disagreements over doctrinal points caused one desertion after another. Laffitte's leadership was a sore point. When Comte died without having named a successor, Laffitte had reluctantly accepted it. However, he believed himself to be the head of the Positivist Society rather than the High Priest of the cult. Many were unhappy with this lack of enthusiasm. Congrave and the English disciples, already on the verge of a split with Harrison and Beesly, sought to replace Laffitte in 1877.[80] They succeeded only in breaking away from the French church and in further fragmenting the English branch. Another rift occurred in 1883 when Miguel Lemos and Juan Enrique Lagarrigue, the heads of the Brazilian and the Chilean churches, broke with Laffitte over what they considered was the latter's betrayal of positivism, the acceptance of a government position as a university professor.[81] Further dissension and sectarianism plagued the movement, reducing its effectiveness and making the utopian dream an impossibility.[82]

The followers who saw positivism as a social gospel of activism did not fare too well either. They also were unable to compromise. As a general rule, whenever they became embroiled in political controversies they alienated the opposition, be they Catholics or communists. And if compromises were reached, their own membership would feel betrayed.[83] If this inflexibility was due to an initial lack of political experience, when they acquired sophistication it was at the expense of the doctrine. This is true of Constant in Brazil, Letelier in Chile, John Morley in England.[84]

In Mexico, Comte's utopian positivism lost its ground to Spencerian, or evolutionary positivism; while in the United States, the utopian experiments of Cedar Vale and Modern Times collapsed and their adherents returned to the Old World. The difficulties in tracing its effects on the American labor movement tend to indicate that they must have been minimal. Still, they should not be disregarded particularly when, once in a while, one finds a warning of the insidious influence of positivism.[85]

Intransigence by the adherents, controversies over interpretation and sectarianism were historical reasons for the decline of the movement. Other reasons can be given, these involving practical difficulties within the doctrine itself. First of all, except for the *Système*, there was no matured plan for what should be done to help set up the positive polity. Comte's version, though definite and precise about the structure of the polity, relied too much on the power of public opinion and on the inevitability of history to prompt the change. He believed that because the polity was a necessary result of historical development it needed no plan of action.[86] But history never compels; and there was no Lenin of positivism. Compared to Marxism, which holds that though communism is inevitable one must still take an active part in the struggle, positivism is a spectator.

Second, once one realizes the scope of Comte's works it is understandable why positivism was not more popular. To fully understand the *Système*, one must read the six volumes of the

Cours, something a layman unfamiliar with science would find hard to do. Even the *Discours* demands too much from the reader and the various catechisms, written for women and the proletariat, did not offer enough, except for excessive regulation and inner contradictions. It smacked of Catholicism.[87] Finally, and probably the most important reason why it failed, positivism had to compete with systems that were intellectually more satisfying—with Marx's own and with Spencer's evolutionism.[88]

We can also cite *philosophical* reasons for the failure of positivism. Granted that the disciples and followers did not achieve their goals; could anyone achieve them? Unlikely, for Comte's program of social reform presupposes some questionable assertions. Briefly outlined, this program consists of three basic tenets:

(1) By means of sociology the scientific laws that describe the behavior of societies can be discovered.

(2) Once these laws have been discovered the scientist can proceed to discover the best social order.

(3) The best social order is, in fact, the positive polity.

Take the third tenet. Comte argues that the positive polity is the last stage of social development. But why? Lester Ward, the sociologist sympathizer of Comte, envisioned a fourth and fifth stage; José Ortega y Gasset, the philosopher, saw a cyclical change; other writers, such as Spencer, posed no limits to growth.[89] Comte's reasons are vague and depend on his belief about the superiority of the polity.[90] He did consider the possibility that this stage might come to an end, but only if the Earth became hostile to human habitation.[91] In this case, our only choice would be to accept the end with dignity. What he did not consider was the possibility that the scientific-industrial states of the future could poison the environment and be themselves a cause for the decline.

When we turn to examine the arguments in support of the positive polity's superiority, we find some serious weaknesses. Why should this particular social structure be the best? Comte offered a number of arguments: first, that the positive polity is the best because it is the result of a developmental law, that is, a law that traces development or evolution from inferior to superior, from worse to better?[2] It, he asserts, is a law that has been verified by history?[3] Yet, this can hardly count as a justification, for to claim that the Law of the Three Stages is developmental—from worse to better—assumes that whatever is at the end of the temporal line is better, i.e., the positive polity. Otherwise it would be only a law of change. Being the temporal end of a chain, developmental or otherwise, however, does not necessarily endow anything with value. A bus depot is the end of a bus line, but this does not make it superior. If the terminus of a series is superior to any element of the series, this improvement must be for some other reason. Comte himself provides us with that other reason: the positive polity is the best because it yields a superior morality—a morality based on benevolent acts and altruistic motives?[4] Apparently, he takes the value of these acts and motives as self-evident, for he never questions nor justifies their superiority.

So far the superiority of the positive polity hinges on acts and motives which not everyone would accept as truly superior, particularly those who would argue in favor of egoism?[5] But Comte advances a third kind of argument. The positive polity is the only kind of government that justifies itself by making an appeal to objective considerations. That is, whatever actions the polity takes, its value will always be verified by observation?[6] This claim presupposes the possibility that a scientist, by studying the facts, can discover the best kind of action and, in general, the best form of government—the second basic tenet of the program. Is this a sound assumption?

With the first tenet—that sociology can discover the laws that describe social behavior—we see no difficulty. It might be rough around the edges, but it is, in principle, acceptable. It is the second one that is unacceptable and in need of clarification. A scientist might have discovered certain facts about society or certain laws that explain the behavior of individuals in that society. In such a case he is entitled to state that *this is the way these people behave*. To justify this argument all he has to do is refer us to the date that gave rise to his claims. On the other hand, if he stated that *this is the way these people ought to behave* he is saying something more. He is declaring that even if people did not behave this way, they should. In other

words, factual claims are reports of regularities in people's behavior which tell us what happened, and to state the opposite
is to make a contradictory assertion. Value claims are injunc-
tions about what people's behavior should be, even though
the opposite kind of behavior is the case. We need such injunc-
tions as reminders of how we ought to, but do not, behave.

Comte is correct when he states that the task of positive
science is to study, discover, classify, make generalizations, explain and predict from the facts, but is seriously mistaken
when he claims that it can justify the superiority of the positive
polity. The qualitative difference between factual premises and
value conclusions prevents any valid justification. If the positive sciences are to be consistent in their logic then they can
never reach value conclusions. This is what is meant by the
requirement that science be value-free. Hence, the discovery
of the best social structure cannot be the province of science.
All that the scientist can do is to present the available alternatives which we, as moral agents, must decide upon—nothing
more, and nothing less.[7]

Yet, Comte is not completely wrong. Science must be
value free, but the scientist is not and cannot be above morality. This is not an untenable position. It is only the requirement
that science be subservient to moral ends, not that it dictate
what these moral ends be. This is a weaker but more acceptable version of Comte's second tenet. After all, science ought
to be our servant, not our master.

We have, so far, explored Comte's conception of the good
society—the positive polity. In the process, we examined the
philosophical foundations and the overarching structure. We
also tried to account for the sociocracy's limited popularity
and followed the works of the disciples, sympathizers and followers. Then we analyzed why it failed, in principle and in
practice, and pointed out some fallacies in the doctrine. Now
we come to the difficult task of evaluating this utopian conception, of passing judgement on its sanity, perdurability, emo-
tionalism, and acceptability as a way of life.

Almost a century and a quarter has passed since the death
of Comte. When we evaluate the polity we have to take into

account that circumstances have changed. His contemporaries might have sharply rejected his utopian visions as insane. We, on the other hand, might be willing to give Comte a more open reception, inured as we are to human suffering and aware of the excesses of Jonestown, of the Pol Pot regime, of Hitler's folkish state and of other "utopian" realities. It is to our discredit that in these hundred and twenty-some years, the ravings of a madman, as some judged the *Système*, have acquired an air of sanity, urbanity, harmony and progressiveness that make it almost attractive.

The positive polity is a child of the nineteenth century. In it we find, characteristically, a respect for scientific investigation, and optimism about the future, a reliance on the power of ideas to convince once principles and means are agreed upon, and even a rationalistic religion. In spite of this, the positive polity stands apart from the rest of that century's dreams. With the exception of Marxism, few utopian conceptions have endured as long as positivism. Whatever the reasons for this longevity—its religious apostleship, its political radicalism, its scientism—Comte's positivism could not have lasted that long unless it filled a social, political and psychological need. And if in comparison to Marxism positivism comes in a poor second, at least Comte was spared the dubious honor of being talked about more than being read.

Inventing utopias seem to be one of those typically human paradoxes. We suffer from the need to speculate quite unrealistically about the life everyone should lead, to dream of more auspicious times and better places in the full realization that they will never exist, but with the contradictory hope that some day they will become a reality. This is what we mean by utopianism—an emotional exercise which misleads our rational faculty and makes us ask for the impossible. Comte also suffered from this malady. The *Système* expressed values not implied in the sociological analysis of the *Cours*. The Religion of Humanity with its calendar, elaborate ritual, pantheon, dogma, barely concealed an underlying utopianism. Yet, this is not completely true, for Comte himself was aware of the power of emotions to keep societies together. Wanting to avoid an overly rationalistic utopia, he sought a place for the emotions in the polity the only way he knew—by religious worship.

Perhaps the most important question that can be asked about any utopia is whether one would be willing to live under such a system. While we would not call the sociocracy a Paradise on Earth, we can still think of worse places to live—Plato's Republic for instance. Admittedly, the positive polity represents a narrow nineteenth-century world, unreal because of its very simplicity. Nevertheless, it possesses a quiet dignity, a respect for others, a civility, and an admiration for intellectual labor that is missing from our own contemporary societies. It also lacks what is commonplace with us: the hopeless poverty, the cult of violence, a lack of respect for human life and for humanity as a whole. In this sense we can look to Comte's utopia as a place, and a no-place, better than our own.

6

Women in Utopias

PATRICIA HUCKLE

Only in us do the dead live.
Water flows downhill through us.
The sun cools in our bones.
We are joined with all living
in one singing web of energy.
In us live the dead who made us.
In us live the children unborn.
Breathing each other's air
drinking each other's water
eating each other's flesh we grow
like a tree from the earth.

from *Woman on the Edge of Time*, Marge Piercy

You can't get there from here. Anonymous

Women, too, have searched for a more perfect world. The quest for utopia (and the difficulty in achieving it) has been as important for nineteenth and twentieth century feminists as it has been for other political and social critics and revolutionaries. It seems appropriate, therefore, to explore the promises and experiments as they affected and still affect women's lives. Much is promised; much is envisioned; much is yet to be achieved.

The nineteenth century utopian communities were developed during a period of rapid social change, a time in which women began to organize to achieve greater social equality. Contemporary communes also reflected change, and many began at the same time that twentieth century women recognized their own need to demand social equity. In both periods of time, the utopian fiction reflects criticism of society and the vision of a more nearly perfect world. My purpose here is to juxtapose nineteenth century social experiments and fiction with more recent communes and feminist science fiction. Each is examined for assumptions and practices in terms of sex role specialization, patterns of relationships, and attempts to achieve new social structures. While the failure to achieve social equality for women and men is evident, and the limitations of utopian ventures varied and many, they nevertheless provide insights, stimulate creative thinking, and clarify the risks and hazards inherent in attempting to remake the world more nearly to our own liking.[1]

Throughout the nineteenth century, both utopian experiments and novels with utopian settings proliferated in the United States. Theoretically, at least, equality for women was an acknowledged goal in both. Many of the novels and communities were based on critical appraisals of the family, and developed new structures designed to foster community spirit as well as equality. Equal rights, at least in terms of marriage and property, were considered appropriate.

Few of the nineteenth century utopian novels were written by women, but Mary Griffith's *Three Hundred Years Hence* (1836) gives credit to women for social reform.[2] The women in Mrs. Griffith's novel "taught their children not to kill; they taught them the true meaning of religion—and so made war impossible." In her pastoral society, women are educated, trained in business, and equal owners of marital property. "In every plan for meliorating condition of the poor, and improving morals, it was woman's influence that promoted and fostered it. It is to that healthy influence that we owe our present prosperity and happiness."[3] The new, ideal world in this view owed much to the special qualities of women. This assumption of women's moral superiority, and a belief in evolutionary change through education were reflected in the general popular literature of the time. Griffith's novel is consistent with the "Cult of True Womanhood," in which women's primary virtues were seen to be "piety, purity, submissiveness and domesticity."[4]

By the end of the century, the movement for women's rights generated activists and theorists. Charlotte Perkins Gilman, social thinker and feminist theorist, wrote three utopian novels: *Moving the Mountain*, *Herland*, and *With Her in Ourland*. *Herland* was published in Gilman's periodical, *The Forerunner*, in 1915, and was reprinted in 1979.[5] The novel serves as a vehicle for Gilman's criticism of women's subordinate role in society, and her prescriptions for achieving a positive transformation. This utopia is a world of women, secluded high in the mountains and discovered by three enterprising male explorers. Their first view is from the air:

> —a land in a state of perfect cultivation, where even the forests looked as if they were cared for; a land that looked like an enormous park, only it was even more evidently an enormous garden . . . clean, well-built roads, attractive architecture . . . ordered beauty of the little town.[6]

The good-natured women of Herland take the men in and educate them. This structure allows Gilman to sketch her ideal world of sharing, physical strength, peaceful and serene surroundings, and to poke fun at the way things are elsewhere. The following passage gives the flavor of her gentle humor:

> . . . There was no accepted standard of what was "manly" and what was "womanly." When Jeff said, taking the fruit basket from his adored one, "A woman should not carry anything," Celis said, "Why?" with the frankest amazement. He could not look that fleet-footed, deep-chested forester in the face and say, "Because she is weaker." She wasn't. One does not call a race horse weak because it is visibly not a cart horse . . . He said, rather lamely, that women were not built for heavy work . . . "I don't understand," she said quite sweetly. "Are the women in your country so weak that they could not carry such a thing as that?" "It is a convention," he said. "We assume that motherhood is a sufficient burden—that men should carry all the others."[7]

Discussing with the women the history of this lovely land, the men discover:

> ... they had no wars. They had had no kings, and no priests, and no aristocracies. They were sisters, and as they grew, they grew together—not by competition, but by united action.[8]

This is a society in which there are no men (an environmental disaster drowned the men and geographically isolated the women). The women discovered parthenogenesis, and have for 1500 years been evolving their cooperative society.

It is a gentle novel, and a gentle world Gilman presents. The only conflict comes from the attempts to escape by the three men, and their final expulsion when one of the men attempts to rape his wife. The point is made that women are morally superior, and capable of bringing about an ideal world in which cooperation, beauty, harmony and peace are realized.

Although the women in Herland perform all the tasks necessary to sustain the society, their special qualities related to mothering seem to echo the views in other works of the period. The controlling force in Gilman's paradise is mothering:

> You see, they were Mothers, not in our sense of helpless involuntary fecundity, forced to fill and overfill the land, every land, and then see their children suffer, sin, and die, fighting horribly with one another; but in the sense of Conscious Makers of People. Mother-love with them was not a brute passion, a mere "instinct," a wholly personal feeling; it was—a religion.[9]

The mothering function is idealized and serves as a building and guiding principle. Gilman is writing after the turn of the century, when feminist demands for property rights, suffrage and economic equality were part of the political context. Her view in *Herland*, however is still consistent with the "separate but equal" claims of the "Cult of True Womanhood." Gilman expects equality for women, and challenges the consequences of male domination. She does so in the most womb-worshipping of fashions, idealizing both the maternal urge and the power of mothering to transform society. The novel reflects a state of yearning and belief in perfectibility as well as being a social critique. There is a quality of the dream in this fleshing out of feminist ideology.

The realities of nineteenth century utopian communities were something else. Whether utopian-socialist or religious in origin, most of the 500 or so nineteenth century social community experiments involved both women and men. From coast to coast, women joined their husbands in these adventures which were meant to bring the ideal future into being.

Most analysts of these utopian communities suggest some working out of equal rights for women. The following is not an exhaustive review, but does illuminate some of the assumed benefits to women from living collectively in these model worlds. For example, it is reported that Rappite communities (Harmonist Society) allowed women the right to vote in community affairs and to receive equal pay for equal work. They were also said to have the right to refuse to have intercourse with their husbands; celibacy was considered necessary to their economic and spiritual survival.[10] The Shaker villages also professed equality for women, and each sex held an equal number of community offices.[11] The Owenites at New Harmony promised equality for women, and Robert Dale Owen was an advocate of women's property rights at the Indiana Constitutional Convention in 1850. The Fourierists also advocated emancipation and equality of women, and Fourier is credited with coining the term "feminism." At the North American Phalanx, Fourierists permitted women to share in policy making, opened all kinds of work to them, and paid them equally with men for their work. Rights to equal pay for equal work are also reported for some economic cooperatives such as Commmunia in Iowa and the Kaweah colony in California.[12]

There were, in addition, several women who were strong leaders in their utopian settlements. Ann Lee's vision led to the foundation of the Shaker villages, although "Mother Ann," as she was called, died in 1784, three years before the first village was established.[13] In a community called Jerusalem, located in western New York, Jemima Wilkinson was spiritual leader and sole trustee of community property for the forty-some families who followed her.[14] Frances Wright was the founder and leader of Nashoba Community, established in 1825, in Memphis, Tennessee. She advocated an end to slavery, and her views of race integration and the apparent sexual freedom at Nashoba were considered scandalous.[15] Loma-Land, a Theosophist community in Point Loma, California, although chronologically twentieth century (1897-1942), was very much in the nineteenth century tradition. It was led by Katherine Tingley, and included among its objectives:

> . . . To help men and women to realize the nobility of their calling and their true position in life . . . [and] To ameliorate the condition of unfortunate women, and assist them to a higher life.[16]

Among the vast literature on nineteenth century utopian communities, only one is mentioned which seems to have been developed by and for women only.[17] Although identified by one source as "utopian-socialist" in philosophy, a 1901 Department of Labor report on "Cooperative Communities in the United States," notes it began about 1876 with a Bible study group started by Mrs. Martha McWhirter, mother of twelve children. The group of women left their husbands eventually, and over time they supported themselves by running two hotels and a steam-laundry plant and by building and renting houses. Although their first ten years were apparently stormy, since the town of Belton, Texas was outraged by their "eccentricities in religion and dress," eventually they were accepted as sound citizens and "When in 1898, they were about to move their Colony to Mt. Pleasant, near Washington, D.C., the whole town begged them to remain." Their move was apparently for retirement purposes, but they continued with another boarding house and farm in the East, and were reported to have eighteen women members in 1906. Their principles were both Christian and communistic, as well as celibate, and they are an intriguing note for historians of utopian experiments.[18]

In general, however, these many communities, some small and short-lived, others sizeable and lasting into the twentieth century, were designed by men and run by them. As Dolores Hayden observes in *Seven American Utopias: The*

Architecture of Communitarian Socialism, "In most nine-teenth century communes 'women's work' remained sex stereotyped ..." Of the seven attempts to build a model commu-nity she surveys, Hancock, Oneida, the Fourierist Phalanx, and Greeley considered in theory that the role of women should be equalized.[19] In practice, whether domestic work was done col-lectively or in isolation, it was generally done by women. Child-rearing, even in communities (like Oneida) where done collectively, was primarily the responsibility of women. Al-most all accepted sex-role specialization, and none suggested men should learn traditional domestic or nurturing skills per-formed by women. Traditional male tasks, including manage-ment and decision-making were retained by men. Although, for example, women held an equal number of positions in the formal structure of Shaker communities, that was because the sexes were completely separated for most community func-tions, and women were needed to supervise women in their domestic tasks.

Most utopian communities attempted to alter family struc-ture, either by adopting a policy of celibacy, or by restricting selection of marriage partner, or by some pattern of "free love." In *Sex and Marriage in Utopian Communities*, Raymond Muncy notes:

> In attempting to create a new social order in which the family no longer occupied the central position, utopians were gener-ally concerned about the new role of women. Practically all of them attempted to demonstrate how their program of economic reform would bring about the liberation of womanhood.[20]

The attacks on the family, and on monogamous marriages, were made to ensure that members of the community (re-ligious or economic) would place the collective interest before personal relationships, rather than to benefit women or to de-velop equal status for them. Domestic reforms, which were among the great innovations of utopian communities, did in fact ease the tasks of collective housekeeping, but the feeding, laundering, cleaning, nursing and child-rearing were done by women. In some instances, where a community might have a "manpower" shortage, women were encouraged to learn "manly" tasks. At Oneida, women were also encouraged to dress in simple clothing, or clothes which permitted more freedom of movement, both to permit their participation in productive activities and to discourage "vanity." But men were not similarly encouraged to adopt positive aspects of "womanly" demeanor or activity. It is true that John Noyes, at Oneida, did advocate equal sexual pleasure for women and men, and suggested that men learn to control ejaculation so that women did not suffer too many pregnancies. However, even this limited form of contraception was controlled by men; only the celibate communities offered some level of sexual autonomy to both sexes. The system of "complex marriage" Noyes developed seemed to owe much to his own personal sexual dynamism, and as Judith Fryer comments, "Despite his stated aims, full sexual equality, what Noyes is actually arguing for here, much like Joseph Smith, is the dominance of women not by one man but by many."[21] As with other attempts to shape community by altering traditional marriage and relationships, both "complex marriage" and the eugenic experiment called "stirpiculture" at Oneida were institutions reflecting the desire of a charismatic leader to control others in the name of community welfare. Speaking of the general hardships of communal living at New Harmony, one woman wondered "if the prospect of paradise on earth were not a treachery played by the male imagination."[22] The dream and reality conflicted sharply in nineteenth century utopian communities, not least of all in terms of life options available to women.

That same set of tensions and unrealized visions is reflected in more recent efforts to build utopian communities. In the late 1960s and 1970s such experiments in group living blossomed in the United States. Hundreds of groups came together with the deliberate utopian goal of establishing "new" ways of relating and living. Some generated as a reaction to observed environmental decline, or to perceived political manipulation. Their orientation might be religious, political and/or rural (sometimes all at once). Some groups developed out of the "hippie" idealism about the power of love to transform structure, or out of a search for personal intimacy. Some were simply avenues of escape from perceived materialism and destructive relationships. A good number of these groups turned to rural settings for fulfillment of their dreams. The issues of economic survival, relationship of individual to community, and how to achieve autonomy and new values troubled these groups as they had the nineteenth century experiments. They also reflect contemporary patterns in male/female relationships and male control of community structure.

Representative of countercultural publications of that period is *Communities: Journal of Cooperative Living*. From 1974 to 1977, the bi-monthly periodical presented articles on the successes of the communal movement, the structure of each in terms of economics, distribution of resources, nature of decision-making, as well as practical articles on building and surviving in the country. Few articles deal with the issue of sex roles or women's liberation. Those that do, confirm the similarity of rural communes of the 1960s or 1970s with the earlier nineteenth century endeavors. In a 1974 article "Women in Communes," the note is made:

> Probably because people in communes do trust and care about each other more, we all try to understand and respect each others thoughts and feelings, and make changes in ourselves when necessary. I am not pleased with the fact that men still do most of the mechanical work and I don't like the fact that only women here see a need to have consciousness-raising.[23]

Open discussion of feelings is a common thread in these communities, but challenge to traditional roles is not taken for granted, and must be initiated by women with limited results.

In the next issue of *Communities*, in an article titled "Women in Community," there is a discussion of the advantage for individual women of living collectively where ". . . childcare and education are dynamics experienced by the entire group, not just the biological parents."[24] But the women having this dialogue also say: "I find that when new people join our community, it's the men who are expected to know how to do all kinds of things."[25] And another acknowledges:

> You know, when it comes down to the nuts and bolts of survival, lots of the things that women traditionally do aren't even

considered skills; those skills become expendable and are not valued.[26]

In his study of *Thirteen Modern American Communes*, Hugh Gardner confirms the general impression of continued sex-role specialization. He comments on "patriarchal elements" in almost all observed communes. Whatever the size, structure or values of the groups he examines, the thread of male superiority is evident:

> Still another result was the fact that women, while otherwise sharing equally in Drop City's vague kind of politics, were almost invariably left with the responsibility for feeding the community . . .[27]

In another instance, he observes that women at Libre often worked beside their men on building, and "were outspoken participants in Councils and other community affairs *when issues fell within their range of interests*" (emphasis added). That range of interests was surely defined by the fact that "Libre women generally assumed traditional household tasks without rotation . . ."[28] In comparing two New Mexico communities (Morning Star East and Reality), he sees women doing traditional domestic work. Noting similar conventional domestic roles at the Maharj Ashram, Gardner does mention that there is a response to the women's liberation challenge, since they did organize the "Grace of God Movement of the Women of America" which a spokesperson characterized as follows:

> Our aim and our ideal . . . is to restore woman to her rightful status . . . where woman will once again be known as the living goddess and put back on her pedestal in the hearts of all men and all mankind the world over.[29]

A more direct reference to the "Cult of True Womanhood" would be hard to find, with the echoes of reverence for woman's passivity and submissiveness as a substitute for individual self-determination.

In other settings, with the passage of time, the presence of feminists began to be felt more strongly in some communes. Concern for the shape of the family, and questions about the best ways for groups to survive often led to claims of equality and aspirations to collective child rearing and non-property sexual relations. One of the best known communal experiments is the Twin Oaks Community, patterned after the community envisioned in Skinner's novel, *Walden Two*. Kathleen Kinkade, a founder and strong presence in that community, addresses the issue of sexism in her book, *A Walden Two Experiment*.[30] In discussing the sexual revolution at Twin Oaks concerning the "ongoing struggle against sexism," she states:

> Sexism is the assumption that one's overall worth is measured in terms of one's desirability to the opposite sex. Outside society is heavily sexist, and women, in particular, suffer from it. We weren't conscious of this problem when we started the Community, but when Women's Liberation consciousness hit the rest of the nation, Twin Oaks naturally started thinking about it, too. We examined our attitudes, and they were not entirely free of sexism.

She acknowledges traditional sexual expectations, and in other areas of community life and decision-making notes:

> Was it true that men did most of the talking in meetings? It was. Was this because the group did not respect women? We thought not. The dismal fact was that many of the women did not know as much as the men . . . The remedy, then, was with the women themselves.

Although there is sensitivity to male dominance, it is taken for granted that the fault lies with women, and that it is women's responsibility to change their behavior, not the responsibility of the community to change. By 1973, Twin Oaks claimed: "We have no sex roles in our work. Both men and women cook and clean and wash dishes; both women and men drive trucks and tractors, repair fences, load hay, slaughter cattle."

Increased sensitivity to the consequences of sex-role expectations and male control of decision-making is evidenced in the later issues of *Communities*. In the May/June 1976 issue, Eric Raimy comments on the difficulties of overcoming traditional patterns:

> Members of some student and counterculture houses believe that their households are unstructured. The housework is accomplished, it is said, in a free-flowing manner by whoever is moved to do a particular job. In reality, these houses usually do have a pretty clear organization—one determined by sex roles.[31]

Further, in the March-April 1977 issue of *Communities*, an article on "Women in Community" comments that "most women who move into community want to leave sex roles and other cultural conditioning behind."[32]

These utopian experiments of the twentieth century echo some of the issues and concerns of earlier communities. There were some advantages to women in the collective life-style, including increased contact with other women, some shared child-rearing and shared domestic labor. Women were still, however, considered less important to the success of communes than the "better skilled" males. Although there was some exploration of non-traditional roles, primarily this meant women learning to do "male" tasks. Women rapidly discovered, as they have in political or religious groups across the spectrum, that the "good life," the simplified "natural" life, meant repetition of sex role specialization and oppression of women. In heterosexual communes they were still sex objects and domestic servants. As "Earth Mothers," they were expected to live in harmony with nature and the kitchen, while men controlled the tools, land and decisions.

Disillusioned, many women left, often to join other women. In 1975, *Communities* reported on one collective in which the men had all left. The article notes:

> Even those who had boyfriends felt relief when the men moved out and we began to call ourselves a "women's farm." . . . We became physically strong. In those times, we were united as only women can be with the knowledge that no man was going to do it for us.[33]

Since the mid-1970s, feminist collective living experiences have also been reported. There is not an accurate estimate of the number in existence, and no overall study has been completed to date, but some themes can be identified. *Country Women*, published by a collective of women in Albion, California, reflects a feminist perspective on rural living. Along with practical advice on tractors, bee-keeping, buying land, etc., this monthly periodical has had issues which focus on the following: Older Women; Children's Liberation; Natural Cycles; Sexuality; Relationships; Politics; Integration of Mental and Physical Health; Food; City/Country; Class; Personal Power; Anger and Violence; and International Women. *Country Women: A Handbook for the New Farmer* was prepared by women who also write for and work on the periodical, and gives practical advice on rural survival. In their introduction, they summarize the goals of many feminists in the rural setting who come together not only to escape male oppression, but also to develop as strong individuals in a collective context.

> In the country, there is room for a women's renaissance. The space and time is there for a total redefinition of ourselves, our relation to the earth, our relation to each other . . . We have the skills, the enthusiasm, the resources to build our dwellings, raise our food, take care of our most basic and real needs.[34]

The reality of the struggle to live out an ideal version of feminist community is like the dream projected in science fiction and also very different. The feminist ideology of equal status can become the "tyranny of structurelessness" in practice.[35] Differences in political strategy have led to bitter factionalism within the women's movement as well as within group living efforts. Belief in the ability of women to do and be anything is often modified by the need for day to day economic survival. Conflicts over the role of mothers and child-rearing attitudes do not disappear in all-woman communities. Nor do the agonies of jealousy and interpersonal power dissolve in lesbian-separatist enclaves. The rural women's communities have offered an opportunity to withdraw, at least for a time, from the urban pressures. They are also inspirational in the sense of

bonding and sharing with other women, and in the opportunity to learn a wide range of skills. They are certainly not
instant blueprints to a perfect future, either at the margin or for
the general population of women and men.

Just as there are links between the nineteenth century
plans for a more perfect world and the visionary novels of the
time, there are connections with experimental communes of
recent decades. The quest for ideal community continues, as
does the political movement toward women's liberation. Unlike nineteenth century utopians, twentieth century feminists
and visionaries do question basic assumptions about the distribution of power based on one's gender. This may be in part
because economic and technological changes, such as the
availability of wage-paying jobs, and more reliable, woman-
controlled methods of contraception permit it. Feminist analysis of society questions and challenges the basic rationale for
sex roles. Further, in looking at oppression on the basis of sex,
many feminists stress the importance of compounding effects.
That is to say, in order to understand the situation of women, it
is important to examine also differences and similarities across
racial, class and age lines. In examining the implications of sexual expectations, it is also important to understand the force of
heterosexuality as it shapes behavior and punishes or rewards
individuals. The dreams of an ideal future in which privileges
based on sex, race, class, sexual preference, age or physical
ability are eliminated, have been presented in feminist ideology and science fiction of the 1970s.

Just as the nineteenth century feminist novelists (like
Gilman) took an imaginative leap beyond the real-life utopias
so, today, feminist writers make up for the deficiencies of actual communal experiments by imagining a utopian world in
which sex roles are eliminated. Much that is creative along this
line is being done in the science fiction genre which,
traditionally, has offered escape into some marvelous other
time and space, in which advanced technology and/or other
life forms shape "man's" destiny. Characteristically, it has been
a genre patterned on dystopian or utopian extensions of industrialized European society. Until recently, relatively little serious attention was paid to imagining futures with different or
no sex role specialization or male dominance. Unlike many in

the male tradition, feminist writers ground their projections for tomorrow in the present reality of oppression in women's lives. Their novels provoke, challenge and inspire creative response to new ways of relating and to new forms for society.

There are, of course, connections between feminist science fiction and the male genre, as well as with the utopian tradition. Current concern with the environment is reflected in the generally pastoral settings. The role of science and technology, although not seen in as hopeful a light as was the case with utopian visions of the nineteenth century, is central in these recent works. As did the utopians, the science fiction writers often take for granted the use of space and time travel as narrative device. These themes, then, are similar. There are, however, crucial differences in perspective and ideology in feminist science fiction. First, the primary characters are female, and provide positive role models. Second, technology is seen as subordinate to the development of a society in which power is shared. These feminist visions of the future take for granted a need to re-order individual and collective priorities. They view the world from the perspective of women, take for granted the need for change, and imagine different ways to get there from here.

Reviews of this new literature include introductory essays by Pamela Saıgaent in her short story collections, *Women of Wonder*, *More Women of Wonder*, and *New Women of Wonder*, and special focus issues of feminist periodicals, *Quest* and *Frontiers*[36] Among interesting novels with a feminist perspective on the future are: Ursula LeGuin's *The Left Hand of Darkness*, with its androgynous, bisexual characters and *The Dispossessed*; Sally Gearhart's *The Wanderground*, in which women's superior psychic abilities and relation to nature are a central theme; Suzy Charnas's *Motherlines*, which creates an all-woman society, deals with parthenogenesis, and raises the issue of the long-term effects of oppression as it affects women relating to women; Dorothy Bryant's *The Kin of Ata Await You*, which emphasizes the psychic abilities of all creatures; Doris Lessing's *The Four-Gated City*, *The Memoirs of a Survivor*, and *Shikasta*, which illuminate a time after the holocaust, where psychic communication is a matter of survival; and Marian Zimmer Bradley's *The Shattered Chain*, which has an Amazon guild, and her *Ruins of Isis*, which speculates on equality and dangers of sex-role reversal on a matriarchal planet.[37] They are valuable for their rich, imaginative projections and for the political/ideological questions they raise. Some are dream-worlds, which can inspire or provide moments of restful optimism; others are challenging creations which give off disturbing images.

For this discussion, two other novels, *The Female Man* by Joanna Russ, and *Woman on the Edge of Time* by Marge Piercy,[38] seem especially useful. They are utopian, in that they provide models for an ideal world. They are also feminist, in that they sharply criticize present society and flesh out possible future directions for women and men, together and apart. Both reflect the assumptions in Firestone's ideological text, *The Dialectic of Sex*, particularly the primacy of reproduction and child rearing as sources of oppression.[39] This contemporary feminist classic attempts to extend class analysis to an examination of women's oppression based on biological functions. Russ extends the question of "What if there weren't any men around at all?" to shape her future vision, articulating a lesbian separatist perspective.[40] Piercy counterpoints a most oppressive and destructive present against a possible balanced and integrated future, in which both women and men are changed.

These novels are utopian in that they provide a vision of an ideal future world. Each acknowledges the uncertainty of attaining that ideal. In common with other utopian works they have the following themes: a high value placed on equitable distribution of resources and authority; options in terms of the nature and place of work in individual lives; status based on individual worth; and a pastoral setting in which there is strong awareness of the inter-relatedness of humans and environment, leading to limited use of technology. Unlike most male utopian or science fiction works, these novels also critique patriarchal power distributions and relationships, where men control resources and decision making, and women are relegated to secondary status at best. They differ from Gilman's *Herland* in their tendency to sharper criticism, as well as in their stronger portrayals of violence and sexuality. They do not assume nurturing is peculiarly the function of the female, nor

do they assume the potential for violence is exclusively characteristic of the male.

Piercy and Russ both follow the ideological issues outlined by Firestone:

> ... the first demand for any alternative system must be: 1) the
> freeing of women from the tyranny of their reproductive biol-
> ogy by every means available, and the diffusion of the child-
> bearing and childrearing role to the society as a whole ... 2)
> the full self-determination, including economic independence,
> of both women and children ... 3) the total integration of
> women and children into all aspects of the larger society, [and]
> ... 4) the freedom of all women and children to do whatever
> they wish to do sexually.[41]

Each novel moves in its own direction, but the dream at some
levels follows Firestone's suggested pattern. For Russ, this
seems to mean creating a world without men, following the
separatist idea that women can only develop full potential in a
society of women. For Piercy, it means creating a society in
which reproduction is controlled collectively.

In Whileaway, the ideal future world of *The Female Man*, a
sophisticated birth technology is essential, since only women
live there. In *Woman on the Edge of Time*, the group balances
deaths with births, selects genetic factors to meet desirable
community traits and needs, and assigns three volunteers of
either sex as mothers. Both women and men breastfeed and
child rear in this society. This is Piercy's working out of
Firestone:

> It was part of women's long revolution. When we were break-
> ing up all the old hierarchies. Finally, there was that one thing
> we had to give up too, the only power we ever had, in return
> for no more power for anyone. The original production: the
> power to give birth. Cause as long as we were biologically en-
> chained, we'd never be equal. And males never would be hu-
> manized to be loving and tender. So we all became mothers ...
> to break the nuclear bonding.[42]

Here again is an echo to Gilman's *Herland*, where mothers are
the primary force in society. Gilman, however, assumed the in-

ate superiority of women as mothers, as therefore better able to build a new society. Piercy, on the other hand, recognizes the central issue of reproduction by saying all must be able to bear children. For Piercy, the end to reproductive specialization is one key to equality for both women and men; for Gilman, mothers simply show the way. Both Russ and Piercy's novels take for granted that sophisticated technology (rather than Gilman's parthenogenesis) controls methods of child bearing. The problems of social control of research and technology are assumed to be resolved.

In these feminist alternative futures power is decentralized and shared. While there is evidence that most historical utopian communities (including the female Woman's Commonwealth) were held together under the domination of a strong, charismatic political or religious leader, that is not the view taken in this fiction. In *The Female Man*, individual self-development is primary, and loose associations or benevolent anarchy replaces formal governmental structure. Piercy shows us a collective, representative democracy where decisions are made by consensus following intensive debate. Leadership is voluntary and rotates, but a strong personal commitment to participation is expected. Tensions and disagreements arise in both future worlds, as was not the case in *Herland* where womanly harmony reminds one of the criticism that socialist utopias would be dull without conflict. If disagreements are strong enough in Whileaway (*The Female Man*), they are resolved by duel; otherwise they are discussed in community meetings and resolved. Each novel also speaks to the issue of violence as social control of women. From *The Female Man*:

> There's no being out too late in Whileaway, or up too early, or in the wrong part of town, or unescorted. You cannot fall out of the kinship web and become sexual prey for strangers, for there is no prey and there are no strangers—the web is worldwide[43]

Since power relationships are equalized and community ties widespread, violent sexual assault is also unknown in Piercy's future world. Frustration and anger have not disappeared entirely, but there are community mechanisms for fostering reconciliation. No one is alone in these futures, except in chosen private spaces. There is respect for both individuality and the collective societal needs.

Each of these two novels reflects sensitivity to the situation of women today. A focus for Russ, for example, is in the fragmented and multi-dimensional aspects of women's lives. Four women characters interact in the novel, across past, present and future. Russ suggests all may be one woman. She suggests that women are the timid, culture-bound, submissive, romantic creature represented by Jeannine. They may also simultaneously be Joanna, struggling: "Let me in, Love me, Approve me, Define me, Regulate me, Validate me, Support me. Now I say Move Over."[44] In each woman is her utopian Amazon, too, living in a world in which there are no sex roles, where there are no men, where women *are*, and have the opportunity to *become*. At yet another level, women are all Alice (or the biblical Jael) with rage and vengeance flaring from their eyes, and destruction inevitable. Russ's shifting back and forth from character to character and time to time is sometimes dizzying and frustrating for the reader, but it does foster an awareness of multiple dimensions and the connections.

The weaving of diverse expectations and limited options is clear in Piercy's novel as well. *Woman on the Edge of Time* begins with grim poverty, violence and racism. Connie, the central character, is confused by the needs and wants generated by her society, her family, and herself. Piercy traces, through this character and the dream connection to the future, the effect on women of systematic social control, particularly by mental health institutions. Piercy suggests that change toward the ideal future state must begin with action here and now, and that those who have the least to lose are likely to be the strongest source of revolutionary change. In this novel, it is the damaged and angry woman of color who uses psychic energy to contact possibly imagined residents of the future, and who begins (however self-destructively) to build toward change in her own present through violent action. In both novels we see the positive possible future joined with the fear of possible destruction.

These, then, are some of the threads of utopian feminist visions. The literature reflects aspirations and ideology. Women are freed from both the power and burden of reproduction. Both children and women are fully integrated into society. The clan or family has been restructured to provide an extended network of friendships and mutual support. The collective needs are worked out cooperatively, with respect for individual talents and preferences. Sexuality is taken for granted as an aspect of people's lives, to be enjoyed in a sharing way. No one owns anyone else, and very few personal belongings are required or wanted, since all is common property and responsibility. There is a recognition of the value of psychic resources, as well as command over advanced technology linked with ecological principles. Status and power in these dreams come from being a valued member of the community, not from sex, class, race or age privilege. Individuals are strong because the community is strong.

These novels work as the best of literature does, to amuse, move, provoke and disturb us. There is laughter, pain, the juice of life and human relationships given shape we can share, at least in imagination. They also provide us with strong female role models or heroines. They say yes, women are active, can grow, develop, take charge of their own lives. Janet Evason, in *The Female Man*, is a bold and shining, fragile and dynamic, fully realized, complex person. In *Woman on the Edge of Time*, we see the sensitivity and compassion of Connie, who struggles both because of and in spite of her oppression. Luciente, that novel's androgynous, multifaceted and talented time traveler, gives us a positive vision of an open, egalitarian society in which women and men nurture and grow in harmony with the natural environment and their community.

Feminist science fiction can be inspirational and provocative. We look at each world created and ask if this is a world we want. Do we agree, disagree? The novels may trouble us; they certainly criticize the world in which we now live. The problem then becomes, how do we get there from here, assuming this is a final ideal world we might prefer? These two novels, for example, take for granted that technology could lead to greater reproductive choice. But serious questions must be raised about this assumption, since that technology is available now but not controlled by women, nor likely to be in the near future. Do we forget that men, not women, control resources and policy decisions? If feminist utopian visions predict violent revolution or some form of holocaust as a prerequisite to social change, then how applicable are they to women's contemporary political options and strategies?[45] The feminist visions of the future are grounded in contemporary values and mores, and posit new and wondrous options. The novels, therefore, are more successful at social criticism than they are at clarifying practical methods for achieving utopia.

All these utopian visions and experiments have common questions: how to build an ideal, harmonious world; how to reconcile the needs of the individual with the needs of the collective; how to balance science and technology with nature and environment. They can be criticized for being "unrealistic," for failing to take into account economic and political obstacles to achievement. Most are designed to be small in scale, and can thus be seen as inappropriate for masses of people. They are pastoral in tone and setting, while the realities are intensively technological and urban. Communal experiments idealize cooperation and democracy, but there is considerable evidence that most operate primarily as benevolent autocracies.

When utopian dreams and realities are examined for their assumptions about and behavior toward women, further criticisms can be made. Ideologically, some nineteenth and twentieth century model communities espoused equality for women without challenging the separation or specialization of the sexes, or questioning male roles in maintaining male power. Although there has been some recognition that women are entitled to economic self-sufficiency, the reality has been a secondary domestic role for women, and an underlying assumption of woman's moral superiority. Even the nineteenth century feminist utopian novel by Gilman idealizes the capacity to give birth or to mother. In the twentieth century communes, women have been expected to learn the important "male" tasks, but men have not often been asked to learn the range of nurturing and supportive skills required of women. Lesbian-separatist, or woman-centered communes were partly a response to that continued sex role separation.

The contemporary feminist novels provide a framework for exploring the consequences of full development of women's potential. They challenge the idea that biology determines options. They propose a collective, cooperative future without oppression, in which lives are fully integrated and meaningful. Both the novels and the social experiments have their problems; neither corrects nor alters the present realities for most of us. Their value, both in the nineteenth century and today, is that they speak to central concerns. No matter that they fail as transformations, or as a perfect plan; more important is that they criticize, raise issues, and envision other ways of relating and surviving. For that, both the fiction and the experiment are worth encouraging.

7

Kurt Vonnegut's American Nightmares and Utopias

KERMIT VANDERBILT

At the turn of the 1960s, our best-known American writers of creative prose summed up the decade in an impressive outpouring of serious best sellers. In Styron's *Nat Turner*, Bellow's *Mr. Sammler's Planet*, Updike's *Rabbit Redux*, Vonnegut's *Slaughterhouse-Five*, Malamud's *The Tenants*, Mailer's *Armies of the Night*, Wolfe's *The Electric Kool-Aid Acid Test*, Roth's *Our Gang*, and other works, our most gifted novelists and "new journalists" responded variously to the incomparable materials of a radical and bewildering time. What seemed remarkable among these writers was that, for all the uniqueness of their individual voices, they shared a strikingly similar skepticism about an age of protest and rebellion. They also shared a closing mood of irresolution and spiritual exhaustion. At the end of a volatile era scarred with antiwar demonstrations, street crusades, drug busts, black rage, sexual liberation, and political lies in high places, the nation these writers depicted was entering a season of spiritual arrest. And what was to be the next step? As readers, we received no reassuring hope of social change or human betterment; in fact, these writers each counseled some form of age-old humility, penitence, meditation, and waiting.[1]

Into the seventies, as the Vietnam War continued to muti-
late the national soul, one continued to ask what was to be
America's redemptive "next step" as the spiritual limbo extended into and beyond the Nixon-Watergate years. The most
celebrated novelists of the sixties, to be sure, kept on writing.
Though Styron had been silent, the others, even including
Joseph Heller, honed the old tools of their experienced and
competent craft. But it was also a practiced sameness. One
turned to the metafiction of the post-modernist fabulators,
only to realize that these virtuoso performances had begun to
lose the edge of shock and novelty. Robert Coover, for one,
worried that his writing had come to share a "blind alley" with
the less experimental "literature of exhaustion." Visions of
apocalypse had also grown wearisome. The more positive,
anti-mainstream consciousness of women and other minority
writers failed to express vital new alternatives for a country in
the political and moral doldrums. Erika Jong's *Fear of Flying*
(1973), she admitted, was finally romantic and traditional.
Ishmael Reed in his parables and Neo-Hoo Doo pursued an
original Afro-American idiom, but the results were unfocused
and largely suggested his Anglo sources. Perhaps excepting
some of Pynchon, Gass, and a few others, virtually nothing
new or significant in American fiction was being written well
into the seventies.

In this literary stalemate, Kurt Vonnegut became the single major writer of the sixties in whom one could detect some
discernible change. The moral miasma of the Nixon years was
apparently good growing weather for Vonnegut. He was grop-
ing his way from the apocalyptic desolation of *Slaughterhouse-
Five*—the Allied fire-bombing of Dresden in 1945 serving as a
bleak correlative of the contemporary "liberation" of
Vietnam—toward something more hopeful. He had begun to
speak and write about a new communal sense of man, of the
writer in his society, and perhaps, too, the discovery of a new
fictional voice to celebrate a future state where life is enjoyed
in accord with utopian ideas. True, in his one major fiction in
the seventies, *Breakfast of Champions* (1973), Vonnegut
seemed to contradict any notion that a decisive shift had occurred in the outlook of the country's foremost dispenser of
black humor. In *Breakfast*, he had served up one more Amer-

ican parable of the helpless American victimized by the rampant idiocy, meanness, and ultimate self-destruction of a nation in love with a runaway technology. In a revealing interview for *Playboy* shortly after, Vonnegut admitted that his latest novel was a decanting of some of the bitter old brew left over from *Slaughterhouse-Five*. But he also insisted that he was moving beyond the theme of self-destruction. "I want to start believing in things that have shapeliness and harmony," he told the reporter. "I've changed. . . . In spite of chain-smoking Pall Malls since I was fourteen, I think my wind is still good enough for me to go chasing after happiness, something I've never really tried."[2] Along with "harmony" and "happiness," he also discussed other traditional utopian ideas in what, to all appearances, would be a remarkable new phase in his now-remunerative and increasingly influential literary career.

Before we look more closely at the opinions he was now offering on public occasions, and the two novels which have since issued from the presumably "new Vonnegut," it will be useful to take a swift backward view into the utopian themes already present in his first seven novels. I apologize in advance to Vonnegut specialists for what must seem in this summary to be a cavalier disregard for the fullness and variety of their author's ideas and literary art. To Vonnegut detractors who may feel that my interpretive paraphrasings show how sophomoric his story-telling antics and satirical lessons really are, I remind them that American utopian thought has been nearly bankrupt for so many years that *any* comic spirit can only be welcome.

Player Piano (1952) was Vonnegut's impressive first book. Commercially, it was something less than a triumph. He had inherited and breathed new life into the turn-of-the-century utopian spirit of Howells's satirical Altrurian romances, as well as the tradition of Edward Bellamy's *Looking Backward* (1888), the classic that had excited more than fifty native imitators a half-century before. Vonnegut claimed that for his immediate inspiration he had "cheerfully ripped off the plot of *Brave New World*, whose plot had been cheerfully ripped off from Eugene Zamiatin's *We*."[3] *Player Piano* is astonishing for the richness of utopian and dystopian matter in this first major outing of the writer who would soon own the best utopian imagination in American literature since World War Two.

Arguably, a novel may be labelled utopian when it includes a smattering of the traditional means and ends for the ideal community of man (or their nightmarish defeat in the dystopian vision). The totally enabling prophetic vision in literature comprehends three stages: the critique of an unsatisfactory present, perhaps influenced by a progressive "hidden prophetic intention" of the past (to quote Whitman) and in which the intimations of a dystopian eschatology may operate as a motive force; a transitional phase, sometimes energized by a cataclysmic event; and climactically, the fulfilling happiness of a peaceful revolution. The new post-industrial civilization will be, customarily, a socialistic commonwealth of rational men and women, with wisely planned urban communities, maximum individual freedom, socially oriented education, material abundance (with wise conserving of natural resources), non-alienating and non-competitive day labor and professional life, self-transcending leisure time for recreation and the arts, effortless virtue, dynamic social stability, permanent peace, and gratifying love. *Player Piano,* rather incredibly, taps all of these elements directly or implicitly, whether utopian or dystopian.

For his dramatic present, Vonnegut depicts an American future fully automated under the leadership of a seemingly rational commonwealth with a titular president and a company of elitist managers and engineers. (He was writing out of his own experience in public relations for General Electric in Schenectady from 1947 to 1950). The central figure is a brilliant, somewhat independent, vaguely disgruntled, protean character named Paul Proteus, who at thirty-five manages one of the nation's production centers at Ilium, New York. Through the recollections of Proteus, the reader discovers how America's utopian transition from the first Industrial Revolution to the second (machines which first had replaced human muscle work now relieve routine work) occurred during World War Two when technology took over much of the routine activity not only of a dwindling labor force at home but also of soldiers on the warfront. Peacetime America has become a miracle of efficient technology, or so believe the elite managers and engineers who enjoy superior economic and social status. They proudly conduct foreign dignitaries on tours about the country to convince them how their nations, too, can become as affluent and fortunate as America—with a necessary assist coming, of course, from American exports. The Shah of Bratpuhr, in particular, plays a role similar to Howells's earlier traveller from Altruria. He observes the human results of this abundant civilization and raises many questions that disconcert his proud hosts.

Proteus is one of several elite managers who are troubled by America's new golden age. We see him at the outset unable to understand

> what seemed so clear to others—that what he was doing, had done, and would do as a manager and engineer was vital, above reproach, and had, in fact, brought on a golden age. Of late, his job, the system, and organizational politics had left him variously annoyed, bored, or queasy.[4]

Proteus fears that, far from accommodating the newest technology to the social needs of the citizenry, the present era has, in fact, rapidly evolved into a nightmarish third Industrial Revolution. Machines are about to replace not only muscle and routine labor but also human thinking and emotional response—a *reductio ad absurdum* of the rational and humanizing utopian commonwealth.

All of the persistent utopian ideals are depicted in the ordeal of Proteus, though Vonnegut's purpose is to describe their inevitable failure in a dystopian present. The urban-industrial life and cityscape of Ilium have been purposefully fashioned, but are so dismal to Proteus that he tries to withdraw to a farm, only to realize his ineptness at manual skills, as well as to learn that the celebrated pastoral world in reality is "coarse and sluggish, hot and wet and smelly. And the charming little cottage he'd taken as a symbol of the good life of a farmer was as irrelevant as a statue of Venus at the gate of a sewage-disposal plant" (p. 246).

The citizens ostensibly enjoy their civil rights, but individual freedom is seen to be problematical. Even the elite members wear classification symbols and the masses, in their regimented appearance, suggest to the visiting Shah that they must be slaves. Furthermore, their rumblings of discontent with the machine takeover have made an incipient police state necessary. Part of the dissatisfaction is with the educational system, which places a premium on the high IQ needed to train the highly competitive elitist corps of managers, engineers, and scientists who will hold the meaningful jobs (there is even a mandatory Doctor of Realty degree). Although the masses are well fed and endowed with creature comforts—Vonnegut wickedly catalogues their countless gadgets—their days are singularly barren of interesting activity. As the visiting Shah's host explains, "any man who cannot support himself by doing a job better than a machine is employed by the government, either in the Army or the Reconstruction and Reclamation Corps," the latter group having dubbed themselves the "Reeks and Wrecks" (pp. 27, 31). The arts and recreational pleasures, rather than allowing imaginative self-transcendence, are passive and automated: the player piano, the computer that wins at checkers, and other electronic amusements. The ingenuous Shah asks a housewife what her life's fun amounts to after her automatic gadgets have quickly liberated her from her daily work:

> Wanda blushed and looked down at the floor, and worried the carpet edge with her toe. "Oh, television," she murmured. "Watch that a lot, don't we, Ed? And I spend a lot of time with the kids. . . . You know. Things."
> "Where are the children now?" asked [interpreter] Khashdrahr.
> "Over at the neighbors' place, the Glocks, watching television, I expect." (p. 160)

The cult of material progress and uncontrolled growth is still alive in America, along with a national aggressiveness visible in a military force that is now subject to the calculated results obtained from a computer named EPICAC. One of the culminating themes of the later Vonnegut also binds much of *Player Piano* together: our frustrated human search for gratifying love, both familial and communal. He shows bickering and hatred in the nuclear family, mutual contempt between and within the two main social classes, the loneliness of a Luke Lubbock who is "the indefatigable joiner," and the automatic, machine-like endearments emptily repeated by the harassed career man Proteus and his ambitiously supportive wife. ("'Anita, I love you.'" "'I love *you*, Paul!'")

The novel pivots on the rather bemused rebellion of Proteus. He allows more forceful visionaries to thrust him into leadership of the insurgent "Ghost Shirt Society." Vonnegut has amply shown the distressing paradox, in which the utopia of progressive thought, when consummated, may well generate restless discontent and become dystopia. Hatred for the recently worshipped Machine provides the impulse for a new revolution that presently destroys the Ilium Works and spreads haphazardly across the nation. To Proteus, however, the result forebodes not linear progress but hopeless cyclic regression. The other leaders view the new "frontiers of their Utopia" with a pride that he cannot share (p. 316). Even though the streets of liberated Ilium glitter with millions of exploded machines and gadgets, from *A*ir conditioners to *Z*ymometers, the gadget-engineers of the future are already rummaging through the rubble to find odd parts to create new machines that will automate their lives into a new emptiness. In a final toast to the new era, Proteus glances at his three satisfied co-conspirators who have just saluted "the record" of their private revolts, undertaken, it seems, with no premeditated, creative goals in view:

> "To a better world," he started to say, but he cut the toast short, thinking of the people of Ilium, already eager to recreate the same old nightmare. He shrugged. "To the record," he said, and smashed the empty bottle on a rock. (p. 320)

The Sirens of Titan appeared seven years later and, at first blush, Vonnegut seems to have radically shifted from serious utopian concerns to a science-fiction romp into outer space. While the utopian texture here is much looser, this second novel can be viewed structurally in terms surprisingly like *Player Piano*. That is, we see the United States bound up tight in false, life-defeating values. A revolutionary army, peopled by American recruits, is trained on Mars. But in the ensuing war on earth, the earthling-Martians are overwhelmed. The victory galvanizes a new human consciousness which is the necessary first condition if man is ever to create his successful utopia.

The story begins at the Newport estate of the affluent Rumfoords, who will reappear in later fiction. Here the richest American, Malachi Constant, who has lived a rakish, loveless existence in Hollywood, has been invited by the haughty socialite, Mrs. Rumfoord, to witness the materialization of her space-travelling husband. Winston Niles Rumfoord has existed as a "wave phenomenon" ever since he ran his private space ship into a sort of time warp (a "chrono-synclastic infundibulum") where he envisioned all of human destiny in a flash and learned that "everything that ever has been always will be, and everything that ever will be always has been."[5] Rumfoord materializes to inform Constant that his destiny includes space-travelling with Rumfoord's forbidding wife Beatrice to Mars, where their son Chrono will be born, and that he will also travel to Mercury, Earth, and Titan. When he presently loses all his wealth, Constant willingly boards a spaceship to join other unhappy earthlings in the Army of Mars. Rumfoord happens to be its financial sponsor and commander-in-chief.

Vonnegut's critique of American life in the present is not so graphic as in *Player Piano*, nor is the rationale for a utopian revolution seriously explored. But the agency is the same: an ugly armed conflict stimulates new expectations for the brotherhood of man on earth. Rumfoord erases the earthly memories of his Army of Mars, implants electronic-control devices in their heads, and presently sends them on their space journey to make war on the earth. The conflict lasts only sixty-seven days and the Martians are nearly annihilated by the sophisticated thermo-nuclear weapons of earth. This disastrous outcome has precisely fitted Rumfoord's perverse utopian scheme. Knowing that we always feel guilt and compassion after the wholesale slaughter of war, he planned the virtual suicide of his liberating army, and now prolongs the American victors' postwar period of horror and repentance by disseminating the shame-inducing sentiment that "Earth's glorious victory over Mars had been a tawdry butchery of vir-

tually unarmed saints, saints who had waged feeble war on
Earth in order to weld the peoples of that planet into a monolithic Brotherhood of Man" (p. 175).

Constant now reenters the plot to play a scapegoat role in
the new utopia. Detoured to Mercury during the war, he returns to earth to become an example of elitist human greed for
the large congregation of Rumfoord's new utopian "Church of
God the Utterly Indifferent." The members are earth-oriented,
generally uncompetitive, peaceful, and loving. They have re-
pudiated special Providence or "luck," and despite the historical manipulations of Rumfoord (himself controlled by emana-
tions of will from the planet Tralfamadore), they live with illusions of self-determination and the rational life. Those born
with special advantages try to minimize them by adopting various handicaps—a rather comic egalitarianism that allows full
play for some of Vonnegut's devilish humor. But he also suggests that they do possess the human capacity to behave with a
wise integrity, even in a crowd—a faint echo of Emersonian
free will and self-reliance, and symptomatic of Vonnegut's
open uncertainty about personal freedom, historical determi-
nism, and the prospects for an eventual utopian humanism.
After Constant has been publicly lambasted by Rumfoord as
one of the immoral plutocrats of a bygone era, the crowd "remained in possession of their own consciences [and] . . . re-
acted in quiet, sighing, personal ways—ways that were by and
large compassionate" (p. 254). In the same crowd scene, the
Martian-earthlings like Constant's Beatrice and Chrono, never
humanized by war guilt and contrition, are hawking wares and
variously trying to cheat the citizenry. All three must be exiled
to Titan, and Rumfoord says to Constant:

> "We will imagine, to our spiritual satisfaction, that you are tak-
> ing all mistaken ideas about the meaning of luck, all misused
> wealth and power, and all disgusting pastimes with you."
> (p. 255)

Finally on Titan, Vonnegut elaborates two of the overarching
ideals in all of his utopian fiction, the saving values of imagination and love for his often-victimized and perenially lonesome
humans. Rumfoord's imaginative lure for Constant, the sirens

of Titan, turns out to be merely three statues embodying a playboy fantasy of feminine beauty. But Constant then grows old
with his earthly Beatrice and conceives a deeply human ideal
in his deterministic odyssey, " 'that a purpose of human life, no
matter who is controlling it, is to love whoever is around to be
loved' " (p. 313).

Even more than *Sirens*, *Mother Night* (1961) seems at first
scarcely inspired by any utopian impulse. It is, to be sure, the
single novel that we can pass over rather swiftly. But it would
be a mistake not to recognize that in the moral debacle of
Nazism experienced by the schizoid Howard W. Campbell, Jr.,
a manipulated American spy and young writer barren of political convictions, Vonnegut explores some of the dark forces in
mankind, Nazis and anti-Nazis alike, that are central to his
evolving meditations on utopia. Vexing mysteries of human nature which can frustrate all visions of social betterment appear
this time, and take the aspect of rationalized hate, mindless
and cyclical vengeance, inadvertent "evil" disguised in self-
deceiving virtue, and more. Perhaps Vonnegut is also suggesting an esthetic lesson for the responsible literary artist. When
the writer avoids gray reality and, like the younger Campbell,
fashions morality plays about disjunctive good and evil or
romanticizes love and death, his moral detachment from the
political affairs of his time and society can lead him into the
Mephistophelian arms of Mother Night.

The nagging issues of human depravity and free will continued to disturb Vonnegut's shaky utopianism. But he preferred to treat them as the conditioned effects of a perverted
political system, warped social ideals, and anti-humanistic science rather than in the problematical terms of quasi-theologi-
cal "evil" in *Mother Night*. And so in *Cat's Cradle* (1963), he
resumes the direct critique of the social present, with its love-
starved and misdirected Americans, and then imagines a more
caring society elsewhere. The main plot stands out in clear outline. Vonnegut's serviceable, recalcitrant hero this time is a
free-lance writer ("Call me Jonah"). He is gathering information on what various people, but chiefly atom-bomb scientist
Felix Hoenikker (from Ilium, New York, of *Player Piano*),
were doing and thinking on the day we dropped the bomb on
Hiroshima. During his assignment, Jonah discovers that Felix

was an amoral scientist and unloving husband and father whose legacy to his three children was an illusory hand trick called "cat's cradle" and, more nihilistically, a catalytic "seed" called "ice-nine." This chemical was intended to freeze the ground for slogging-through-the-mud American marines. It can also freeze the entire world. Within this ostensible story of the scientist's moral irresponsibility, Vonnegut indulges the utopian critic's penchant for cultural satire. Interviewing one of Felix's fellow scientists, Jonah runs the gamut of utopian themes:

> . . . we talked about the Pope and birth control, about Hitler and the Jews. We talked about phonies. We talked about truth. We talked about gangsters; we talked about business. We talked about the nice poor people who went to the electric chair; and we talked about the rich bastards who didn't. We talked about religious people who had perversions.[6]

Vonnegut returns also to the urban ugliness of Ilium, the dull mentalities and the "deathlike jobs" (especially for women), the police-state safeguards against Communism, and above all, the pathetic quest for love in American life, indeed for any forms of human connectedness, be they identical last names or " 'We Hoosiers got to stick together,' " or " 'You call me "Mom," ' " or " 'Three Cornellians—all in the same plane!' " (pp. 56, 67, 92)

Jonah's nihilistic book peters out, and Vonnegut moves the story through a second plot that complements the social criticism of part one. Jonah accepts a magazine assignment to go to the Caribbean for a story on an American millionaire, Julian Castle, a Schweitzer figure who has founded a free hospital in a jungle on the island of San Lorenzo where his grandfather established Castle Sugar Company. (The Hoenikker heirs of ice-nine will reappear in this co-plot.) The main education for Jonah comes not from Castle but another source: he discovers the life and career of a would-be utopian, the black Lionel Boyd Johnson. "Bokonon," as he is called by the islanders, left Tobago in the West Indies for a London education and service in the First World War. After a postwar stint with followers of Ghandi, plus various escapades at sea, he met a

"brilliant, self-educated, idealistic Marine deserter" named
Earl McCabe (p. 77). En route to Miami in 1922, the two were
shipwrecked on San Lorenzo so that, naked and reborn,
Bokonon (Johnson) and his shipmate played Prospero on the
disease-ridden island that had been dominated by Castle Sugar
and the Catholic Church. As Jonah reads of the island's history:
"McCabe and Johnson dreamed of making San Lorenzo a Utopia. To this end, McCabe overhauled the economy and the
laws. Johnson designed a new religion" (p. 90). Johnson, now
Bokonon, codified the new religion in *The Books of Bokonon*,
that include calypso poems:

> I wanted all things
> To seem to make some sense,
> So we all could be happy, yes,
> Instead of tense.
> And I made up lies
> So that they all fit nice,
> And I made this sad world
> A par-a-dise. (p. 90)

Bokonon's comforting religious untruths notwithstand-
ing, San Lorenzo does not become the earthly paradise. Vonnegut's Prospero figures hold no magic powers to transform
the muck-ridden, overpopulated port city of a country "as unproductive as an equal area in the Sahara or the Polar Icecap"
(p. 94). Socialistic sharing in such a society is farcical, its historian notes:

> During the idealistic phase of McCabe's and Johnson's reorga-
> nization of San Lorenzo, it was announced that the country's
> total income would be divided among all adult persons in equal
> shares. The first and only time this was tried, each share came to
> between six and seven dollars. (p. 94)

Bokonon maintains the utopian purpose, however, by disap-
pearing to become a legendary holy man who spreads his ap-
pealingly human-centered religion in designed opposition to
the assumed political tyranny of McCabe.

Jonah becomes a convert to Bokononism, absorbing such
imaginative concepts as *karass*, or fated ties with other people;

wampeters, or pivotal objects and ideals that bind a true *karass*; *granfalloon*, or an irrelevant, false *karass*; *foma*, or workable, life-enhancing, harmless untruths; and *boko-maru*, a face-to-face foot-touching ceremony that engenders familiar and universal love. When Jonah falls into the presidency of San Lorenzo, he becomes a version of the manipulated Paul Proteus or Malachi Constant, though he does undertake a real command. He weighs the possibility of renewing the utopian dream by bringing Bokonon back to public life:

> But then I understood that a millenium would have to offer something more than a holy man in a position of power, that there would have to be plenty of good things for all to eat, too, and nice places to live for all, and good schools and good health and good times for all, and work for all who wanted it—things Bokonon and I were in no position to provide. (p. 152)

Since the people, like the land, appear inimical to scientific or industrial development, they are left only with whatever consolations can be gathered from the doctrines of wise resignation, pleasant illusions, and world love urged in the wayward sayings of Bokonon.

Vonnegut then erases even these fragile consolations, for ice-nine (like the nature-altering atomic bomb) falls into irresponsible hands, San Lorenzo freezes over in a reverse holocaust, and Jonah remains to meditate with fellow survivor Newton Hoenikker upon the depressing paradox of Bokonon's "heartbreaking necessity of lying about reality, and the heartbreaking impossibility of lying about it" (p. 189). The novel closes on Bokonon's undeceived rejection of utopia. Jonah is discussing with Newton the chances for a new beginning after the great freeze:

> I directed our conversation into the area of Utopias, of what might have been, of what should have been, of what might yet be, if the world would thaw.
>
> But Bokonon had been there, too, had written a whole book about Utopias, *The Seventh Book*, which he called "Bokonon's Republic." In that book are these ghastly aphorisms:
>
> The hand that stocks the drug stores rules the world.

> Let us start our Republic with a chain of drug stores, a chain of grocery stores, a chain of gas chambers, and a national game. After that, we can write our Constitution. (p. 190)

Jonah curses this pessimism, but our final glimpse is of the cynical old Bokonon, dying of ice-nine, regretting only that he can't climb the nearby mountain with a "history of human stupidity" in hand to become an ice-nine statue "lying on my back, grinning horribly, and thumbing my nose at You Know Who" (p. 191). Vonnegut's literary idol Mark Twain, he of the sayings of Pudd'nhead Wilson and the historical satire of *The Mysterious Stranger*, would have loved that irreverent finale.

Soon after *Cat's Cradle* came another darkly comic novel, *God Bless You, Mr. Rosewater or Pearls Before Swine* (1965). The story, accompanied by Vonnegut's usual grotesqueries and extended jokes, moves again from a critique to an awakening and thence to a somewhat clownish version of utopia with serious overtones. A simple plot binds it all together. Norman Mushari, fresh out of Cornell Law School, and impelled by idols Joseph McCarthy, Roy Cohn, and Barry Goldwater, goes to work for a law firm that oversees the millions of dollars of the Rosewater Corporation and Foundation. If he can manage to have the chief heir, Eliot Rosewater, declared insane, Mushari hopes to become rich as counsel for an unknown second cousin, Fred Rosewater of Rhode Island, who happens to be next in line to inherit the fortune.

Eliot, the addled president of the family Foundation, has been dispensing the family fortune for seventeen years in support of birth control, medical research, and curbs to race prejudice and police brutality. Now he is running a one-man relief agency for the miserable and poor in Rosewater County, Indiana. He has returned to the region where, years before, the Rosewaters built an ambitious canal, and among the losing investors in that venture was "a Utopian community, New Ambrosia."

> They were Germans, communists and atheists who practiced group marriage, absolute truthfulness, absolute cleanliness, and absolute love. They were now scattered to the winds, like the

worthless papers that represented their equity in the canal. No one was sorry to see them go.[7]

In Eliot's time, the only visible reminder of their utopian dream appears on the label of the beer cans from their still-surviving brewery, "a picture of the heaven on earth the New Ambrosians had meant to build. The dream city had spires. The spires had lightning-rods. The sky was filled with cherubim" (p. 38).

Meanwhile, Mushari has been reading confidential documents in his law firm's vaults. He finds a clinching piece of evidence in Eliot's interpretive history of the Rosewater fortune, to be opened by the next heir. Mainly, it is a scathing account of how the wealthy Rosewaters have perverted the American Dream. Some excerpts:

> When the United States of America, which was meant to be a Utopia for all, was less than a century old, Noah Rosewater and a few men like him, demonstrated the folly of the Founding Fathers in one respect. Those sadly recent ancestors had not made it the law of Utopia that the wealth of each citizen should be limited. (p. 12)
>
> Thus was the savage and stupid and entirely inappropriate and unnecessary and humorless American class system created. Honest, industrious, peaceful citizens were classed as bloodsuckers, if they asked to be paid a living wage. (p. 12)
>
> *E pluribus unum* is surely an ironic motto to inscribe on this Utopia gone bust. . . . (p. 13)
>
> [Samuel Rosewater's doctrine]: *Anybody who thought that the United States of America was supposed to be a Utopia was a piggy, lazy, God-damned fool.* (p. 13)
>
> And Eliot became a drunkard, a Utopian dreamer, a tinhorn saint, an aimless fool. (p. 14)

The document, and especially the last comment, shows that Eliot is both dangerously schizophrenic and subject to moments of sober self-awareness ("he had no illusions about the people to whom he was devoting his life" [p. 90]). Mushari assumes the former, and adduces further proof from Eliot's foolish, closing injunction: "Be generous. Be kind. You can safely ignore the arts and sciences. They never helped anybody. Be a sincere, attentive friend of the poor" (p. 15).

Eliot's humanitarian outlook is blurred by alcoholic senti-mentality and aimless generosity. He wishes to correct eco-nomic inequities in America and also offers uncritical love and sympathy (sometimes absently, sometimes genuinely) to the lumpish, miserable townspeople who look for compassion and handouts from his grubby little office. Eliot's crack-brained, incomplete utopian dream is instructive for what he leaves out. He does not envision a planned community, en-lightened education, fulfilling work and leisure, ecological harmony, and so on. To the depressed, his favorite advice is, " 'Dear, I tell you what to do—take an aspirin tablet, and wash it down with a glass of wine' " (p. 78). His father, a right-wing senator, becomes an effective foil and a corrective with his conservative clichés about private enterprise and human de-pravity. When he asks Eliot's erstwhile psychiatrist, " 'Eliot is bringing his sexual energies to what?' " the reply is, " 'To Utopia' " (p. 73).

But there is some reason in Eliot's madness, for America is suffering an unrelieved epidemic of unhappiness and perverted love. Seemingly all the young people are as sexually warped as adult America, both in Eliot's Indiana and in Fred's Pisquontuit, Rhode Island, where "Utopian lanes" (p. 116) lead to expensive suburban homes in which soul-rot and failed marriages are producing disturbed, unloved children. Eliot re-ceives partial credibility, too, from his favorite author, the no-toriously third-rate utopian novelist Kilgore Trout, whose "favorite formula was to describe a perfectly hideous society, not unlike our own, and then, toward the end, to suggest ways in which it could be improved" (p. 20). Trout's criticism is usually more on target than his various schemes for social im-provement, though both suffer from his flat-out inability to create literary art. He appears briefly at the end to vouch for Eliot's sanity and pronounce an elaborately hopeful verdict on Eliot's utopia of uncritical love:

> It means that our hatred of useless human beings and the cruel-
> ties we inflict upon them for their own good need not be parts of
> human nature. Thanks to the example of Eliot Rosewater, mil-
> lions upon millions of people may learn to love and help
> whomever they see. (p. 187)

Eliot has more or less recovered his wits after a traumatic war-flashback, and his final act is a typically quixotic dispensation of love and the Rosewater fortune. Since he has lately been accused by scores of greedy women in Rosewater of fathering their babies, Eliot makes his last utopian gesture by endowing a quasi-extended family of every child alleged to be his: "Let their names be Rosewater from this moment on. And tell them that their father loves them, no matter what they may turn out to be" (p. 190).

For *Slaughterhouse-Five* (N.Y.: Dell, 1969), Vonnegut returned to the effects of World War Two, the historical event which catalyzed the transition to utopian possibilities in *Player Piano*, *Cat's Cradle*, and even *Rosewater* (on two pivotal occasions, Eliot suffers from war neurosis). Now he fully explored the decisive impact of the war, particularly the Allied fire-bombing of Dresden, on the fantasy-prone, passively suffering Billy Pilgrim. Dissatisfaction with the callousness of present American society also continued to fester, as we discover in the depiction of gentle Billy's joyless postwar life after being a mental patient in a VA hospital with Eliot Rosewater. Billy takes occasional "trips" to a comically limited, utopian "no-place," the planet of Tralfamadore. There he lives with a siren this time materialized, a Vonnegut dream girl named Montana Wildhack. If it were not for this life-saving illusion of a place where everyone lives in peace and accepts the absurdity of the cosmos ("So it goes"), he could not periodically sustain a desire to live. The Alcoholics Anonymous serenity prayer also helps the impotent Billy survive the vicious realities of the late '60s. Vonnegut said that he finished decanting this acidic brew in *Breakfast of Champions*. Taken together, the two novels constitute an indictment of American culture so searing and inclusive that he could well have felt in 1973 that he must have emptied his spleen of social bitterness.

In *Slaughterhouse-Five*, Vonnegut relates the unsavory and confused "children's crusade" of GI's at war to social conditions back home, and he stresses everywhere the self-righteous aggressiveness of Americans. His alternating story, the postwar horrors of "peacetime" America, directly concerns us here. Billy Pilgrim comes home to Ilium, New York, marries and becomes rich in the optometry business of his conservative father-in-law, a John Birch Society advocate of law and order. Billy placidly drives his Cadillac through Ilium's riot-torn, burned-out black ghetto to attend Lion's Club meetings (he is past president) where, by 1967, the speaker is a Marine officer in favor of the saturation bombing of North Vietnam. Both the drive and the speech remind Billy of America's compulsive destructiveness and penchant for violence. He returns to his gadget-filled house, turns on the "Magic Fingers" vibrator in his mattress, and quietly weeps.

Other characters reappear in this fiction to help Vonnegut deliver his verdict on American civilization. Howard Campbell, the American spy of *Mother Night*, writes an anti-American propaganda monograph for the Germans explaining (all too accurately) how American wealth is cornered by the few, and the poor are encouraged to despise themselves. Eliot Rosewater introduces Billy to Kilgore Trout's science-fiction parables of Christian cruelty. One of the Rumfoords (see *Sirens*) is a Harvard historian who justifies the practical necessity of the Dresden bombing. Billy decides that America's only salvation lies in the passive, Bokonon-like doctrines of Tralfamadore. He drives to New York City, hoping to appear on television. There he experiences American civilization in a dehumanized Babylon replete with the reality of crime, death, corrupt power, peep shows, and climaxed by fatuous literary conversation on the death of the novel—this last on a radio talk-show where Billy intrudes and, when allowed to speak, discourses on the pleasures of Tralfamadore. He is expelled during a commercial break. We are told that he is murdered in Chicago in 1976 where he has come to speak, again on outer space—the escape therapy of Billy's disengaged and finally non-utopian imagination.

Though Vonnegut had been considering *Slaughterhouse-Five* to be his final summing-up as a novelist, he added more bile to his Vietnam-era diagnosis and satire of what was passing for "culture" in America by publishing a companion, postmodernist anti-novel, *Breakfast of Champions*, in 1973. In the process, he left behind the pivotal impact of World War Two that had dominated his four novels of the sixties and this time did not entertain so much as a comically flawed utopia. *Breakfast* reached a high-water mark in his nihilism and black humor. He assailed everything from the nation's consuming preoccupation with sex, to boys' military academies, racial injustice, junk food, self-help fads, automated technology, and alcohol ("the breakfast of champions"). The simple plot alternated between chapters on Kilgore Trout's westward journey to the Midland City Arts Festival "on a planet which was dying fast," and chapters on the sick behavior of Dwayne Hoover, Midland City's Pontiac dealer. The plots come together when Hoover goes berserk after meeting Trout and personally acting on a poisonous idea in Trout's science fiction that suggests to Hoover that he is the wilful master of the world because everyone else acts like robots. Vonnegut lends credence to Hoover's fantasy by presenting himself as an ingenuous narrator who tries to explain, with absurdly innocent definitions and sketches, how Americans behave like socially conditioned machines while they pollute their systems with chemicals. They also pollute their minds with self-deceiving ideas, including the "gibberish" of the national anthem and the "vacant motto" *E Pluribus Unum*. He observes that "it might have comforted them some if their anthem and their motto had mentioned fairness or brotherhood or hope or happiness, had somehow welcomed them to the society and its real estate."[8]

Vonnegut portrays Trout leaving a sooty and littered New York City after a night among porno bookshops and theatres, whores and muggers. Picked up by a lonely truckdriver, he rides across "the poisoned marshes and meadows of New Jersey" (p. 84), over Philadelphia's Walt Whitman Bridge "veiled in smoke" (p. 102), and into West Virginia where "the surface of the State had been demolished by men and machinery and explosives in order to make it yield up its coal" for industries like the Rosewater Coal and Iron Company (pp. 119, 125). Arriving at Midland City, Trout wades across a creek thickly polluted with plastic wastes from a company manufacturing anti-personnel bombs, and then crosses an "asphalt desert" parking lot to a standardized Holiday Inn. In the bar, Hoover snatches from Trout and reads the novel that gives him the illusions of omnipotence.

Hoover has migrated to the bar after a bizarre day in his life as a well-to-do American businessman. After his wife's suicide from eating Drāno, Hoover has lived unhappily in a suburban "dream house" where he talks to his dog, employs a woman domestic whose people were American slaves, suffers from hallucinations, and contemplates his own suicide. He mistreats his mistress-secretary, Francine Pefko (from *Cat's Cradle*), insults his transvestite car salesman, and avoids his homosexual son. He is Vonnegut's most devastated victim of America's bungled civilization. When Trout's book fills him with delusions of superiority, he goes on a savage spree, brutalizing both women and men and hospitalizing eleven people, including Trout. In the aftermath, lawsuits will leave Hoover a destitute bum.

As for Trout, he emerges from the hospital to meet his fictional creator and be set free from future services as a writer of science-fiction parables inspired by the absurdities of American life. Why has Prospero-Vonnegut freed his Ariel? Presumably because many pages earlier, Vonnegut had begun his creative self-liberation from chaos by accidentally inventing a second-rate minimal painter who attached sixteen feet of orange reflecting paint on an enormous canvas of green wall paint and persuaded Vonnegut to respond to it as a message from St. Anthony that all creatures own a sacred band of light, an awareness that emanates from the "immaterial core" of their being. Vonnegut's artistic accident, he proclaims without apparent irony, has "made me the serene Earthling which I am this day" (p. 220). Trout and all the others, therefore, have completed their services to his social satire and nihilistic humor. He informs Trout, " 'I am cleansing and renewing myself for the very different sorts of years to come' " (p. 293). Phrased in the continuing dialectic of utopian good warring with social evils of the past and present, Vonnegut's rather sudden optimism seems to affirm that the redeeming Good Idea of human aspiration may yet triumph over the Bad Idea of human impotence. The nightmare of present history will be overcome.

What different direction was Vonnegut in the process of moving within this "cleansing and renewing"? We presently had the fictional answers in *Slapstick* (1976) and to close the decade—or enter the '80s—his *Jailbird* (1979). But indispensable revelations lie elsewhere, too, during the period of *Slaughterhouse-Five* and *Breakfast of Champions*. As a writer-citizen in the public arena, Vonnegut was preparing the ground that has brought him to the two recent novels.

After the brilliant success of *Slaughterhouse-Five*, Vonnegut gained a wider following as a journalist and public speaker, thanks to his new celebrity status. His writings and speeches lent further evidence of what now seems clear after the survey of his first seven novels, that Vonnegut has been our one writer closest to the reform-minded meliorism of the earlier decades of the century, and that the upheavals of the sixties had powerfully goaded his socially oriented, historical consciousness. He was now turning increasingly to the public platform for the more didactic privileges that had not been available to his literary art. He then arranged these pronouncements into a chronological record with the self-disparaging title, *Wampeters, Foma & Granfalloons* (1974, cited earlier). His subjects ranged, apparently without discrimination, among space-shots, the fall of Biafra, the counter-culture, Melvin Laird, the Hesse cult, Middle America, American massacres in Vietnam, and the Nixon convention of 1972. But coming through forcefully amid all of this topical variety was the familiar voice of outrage over the moral hypocrisy and fatal ignorance of those in command of our national life. And other inflections and overtones rather abortively sounded in the novels became more insistent. Now Vonnegut was unabashedly celebrating community over loneliness, social generosity over private greed, sensitized consciousness over old blindnesses, and the implied triumph of life and hope over suicidal despair and cosmic doom.

In the preface of *Wampeters*, he debunked public speaking as a source of easy money and flattering applause for the lionized novelist of the hour. But the public platform could also afford a serious opportunity for the popular writer. "I do think," he said, "that public speaking is almost the only way a poet or a novelist or a playwright can have any political effectiveness in his creative prime" (p. xvi). He had spoken publicly, especially to campus audiences, in the days before *Slaughterhouse-Five*. But he had studiously avoided the weighty moral accents of a Truth-Teller come from the "real" world outside. In 1969, however, he shifted his tactic as a campus speaker. In those dark months of futile protest against a wasteful military-industrial Establishment and unresponsive White House, he realized that students wanted a large dose of moralizing. As he told a group of physicists in that year:

> So now when I speak to students, I do moralize. I tell them not to take more than they need, not to be greedy. I tell them not to kill, even in self-defense. I tell them not to pollute water or the atmosphere. I tell them not to raid the public treasury. I tell them not to work for people who pollute water or the atmosphere, or who raid the public treasury. I tell them not to commit war crimes or to help others to commit war crimes. These morals go over very well. They are, of course, echoes of what the young say to themselves. (p. 100)

Vonnegut's optimism, implicit within such counsel, appears to have been quite precarious just then. In the months immediately after came more weary street marches, the Cambodian invasion, and then the climactic tragedies of Kent State and Jackson State. In mid-1970, when he addressed the graduating class at Bennington College, he chilled his young audience with an apparent return to his doomsday pessimism. He publicly despaired over the American military's unabated contempt for human life, and the massive global problems of waste disposal, birth control, and non-humanistic science. "My wife begged me to bring you light," he said, "but there *is* no light. Everything is going to become unimaginably worse, and never get better again" (p. 162). Still, he allowed a flicker of hope for the idealistic young. He puckishly advised that they "become an enemy of truth and a fanatic for harmless balderdash" by acquiring "the most ridiculous superstition of all: that humanity is at the center of the universe" (p. 163). From this humanistic premise, Vonnegut drew a conclusion that was more than casually political:

> I suggest that you work for a socialist form of government. Free Enterprise is much too hard on the old and the sick and the shy and the poor and the stupid, and on people nobody likes. They just can't cut the mustard under Free Enterprise. They lack that

certain something that Nelson Rockefeller, for instance, so abundantly has. (p. 168)

In 1971, one hears again a determined optimism within Vonnegut's grim prospects for the rest of the century. To the National Institute of Arts and Letters, he spoke of the happiest day of his life, in October 1945, when he was an ex-GI admitted to the program in anthropology at the University of Chicago. (They rejected his postwar Master's thesis, but in 1972 liberally awarded him the degree for *Cat's Cradle*). There he learned from "the most satisfying teacher in my life," Robert Redfield, how a folk society once lived with their natural environment and each other in deeply personal terms. Unfortunately, there are no folk societies any more. Yet we are "chemically engineered" to be gregarious, and Vonnegut affirmed that our society might be reconstructed on the model of the "extended family." He then playfully disparaged the suggestion as "this biochemical-anthropological theory of mine" (p. 178).

This crippling loss of human community in America became an obsession both in his speeches and in writings for the serious and popular magazines. He agonized over his countrymen who pursue relief from oppressive loneliness through Halfway Houses, church-centered Appalachian communities, art colonies in New York City, the recent rural communes of the young, Group Sex, Group Food, the Jesus-Freak movement, the youthful Drug Cult, the Charles Manson family, Alcoholics Anonymous (whose meetings are also attended by lonely teetotalers), and other poignant and baffled variations of the extended family—the Lions Club, the Loyal Order of the Moose, the War Dads of America, the various professional societies, and even the academic departments of the American university. (In this last case, Vonnegut himself had hoped to experience a close, like-minded family but was unable to find one).

After the *Wampeters* collection, Vonnegut was to make what now seems a climactic public speech in his progress of more than two decades toward a utopian vision of America. He gave the graduation address at Hobart and William Smith Colleges in Geneva, New York, in May of 1974. There he spoke

once more of the need for community in the face of devastating
loneliness in America. (President Robert Skotheim of Whitman
College was then provost at Hobart-Smith and generously supplied me with a copy of the address. It can now be found in
Vonnegut's latest potpourri, *Palm Sunday* [Delacorte, 1981,
pp. 195-210].) Although Vonnegut's remarks may have seemed
his customary ramble, thrown together with bits and pieces
from his recent *Playboy* interview and other sources, he had in
fact conceived his speech carefully in three parts. First was a
sounding of the hollow present; then, a humanistic remedy in
the dream of a future community; and finally, an optimistic
conclusion that we are on the way to realizing this utopian
dream.

He first diagnosed the nation's current hollowness at
heart. He isolated two symptoms of recent years for brief comment. First was the Loud Family of Santa Barbara, California,
whose affluent and pathetically confused lives as a nuclear
family had been observed by millions in the recent television
documentary. "Christianity could not nourish the Louds,"
Vonnegut observed. "Neither could Buddhism or the profit
motive or participation in the arts, or any other nostrum on
America's spiritual smorgasbord. So the Louds were dying before our eyes." He found the other public drama of America's
moral stagnation in the recent White House Prayer Breakfasts
of Richard Nixon: "I think we all know now that religion of
that sort is about as nourishing to the human spirit as po-
tassium cyanide."

What America clearly needed in the wake of the Louds and
Richard Nixon, said Vonnegut, was a "new religion" to hu-
manize our relationships and our knowledge overload. The
subject in the second part of his address was his continuing
campaign to establish the basis for a utopian future. His "new
religion" was a return to old-fashioned caring through society
conceived as an "extended family." He explained how this utopian idea could work. We all would share urgent environmental goals for the survival of the race and become so like-minded
and self-relying that a society of extended families could even
police itself. If any planet polluters and planet gobblers were
still around, they would be thwarted by the moral suasion and
inevitable contempt of their communal family. Though he had

the Depression families of the thirties in mind, Vonnegut also recounted his recent eye-witness experience of the closing days of the Nigerian Civil War, and the last-ditch survival of starving Biafrans, impressive to him because each "was a member of an extended family," and each family was taking care of their own wounded and starving. He digressed that with this extended-family dream in mind, he happened to meet in 1972 a campaigning Sargent Shriver, whom he knew slightly. (He recalled this occasion, too, in the *Playboy* interview the year before.) Shriver asked Vonnegut if he had any ideas.

> I told him, and I am afraid he didn't listen, that the number one American killer wasn't cardio-vascular disease, but *loneliness*. I told him that he and McGovern could swamp the Republicans if they would promise to cure that disease. I even gave him a slogan to put on buttons and bumpers and flags and billboards: "LONESOME NO MORE!"
>
> The rest is history.

At the close of this speech in 1974, Vonnegut presented himself to the Hobart-Smith students without apology as an optimist even with regard to the hideous dilemmas of the present which he had already bemoaned in his earlier remarks. There is a new spirit across the land, he proclaimed. Citizens everywhere have begun to denounce American acquisitiveness and technology. They are now saying no to the factories and repudiating the zealots of a rising Gross National Product. In his remarkable closing words, the recent author of *Slaughterhouse-Five* and *Breakfast of Champions* seemed clearly to embrace a radical new utopian optimism:

> We were once maniacs for possessions, imagining that they would somehow moderate or somehow compensate us for our loneliness. . . . There is a willingness to do whatever we need to do in order to have life on the planet go on for a long, long time. I didn't used to think that. And that willingness has to be a religious enthusiasm, since it celebrates life, since it calls for meaningful sacrifices. . . . Thank God we are beginning to dream of human communities which are designed to harmonize with what human beings really need and are.

The question for Vonnegut watchers was whether he would discover the craft, along with the desire, to present an artist's utopian vision of this revitalized community and ecological reverence on a dying planet. In his fiction of the sixties, he touched on the responsibility of the literary artist, usually to rebuke the writer who does not engage his imagination in the urgent crises threatening life in his society. We have seen the implicit rejection of Howard Campbell in *Mother Night*, with his romantic distancing and polarizing of good and evil. In *Cat's Cradle*, Chapter 103 ("A Medical Opinion on the Effects of a Writer's Strike"), Jonah asks San Lorenzo's Schweitzer, Julian Castle, about the possibly fatal effects if writers should call a moratorium on new literary creations:

> "Sir, how does a man die when he's deprived of the consolations of literature?"
> "In one of two ways," he said, "petrescence of the heart or atrophy of the nervous system."
> "Neither one very pleasant, I expect," I suggested. (p. 156)

Vonnegut's irony, particularly for those who missed it here, was less subtle in *Rosewater*. We recall in Eliot's open letter to his successor the advice, "You can safely ignore the arts and sciences. They never helped anybody" (p. 15). And more pointedly to a convention of science-fiction writers, Eliot says,

> "You're the only ones with guts enough to *really* care about the future, who *really* notice what machines do to us, what wars do to us, what cities do to us, what big, simple ideas do to us, what tremendous misunderstandings, mistakes, accidents and catastrophies do to us." (p. 18)

Billy Pilgrim and Eliot Rosewater are Kilgore Trout enthusiasts in *Slaughterhouse-Five*, since "both found life meaningless, partly because of what they had seen in war. . . . So they were trying to re-invent themselves and their universe. Science fiction was a big help" (p. 87). At the end, Billy's short-term radio career happens on a program where dilettantish critics discuss what "the function of the novel might be in modern society." The vacuous opinions include " 'To provide touches of color in rooms with all-white walls,' " " 'To describe blow-jobs artistically,' " " 'To teach wives of junior executives what to buy next and how to act in a French restaurant' " (p. 178). Yet Billy's severely limited utopian imagination offers little more than the surviving strategy of a passive, if entrancing, hedonism. In *Breakfast of Champions*, Kilgore Trout is invited to join a symposium at the Arts Festival to discuss "The Future of the American Novel in the Age of McLuhan." Trout had planned to say, "'I don't know who McLuhan is, but I know what it's like to spend the night with a lot of other dirty old men in a movie theater in New York City. Could we talk about that?" (p. 55). But Trout is unable to translate his satirical awareness into imaginative visions of a better society. So at the end of *Breakfast*, a self-cleansed and renewed Vonnegut liberates Trout, the faithful agent of his creator's recent purgation.

While he was writing these last two novels, Vonnegut suggested on several public occasions the same progress of his imagination (see again the *Wumpeters* collection). Mordant social criticism, deterministic gloom, and desperate fictions of creative escape were slowly giving way to emergent new beginnings of utopian activism. During the dark time of 1969, he spoke to the American Physical Society on the special service of the writer's critical insight and imagination within a society and offered his "canary-in-the-coal-mine" theory of art. In this analogy, the artist is valuable to the degree that, like the canary in the mine, he is more sensitive than the endangered humans with whom he shares breathing space. Not meliorists of mining conditions, writers and their fellow artists are, instead, "supersensitive" indicators of impending doom. "They keel over like canaries in coal mines filled with poison gas, long before more robust types realize that any danger is there" (p. 92). Not surprisingly, after this dark variation on Pound's "artists are the antennae of the race," Vonnegut went on to commend George Orwell as "a man I admire almost more than any other man" (p. 94).

He rallied from this dystopian gloom on subsequent occasions and by 1973, in an address to fellow writers at the PEN conference in Stockholm, he described the special responsibility of the artist in a significant new metaphor. Beyond their being supersensitive, martyred canaries in the coal mine, the artists can be "specialized cells in a single, huge organism, mankind." Echoed here is the tradition whose American origins reach back at least to Emerson's and Whitman's transcendental poet within the social organism, a social-esthetic engagement that culminated in Steinbeck and the best political novelists of the thirties. Vonnegut continued: "The best of our stuff draws information and energy and wholeness from outside ourselves." Those signals come from "other specialized cells in the organism. Those other cells contribute to us energy and little bits of information, in order that we may increase the organism's awareness of itself—and dream its dreams" (p. 228). He could well have been reading, just before, Emerson's essay on "The Poet" or the Preface to Whitman's 1855 *Leaves of Grass*.

For *Playboy*, also in 1973, Vonnegut further explained his conviction of the writer's ultimate service. "My motives are political," he reiterated. "I agree with Stalin and Hitler and Mussolini that the writer should serve his society. I differ with dictators as to *how* writers should serve. Mainly, I think they should be—and biologically *have* to be—agents of change. For the better, we hope" (p. 237). Some months later, however, he voiced the esthetic worry that has been acknowledged by novelists from Tolstoy and Howells to John Barth and fellow moderns: when the writer "tries to put his politics into a work of the imagination, he will foul up his work beyond all recognition" (p. xvi). Yet Vonnegut clearly intended to be an agent of change, and he did not choose to go the route of the New Journalism. "I have wavered some on this," he admitted, but he had come down once more on the side of imaginative showing over explaining. "I am now persuaded again that acknowledged fiction is a much more truthful way of telling the truth than the New Journalism is. . . . The New Journalist isn't free to tell nearly as much as a fiction writer, to *show* as much" (pp. xix-xx). He had, in short, discovered a new faith in the practical power of art: "I now believe that the only way in which Americans can rise above their ordinariness, can mature sufficiently to rescue themselves and to help rescue their planet, is through enthusiastic intimacy with works of their imaginations" (p. xxvii).[9]

At the PEN congress in Vienna in 1975, an interviewer caught Vonnegut in a doleful mood. "The biggest truth now—what is probably making me unfunny now for the remaining one-third of my life—" Vonnegut said, "is that I don't think people give a damn whether the planet goes on or not. . . . I know of very few people who are dreaming of a world for their grandchildren." In view of this self-absorbed passiveness—an advancing state of mind in the seventies, it should be added, that his previous Billy Pilgrim fantasies iron-ically had indulged, if not encouraged—Vonnegut mused that it might be time to pack it in as a writer. Perhaps he would look for a different career.[10] But there were more books to come. The next year brought the awaited new novel, ominously titled *Slapstick* and dedicated to the memory of Laurel and Hardy. Still, his subtitle bore the hopeful utopian slogan he had proferred the McGovern-Shriver campaign of 1972: *Lonesome No More*! Nor did one read very far to discover that Vonnegut had indeed assumed his precarious double role of canary in the coal mine and evolutionary cell in the social organism.[11]

The story, he promised on the opening page, would be his most autobiographical. He had also written what the reviewers again consistently overlooked, namely a novel which, un-scrambled, could be seen to have a predominantly utopian time frame and thematic structure. Flying to Indianapolis with his scientist brother to attend the funeral of a lonely alcoholic in his nuclear family, he thought of his deceased sister, a tall, gritty, responsive and intuitive woman who had been the spe-cial audience of his earlier writing. He thereupon fell into the utopian dream of *Slapstick*, though he called it a funereal story "about desolated cities and spiritual cannibalism and incest and loneliness and lovelessness and death, and so on. It depicts myself and my beautiful sister as monsters, and so on" (pp. 18-19). Clearly, the doomsday terrors of *Slaughterhouse-Five* and *Breakfast of Champions* had returned once more.

Vonnegut's narrator is Dr. Wilbur Daffodil-11 Swain, the hundred-year-old last president of the United States. He lives on an isolated, futuristic Manhattan ravaged by a plague of or-ganisms termed "The Green Death." Wilbur recounts how he and his twin, Eliza, grew up in present-day America as rich, unloved, grotesque but telepathically ultra-intelligent children. Wilbur's is the rational mind and Eliza's the harmonious, unifying intuition. No one knows that the monster-twins possess this cooperative genius. They are sent to an estate in Vermont to enjoy a presumably short life by parents who are "fabulously well-to-do, and descended from Americans who had all but wrecked the planet with a form of Idiot's Delight—obsessively turning money into power, and then power back into money again, and then money back into power again" (p. 28).

Vonnegut's creative anger over the American present seems to be somewhat played out, however, and after nine rather dull chapters developing this autobiographical tribute to his own sister and implying that humans might display more "decency," if not love, toward each other, he has the children, at a fifteenth birthday party, confess their paired genius to shocked and unbelieving parents. Eliza is hospitalized, gains some family money, and ends up in a condominium in Peru. Reportedly, she dies in an accident at a Chinese colony on Mars. Within these slapstick contingencies, Vonnegut manages the semblance of a forward-moving plot. Wilbur and Eliza as precocious children hatched, among other projects, a manual on child-rearing; an essay on gravity that becomes especially interesting to advanced Chinese scientists; and "a utopian scheme for creating artificial extended families in America by issuing everyone a new middle name. All persons with the same middle name would be relatives" (p. 107). (In the *Playboy* interview of 1973, Vonnegut had casually attributed this idea to the overly active imagination of Kilgore Trout.) In a triple sequence, then, first Wilbur goes to Harvard to become a pediatrician. But gravity inversions (caused by Chinese wizard-scientists) create catastrophic, world-wide damage, and "the world would never be the same again" (p. 154). So Wilbur leaves his medical practice to step into this ravaged new era as a presidential candidate who successfully runs on the slogan, "LONESOME NO MORE!" His campaign promise: to create artificial extended families through government-issue middle names and thereby alleviate American loneliness. ("It was the only subject I needed for victory, which was lucky. It was the only subject I had" [p. 160].)

These devised "families," of course, are the fictional version of Vonnegut's "sunny little dream" of utopian community. The gravity disasters suggest, however, that he continues to believe that any transition to utopia will have to be aided by powerful events unrelated to wilful social planning. Wilbur's America does come to enjoy haphazardly certain utopian benefits. But stable government, education, work, and abundance are not among them because of the gravity inversions. Technology is threatened by an energy shortage, though the industrial urban world at least is not therefore generating new schisms of wealth, power, and social status. So "Americans were happier than they had ever been" (p. 187). They are encouraged to feel closer to nature by their computerized middle names that denote vegetation, wild life, or minerals. (In *Breakfast of Champions*, on the other hand, one character had proudly announced, "We're a Pontiac family!") They are expected to perform decent favors for their family members. Some, of course, resist Wilbur's utopia. His wealthy wife, Sophie Rothschild, refuses to join the "Peanut-3" family and wears, with others, the button "LONESOME Thank God!" But others bind together, issuing family newspapers with helpful want ads, free-enterprise tips, human interest stories, and "one interesting essay," Wilbur recalls, "either in the *Daffy-nition* or *The Goober Gossip*, which said that families with high moral standards were the best maintainers of law and order, and that police departments could be expected to fade away. 'If you know of a relative who is engaged in criminal acts,' it concluded, 'don't call the police. Call ten more relatives' " (p. 180). Leisure activities are plentiful for young and old at the family clubhouses, some of them the former haunts of wealthy Americans.

Once the extended families are formed, the American utopia of President Wilbur Daffodil-11 Swain develops without his federal leadership; in fact, he is permanently on tranquilizers and somewhat bemused by it all, anyway. Suddenly, a second disaster hits America in the form of "The Albanian Flu"—the "germs" actually well-meaning tiny Martians—followed by the Manhattan "Green Death," the organisms being microscopic, peace-loving Chinese. Wilbur's national government officially collapses. The decentralized nation, including New York City,

is now run by extended families, some of whom organize natural communes and cultivate the earth, while others, inevitably,
line up behind aggressive State leaders who direct regional
skirmishes and local feuds. But the weapons are old-fashioned
and the fighting does not escalate into callous massacre. After
all, a Daffodil of one State must care for a Daffodil from another.

Vonnegut climaxes his utopian caper with Wilbur's memory of a visit to his Daffodil family members in Indianapolis. An
embattled group, they had lost by then most of the ostensible
joys of utopia. But the moral foundation of the extended family
remained. Wilbur attended a weekly family meeting where
everyone respected Robert's *Rules of Order*. Selected by lot,
the chairperson was pointedly youthful (eleven years old),
black, and female. She presided skillfully over such matters as
feeding and sheltering Daffodil refugees of a local battle and
reminding each other of domestic obligations to their children
and dogs. "And so on," the reader is inclined to add, quoting
one of Wilbur's mocking tag-lines as he is dying on quaran-
tined Manhattan. Another put-down is "I had to laugh," as
though his artificial extended families are, after all, just *granfalloons*. No doubt these refrains are necessary to Vonnegut's
absurd-slapstick approach, an esthetic that shuns intrusive
preaching and avoids at any cost the serious resolution. The
tactic also denies the reader a sustained and responsible vision
of utopian community, assuming Vonnegut had one to disguise. Perhaps because he raised our hopes for a significant
new turn in his fiction, *Slapstick* becomes the most disappoint-
ing of all his novels.

His recently published *Jailbird* (1979), on the other hand,
comes closer to the transitional novel one expected in the middle 1970s. A different seriousness is signalled at the outset by
the plain subtitle: *A Novel*. The twenty-three chapters and Epilogue are separately extended fictional treatments of American
social history in the twentieth century, together with a respon-
sibly conceived turning point, and finally a critical glimpse,
with plentiful moments of satirical but not black humor, into
the possible middle terrain between our historically flawed
economic and social arrangements and an eventual American
commonwealth of decent, unselfish citizens. That Vonnegut's
utopian future does not finally materialize on these pages is

neither so exasperating nor depressing as the deferred hopes of *Slapstick*.

Vonnegut's favorite utopian protagonist, the recalcitrant idealist, now is named Walter F. Starbuck. The year is 1980, and Starbuck is writing memoirs that become a cavalcade of crucial moments in twentieth-century American life. He is the son of a chauffeur whose employer, a millionaire-industrialist, sent Walter to Harvard in the thirties. There Walter became a Depression-era, card-carrying Communist, met a fellow visionary named Mary O'Looney, and both came under the spell of Kenneth Whistler, an anti-capitalistic Harvard alumnus. After Harvard, Walter held government jobs in the New Deal, at the Nuremberg War Trials, and in the Truman administration. But his government career was over several years after he played a Whittaker Chambers role for young Richard Nixon's witchhunts in 1949. After his blacklisting, he does not return to government service for nearly twenty years, and then to become Nixon's idealistic advisor on youth affairs. Walter still cherishes his 1930s dream, "a possibility that there will one day be one big happy and peaceful family on Earth—the Family of Man." [12] Then comes Watergate. Illegal contributions are stored in Walter's subterranean office and when they are discovered, he is indicted for embezzlement, perjury and obstruction of justice. He goes to a minimum-security prison in Georgia until 1977.

This paraphrase typically misses the art with which Vonnegut enriches the drama of history with deceptively casual byplay of supporting characters and apparently random idiocies of setting and plot. Nor have I suggested the range of his critical odyssey into the past. The book embraces almost a century of agonized national experience, including turn-of-the-century labor clashes, World War One beggar-veterans, Sacco and Vanzetti, Prohibition, the Crash and Depression, Nazi death-camps, the Korean War, Kent State, and then Watergate. As if to assault the present decade's advanced "narcissism" (to borrow the new intellectual buzz word), Vonnegut imaginatively summons the muse of history more urgently than in any of his past fiction. He announces on the first page of this autobiographical novel-as-history, "Pay attention, please, for years as well as people are characters in this book, which is the

story of my life so far" (p. 1). Indeed, the book can be read as
The Education of Kurt Vonnegut, his continuing effort as a utopian writer to clarify his troubled perception of history and
human will. Is there an evolving, linear course of good and
evil, now blind, now humanly directed, among and within the
historical events of his "years"? Or is history a cyclical
stalemate? Or Emersonian-circular progress? Or is a hopeful
previous time and place of any value except to serve nostalgic-
pastoral dreams? As in all his previous eight novels, the
treatment of time is linked to his wavering view of free will (at
best illusory? or sometimes, somehow potential?) and usually
depends on whether his cynicism or optimism is holding sway
at the moment. In *Jailbird*, the ambivalence about progress
and free will is Vonnegut light- rather than dark-gray. Despite
apparent evidence to the contrary, we are *not* doomed to re-
peat the past nightmares, because Vonnegut will not let us forget how our human freedoms have been jeopardized in the
cases of Sacco and Vanzetti and Richard Nixon. The defeated
social dreams of the somewhat simpler thirties *can* be recovered and reenacted to some good purpose in the present
and perhaps enjoy eventual success the next time around.

The novel periodically returns to the post-1929 years as
the valid turning point in American history, when the mistakes
of the past were realistically appraised and the nation was for a
first time united and kind and visionary. In his Prologue, Vonnegut features Powers Hapgood as the model for Kenneth
Whistler in the novel and prepares the reader for the signifi-
cantly pivotal utopian "character" of those "years" in the
1930s. For his story, he links that decade to the late 1970s in a
manner similar to the dual focus of the '40s and '60s in *Slaughterhouse-Five*, but this time the cyclical analogy recalls social
hope rather than heartless militarism. Starbuck, out of prison
in 1977, is wandering the streets of New York City, as deso-
lately jobless as any victim of the Depression years. Suddenly
he is set upon by a fellow derelict in the form of a little home-
less woman in oversized basketball shoes carrying her scav-
engings in six shopping bags while she loudly curses the
wealthy, aloof passers-by. This feisty woman is Mary
O'Looney, Walter's fellow radical of the thirties who, more
than he, still cherishes the socialist ideals of justice and equal-

ity during that earlier period. In extended flashbacks, Vonnegut recreates those earlier dreams of Walter and Mary.

They had been nourished by the eloquence of Whistler, the labor organizer who died not long after in a Kentucky mine disaster where he insisted on working alongside the day laborers. Walter recalls the night when he took Mary to hear Whistler, come to Cambridge from Kentucky to address a meeting of laborers who had been fired for joining a union. Whistler spoke mainly on two subjects: the gruesome injustice in the American past that was typified by the Sacco-Vanzetti executions just before the Crash of the late twenties; and the prospects in the thirties for a fulfillment of utopia. With typical blunting of his didactic purpose, Vonnegut reverses the logical sequence of Whistler's critique and prophecy. The searing lessons of the Sacco-Vanzetti case, we infer, became one of the influences on the heightened utopian conscience of the thirties that Mary and Walter are now rekindling in the late seventies. Walter recalls Whistler's prophetic speech, and it carries Vonnegut's utopian message virtually in one breath:

> Kenneth Whistler promised us that the time was at hand for workers to take over their factories and to run them for the benefit of mankind. Profits that now went to drones and corrupt politicians would go to those who worked, and to the old and the sick and the orphaned. All people who could work would work. There would be only one social class—the working class. Everyone would take turns doing the most unpleasant work, so that a doctor, for example, might be expected to spend a week out of each year as a garbage man. The production of luxury goods would stop until the basic needs of every citizen were met. Health care would be free. Food would be cheap and nourishing and plentiful. Mansions and hotels and office buildings would be turned into small apartments, until everyone was decently housed. Dwellings would be assigned by means of a lottery. There would be no more wars and eventually no more national boundaries, since everyone in the world would belong to the same class with identical interests—the interests of the working class.
>   And on and on.
>   What a spellbinder he was! (pp. 170-71)

But what to do in advancing the utopian revolution now in the late 1970s? One international conglomerate, RAMJAC, currently has gobbled up the *New York Times*, *Playboy*, *Time*, Youngstown Steel, hotels, car rentals, and even McDonald's and Colonel Sanders fast-food chains. True, but there is a good fairy in Vonnegut's utopian tale. The widow of the founder of RAMJAC and majority stockholder whom nobody on the Board ever sees—this happens to be Mary herself! (She lives in an abandoned area below Grand Central Station.) When Walter assures her that good people do still exist and have recently been kind to him, she promptly orders that they become vice-presidents in various companies of RAMJAC. Like her fictional predecessors Rumfoord and Rosewater, Mary uses her capitalist wealth to invent a new commonwealth. Dying, she tells Walter that a will is in her left shoe: "I leave the RAMJAC Corporation to its rightful owners, the American people" (p. 219). America can thereby dismantle the apparatus of industrial capitalism and create the beneficent society dreamed by Whistler and his latter-day disciples Mary and Walter. The book ends happily on this fanciful prospect.

But there is an Epilogue. The utopia did not come into being after all. To prevent the sudden confusion and collapse of RAMJAC, Walter buried Mary secretly and placed the will in a safety-deposit box. He then managed effectively his own subsidiary, Down Home Records, throwing lavish parties for the artists and proving himself an efficient businessman, though with no eye to funnelling the profits into the public coffers. Then came the discovery of Mary's body and her will, and for concealing the latter, Walter must go to prison once more. Mary's bequest of RAMJAC— only 19 percent of the nation's corporate wealth, one should note—is being processed by an army of twenty thousand new bureaucrats and her peaceful revolution has misfired. Walter thinks he can explain why: "For one thing, the federal government was wholly unprepared to operate all the businesses of RAMJAC on behalf of the people. For another thing: Most of those businesses, rigged only to make profits, were as indifferent to the needs of the people as, say, thunderstorms" (p. 231). So the spirit and the dream of Whistler, renewed four decades later, are laid to rest as the impractical stuff of harmless illusion and nostalgic regression? Perhaps not quite. At his bon voyage party before returning to prison, Walter is reconciled with his estranged son while friends play the record of his 1949 testimony before Nixon's anti-communist committee. Why, asked Nixon, had a privileged man like Walter not embraced the existing American economic system? Walter had plagiarized a reply of his college hero (and Vonnegut's Powers Hapgood, p. xix):

> Whistler had been a witness at a trial of strikers accused of violence. The judge had become curious about him, had asked him why such a well-educated man from such a good family would so immerse himself in the working class.
>
> My stolen answer to Nixon was this: "Why? The Sermon on the Mount, sir." (pp. 240-41)

On this gentle but decisive note at the close of an essentially affirmative novel, Vonnegut may be entering the 1980s with the promise that his next protagonist will renew more neglected or forgotten dreams of our idealistic past and create from them new utopian vistas of harmony, peace, and decency that belie Orwell's prophesies of 1984. If so, who will be around to play the practical canary in the coal mine of the present? No doubt Vonnegut will be there, too.

8

The Utopian Vision: A Selective, Annotated Bibliography of Works in English

JULIO A. MARTINEZ

When I was asked to prepare an annotated bibliography on utopias for the educated reader, I assumed the responsibility with the suspicion that my labor would not be altogether original. Surely, I thought, since utopian literature had been at the center of intense humanistic disputation and concern, annotated bibliographies of its foremost advocates and movements would not be difficult to find. As I began searching for bibliographies similar in format to the one I intended to prepare, I realized that no such work existed. Several monumental unannotated bibliographies on utopias have, of course, been published. However, these works are so scholarly in scope and so detailed in their coverage that they are of little help to the reader who wants to be initiated into the field, not overwhelmed by it. Furthermore, none have been annotated adequately.

I quickly discovered that the best works in languages other than English had been translated into English. Therefore, in limiting this bibliography to books in English, I am reasonably confident that no major utopian work will be eliminated. I have deviated from the linguistic criterion in only three instances. Etienne Cabet's *Voyage to Icaria* is available only in French, but is so important that to leave it out would be scandalous. I have also included a critical evaluation of Emile Zola's *Work*; it is a major piece of research indispensable to anyone interested in Zola's Fourierian fiction. In the case of Moses Hess, I have included a critical evaluation of his utopian thought because of its early influence on Karl Marx's utopian vision, although his original utopian writings remain untranslated.

In addition to including the most widely known authors, a few writers who have emphasized idiosyncratic utopian constructs will also be found in this bibliography, e.g. works dealing with feminist and objectivist utopias. The contemporary appeal of the issues they discuss amply justifies, it seems to me, their inclusion. I have not followed in every case the usual bibliographic practice of citing first editions. Rather, whenever possible I have cited editions which are easily available or have been published at moderate prices. My primary concern in choosing critical publications on the authors or subjects covered has been to select monographs or essayists capable of engaging the attention of the educated lay person, but, needless to say, I have preferred those which combine this feature with sound scholarship. Finally, I should like to caution the reader that there are many alternate spellings of Evgveni Ivanovich Zamiatin's name. I have chosen Eugene Zamyatin because it seems to be the most prevalent.

General Bibliographies

Bentley, Wilder. *The Communication of Utopian Thought: Its History, Forms and Use*, Vol. 1. *The Bibliography*. San Francisco: San Francisco State College Bookstore, 1972.

Like its predecessor, *Utopias: A Bibliography* by Buell G. Gallagher (now dated and unserviceable), published in 1946, this poorly annotated checklist of utopian works and studies on utopian thought, makes no pretension of completeness or even accuracy, since many of the original publications were unavailable to the compiler. Titles are entered under five categories: I. Communication and the American Cultural Community. II. Utopian Thought—Its History, Forms, Uses and Abuses (books about Utopias). III. The Great Religious and Secular Utopias. IV. A Miscellany of Minor Utopias of Many Persuasions, Whether Publicly or Privately Held, and V. A Prospectus and Conspectus of Seven Archetypal Utopian Symbols and Their Influence on the Contemporary Situation in the American Cultural Community.

Negley, Glenn. *Utopian Literature: A Bibliography: With a Supplementary Listing of Works Influential in Utopian Thought*. Lawrence, Kansas: The Regents Press of Kansas, 1977.

This unannotated bibliography provides the titles of approximately 1,200 utopian and dystopian works of fiction. They describe a particular state or community, which "may be as limited as a small group or so extensive as to encompass the world or the universe" (thus a statement of principles or procedural reforms is not a utopia). Each has for its theme the political structure of that fictional state or community (thus a mere Robinsonade, adventure narrative, or science fantasy does not qualify as utopian). The works considered seem to be only American and European, beginning with those of the 17th century up to the present. The entries indicate in which of the eleven libraries in Europe and the United States, known for their large holdings of utopian works, a title can be found in its earliest edition. Pseudonyms and anonyms are profusely represented with references to probable authors. By almost any standard, this is the most extensive bibliography on fictional utopias and is highly recommended as a research tool.

Roemer, Kenneth M. "Bibliographies," In *The Obsolete Necessity: America in Utopian Writings, 1888-1900*. Kent, Ohio: Kent State University Press, 1976.

By far the most useful of the short bibliographies on American utopian, anti-utopian and partially utopian fiction. The first section is an annotated listing of bibliographies that were very useful to the author in compiling the sample of utopian works included. Besides these titles, it lists bibliographies focusing on specific authors, special collections and subject card catalogue listings at Duke University Library's collection on utopian literature, book reviews and advertisements in utopian journals, and, finally, general bibliographies. The annotated listing of primary sources follow the bibliography. They include separate annotations of the 160 works that constitute the sample of utopian literature examined in this work. It should prove indispensable for those interested in learning more about utopian literature in the United States.

Sargent, Lyman Tower. *British and American Utopian Literature, 1516-1975: An Annotated Bibliography*. Boston: G.K. Hall, 1979.

This briefly annotated—about a line long—bibliography is divided into three major sections: (1) A chronological list of utopias in English printed between 1516 and 1975, (2) A list of secondary works on utopian literature and (3) author and titles indexes to the chronological list. The first edition is given whenever possible. A symbol is given beside each entry which locates the library or libraries in which the compiler saw the book. Section (2) contains many citations, in foreign languages as well as in English, on utopianism in general and on some continental utopias. The chronological approach makes the location of specific works needlessly time consuming, because the author index simply correlates an author with the year in which the work was published. A selective list of Ph.D. dissertations and M.A. theses is provided.

General Works on the History and Concept of Utopia

Berneri, Marie Louise. *Journey Through Utopia*. New York: Schocken, 1971.

The author provides a general survey of utopian writings from the time of Plato to the present day. She has attempted to include those writings which have enjoyed the most popularity or which have had the greatest influence on utopian thought. Excerpts from the various works are included to document her conclusions. Anti-utopian writings, such as Huxley's *Brave New World*, and satires, such as Richter's *Pictures of the Socialist Future*, have been included. In much of her analysis she emphasizes the intolerant and authoritarian aspects of some utopian works. The work concludes with a bibliography of utopian writings, which includes precursors and critical writings of utopian thought. Originally published in 1950, this publication has not been updated.

Donner, H.W. *Introduction to Utopia*. Uppsala, Sweden: Sidgwick & Jackson, 1945.

This essay is designed as an introduction to the study of Thomas More's *Utopia*. The author's thesis is that More's work is not, as the socialists have believed, a plea for communism, nor as some German scholars have claimed, an incipient defense of British imperialism. Instead, he maintains, this work is a picture of the state society can attain without revelation; an appeal to mend our ways and ease the burden of our fellowmen. It does not describe an ultimate ideal, but one that is practicable enough to warrant serious consideration. Although this theological interpretation of *Utopia* is controversial, the book succeeds in summarizing the most distinctive features of this classic. For a more scholarly defense of this interpretation see Chambers, R.W.

Egbert, Donald Drew and Stow Persons, eds. *Socialism and American Life*. 2 vols. Princeton, N.J.: Princeton University Press, 1952.

Although not devoted to utopian socialism, this volume provides a generally reliable account of the utopian movement in America, particularly of the Owenites and the Oneida Community. Included are many sources on the less known colonies, such as Amana, Ephrata, and Icaria, as well as those founded by religious sectarians, i.e. the Rappites, Shakers, and Mormons, all of which are listed in the bibliography.

Elliott, Robert C. *The Shape of Utopia: Studies in a Literary Genre*. Chicago: University of Chicago Press, 1970.

Elliott argues that utopian literature is a distinct literary genre, having its origins, not in Plato's *Republic*, but in the myths of the Golden Age, as passed down in the satires of the Saturnalia of classical and medieval times. They are said to expose social shortcomings and point to professed but unfulfilled ideals. This strong satiric element is then traced in utopian and dystopian works, such as More's *Utopia* and Huxley's *Brave New World*. The moot claim that utopian literature is essentially a form of satire is engagingly presented and, if not the whole truth, is deserving of serious consideration.

Ernst, Morris Leopold. *Utopia Nineteen Seventy-Six*. Westport, Ct.: Greenwood, 1955.

Originally published in 1946, this work is a "prophetic" view of life in 1976, described in detailed and mildly utopian terms. It will interest those bemused by the naive progressive optimism still alive in the forties in this country.

Eurich, Nell. *Science in Utopia: A Mighty Design*. Cambridge, Mass.: Harvard University Press, 1967.

Devoted to utopian thinkers of the XVII century, i.e. Tomasso Campanella, Johann Valentin Andrea, Sir Francis Bacon, and other less known writers, such as Cowley and Glanvill, this book attempts to show how science and technology played an important role in the utopian schemes of that century. In the last chapter, entitled "A Look to the Future," the author argues that society's future technological changes will be along the lines the utopian thinkers of the seventeenth century envisioned.

Ferguson, John. *Utopias of the Classical World*. Ithaca, N.Y.: Cornell University Press, 1975.

Beginning with Homer, this book attempts to show how the ideal common-wealths of Plato and other Hellenistic thinkers converged and were incorporated into Roman and Christian religious utopianism, exemplified in such works as St. Augustine's *The City of God*. Although written in a dry-as-dust style, this work will prove useful for those interested in tracing the earliest visions of the good life in the Western world. It is copiously footnoted and provides a critical, annotated bibliography.

Fogarty, Robert S. *American Utopianism*. Itasca, Ill.: Peacock, F.E., 1972.

This book, from the series *Primary Sources in American History*, collects some of the most important utopian documents published between 1732 and the present. It is ideally suited for the beginning student of utopian literature who wants to know the essentials of what the seers and leaders of the movement have said on the subject.

Fuller, R. Buckminster. *Utopia or Oblivion*. New York: Overlook, 1972.

First published in 1969, this series of talks deal with the author's ideas on how to cope with the problem of material scarcity in the world. He proposes the harnessing of information resources and technology, so that "less will yield more." This vague technocratic approach to social evils exemplifies the perennial American hope that technological change is the road to vastly improved socio-economic conditions. The author uses the term "utopia" with some looseness, since he does not advocate a radically new political and social order.

Hansot, Elisabeth. *Perfection and Progress: Two Modes of Utopian Thought*. Cambridge, Mass.: MIT Press, 1974.

The author advances the thesis that while the classical utopian mode viewed utopia as a static social condition that reflects man's innermost nature and craving for perfection, the modern utopian mode conceives utopia as a dynamic social setting, and mankind's perfectibility as an unending process. The contrast between the two modes is developed with ingenuity and precise analytical power. Six utopian commonwealths are examined: Plato's *Republic*, More's *Utopia*, and Andreae's *Christianopolis* serve as examples of classical utopian thought, while Bellamy's *Looking Backward*, Wells's *A Modern Utopia*, and Howell's *A Traveler from Altruria* and *Through the Eye of the Needle* serve as examples of modern utopian thought. The author includes a bibliography of utopias and commentaries on utopias which have been cited in the footnotes.

Hertzler, Joyce Oramel. *History of Utopian Thought*. New York: Cooper Square, 1923.

The first part of this history is a non-evaluative review of "utopian" ideals, beginning with the Hebrew prophets and ending with the writings of Bellamy, Hertzka and Wells. The second part is a critical appraisal of various utopian works, the contributions they have made to civilization, and their alleged shortcomings. This work not only relates utopian works to the historical times in which they were produced, but also provides useful biographical data on utopists. Although less engaging than Lewis Mumford's survey (see), this work is an excellent piece of research in an area of historical scholarship which hitherto has not been well covered.

Hertzler, Joyce Oramel. "On Golden Ages: Then and Now." *South Atlantic Quarterly* 39 (July 1940), 318-329.

Hollins, Dorothea, ed. *Utopian Papers: Being Addresses to the Utopians*. London: Masters, 1908.

Hughes, David Y. "*The Mood of A Modern Utopia*." *Extrapolation* 19 (December 1977), 59-67.

Johnson, J.W., ed. *Utopian Literature: A Selection*. New York: Modern Library, 1968.

This anthology is comprised of selections chronologically arranged from the past to the 20th century, which show the historical development of utopian thought. Each chapter covers a broad historical period. An introductory essay provides added perspective to these selections. The coverage includes prehistoric myths, religious excerpts, classical political myths, as well as contemporary utopian thought. Some selections, e.g. the prophetic sections of Isaiah, Strabo's *The Scythians* and Dante's *Purgatory*, can be considered "utopian" only in the most liberal sense. Some of the major utopian fictional writers are included, but not one of the French utopian thinkers! Each chapter concludes with a list of primary sources. The "Suggested Additional Readings" and "Questions for Research and Discussion" at the end of each of the nine chapters are two valuable didactic and bibliographic aids that enhance the usefulness of this work.

Kaufmann, Moritz. *Utopias: or Schemes of Social Improvement, from Sir Thomas More to Karl Marx*. London: Paul, C.K., 1879.

The main value of this work is that it seems to have been the first study of utopianism which viewed Karl Marx's philosophy as the articulation of an utopian vision. It should be read with caution since it does not present a sophisticated analysis of Marx's ideas and in some cases distorts them.

Kateb, George. "Utopianism. I. Utopia and Utopianism." In *International Encyclopedia of the Social Sciences*, edited by David L. Stills. New York: Macmillan & The Free Press, pp. 267-271, 1968.

This is both a general and a theoretical introduction to the concept of utopianism and its varieties, by one of its most reputable scholars. The beginning student of the subject would do well to read it. For those wishing to deepen their basic understanding of the concept, Karl Mannheim's article, "Utopia" in the *Encyclopedia of the Social Sciences* (see), published in the thirties, is recommended.

Krutch, Joseph Wood. "Danger: Utopia Ahead." *Saturday Review*, August 20, 1966, pp. 17-18.

Levin, Harry. *The Myth of the Golden Age in the Renaissance*. Bloomington: Indiana Unviersity Press, 1970.

The unifying theme of this erudite volume is that the myth of the Golden Age, emphasizing free will, a life of undisturbed pleasure and the pursuit of beauty, became an attractive vision for the Renaissance. The author draws comparisons from analogues of the myth in the eighteenth, nineteenth, and twentieth centuries (the utopian, pastoral and travel literature to exotic and often imaginary islands). Those interested in comparing the fundamental similarities between the Golden Age myth and utopianism will find this study to be indispensable reading. The appendix, "Paradises, Heavenly and Earthly: Some Paradoxes of Utopia: A Note on Iconography," will be of particular value to those interested in the paradoxical nature of some utopian visions.

Mannheim, Karl. "Utopia" in *Encyclopedia of the Social Sciences*, Vol. 15. New York: Macmillan, 1935.

This is a scholarly, if somewhat dated, introductory article to the concept of utopia by the eminent German sociologist. It should be read in conjunction with George Kateb's "Utopianism. I. Utopia and Utopianism" in the *International Encyclopedia of the Social Sciences* which reflects recent scholarly interpretations of the concept.

Manuel, Frank E. and Fritzie P. Manuel. *Utopian Thought in the Western World*. Cambridge, Mass.: The Belknap Press of Harvard University Press, 1980.

This ambitious and elegantly written history of "the utopian thought of the literature classes in Western society" from ancient times to the present, classifies utopias into seven major historical groupings. Each grouping or constellation, e.g. the French Enlightment, aims to exhibit similarities with other groupings, so generalizations about the utopian propensity may be drawn. The emphasis of the book is on the contributions that utopian writers have made to the notions of equality, freedom, work, pleasure, love and community, not on the social conditions which stimulated them to devise their alternate melioristic social programs. The impact that utopian thought had on social reform is also deftly illuminated.

Moment, Gairdner B. and Otto F. Kraushaar, eds. *Utopias: The American Experience*. Metuchen, N.J.: Scarecrow Press, 1980.

The thirteen essays comprising this anthology are an outgrowth of a series of lectures given on American utopias during the American Bicentennial. Although this book is marked by a lack of a unifying theme and includes articles that should have been better edited or excluded altogether, the student of utopianism will find several contributions. e.g. on unconscious sexual stereotyping in utopias; town planning in the XIX century Harmony Society and women in utopia, which are quite rewarding both from an informative and a scholarly point of view. However, an article on Jim Jones's People's Temple seems out of place in a collection whose avowed aim is to discuss American utopias. The work is also marred by the lack of a bibliography and by the brevity of its index.

Manuel, Frank E. and Fritzie P. Manuel. *French Utopias: An Anthology of Ideal Societies*. New York: Free Press, 1966.

The 26 selections included in this anthology are drawn from sections of various utopian works—written in the last 400 years—that describe the ideal society or advance a program for organizing such a society. All major writers usually identified as utopian are included, i.e. Rabelais, Cyrano de Bergerac, Fenelon, Restif de la Bretonne, Saint Simon. Fourier, Comte and many others. It presents a balanced and representative picture of French utopian literature.

Manuel, Frank E. "Toward a Psychological History of Utopias." In his *Freedom from History and Other Untimely Essays*." New York: New York University Press, 1971, pp. 115-148.

Manuel, Frank E. *Utopias and Utopian Thought*. Boston: Houghton Mifflin, 1966.

This collection of sixteen essays by leading scholars in many fields explores man's yearning for utopia or questions its feasibility and attractiveness. Included are general discussions by George Kateb, Paul Tillich, Lewis Mumford, Judith Shklar, Frank Manuel, and Northorp Frye, among others, as well as essays treating specific utopian movements such as Oneida.

Molnar, Thomas, *Utopia; The Perennial Heresy*. New York: Sheed and Ward, 1967.

This book professedly sets out to denounce utopianism as a "delirious ideal stamped with the madness of logic." The dream—utopia—leads, according to the author, "to the denial of God and self-divinization—the heresy." Contrasted to utopia is the view that society is always unfinished and imperfect and that its essential problems can never be solved by social engineering. Elegantly written by a conservative thinker who concludes that utopia is the panacea for a "lawless and sorry herd."

Morgan, Arthur E. *Nowhere Was Somewhere: How History Makes Utopias and Utopias Make History*. 1946 Reprint. Westport, Ct.: Greenwood, 1976.

The theme of this book is that More's *Utopia* actually existed at one time. The author concluded that it is a description of the Inca civilization, based on accounts brought by European travellers. The author, a former social planner, thinks utopias are basically good, but cannot be achieved without a spiritual rebirth. In spite of the good credentials of the publisher, the work reflects a shallow optimism and questionable scholarship. Nonetheless, it provides useful, succinct discussions of utopias, from the Old Testament to Edward Bellamy.

Morton, A. L. *The English Utopia*. London: Lawrence and Wishart, 1952.

This is a reliable study of English utopianism, although a bit dated. It covers English utopias in more detail than do general introductions to the topic.

Mumford, Lewis. *Story of Utopias*. New York: Peter Smith, 1941.

Originally published in 1922, it holds that utopias serve several purposes: to record men's reactions to the environment and their efforts to shape reality in accordance with the ideal; to forecast how their vision will some day be partially realized. Mumford considers a number of important thinkers, from Plato to H. G. Wells, and divides their works into "utopias of escape" and "utopias of reconstruction." The former represent a complete break with immediate, pedestrian reality, while the latter "lead outward into the world" and dispose men to make social changes. Mumford writes skillfully and displays a thorough familiarity with the literature. It should appeal to lay persons and scholars alike.

Negley, Glenn Robert and John Max Patrick, eds. *Quest for Utopia: An Anthology of Imaginary Societies*. New York: Schuman, H., 1952.

This anthology contains either the whole or excerpts of 33 utopian works, ranging from the well known, such as Tommaso Campanella's *City of the Sun* and H. G. Wells's *Modern Utopia*, to the less known, such as Ludvig Holberg's *Niels Klim's Journey Under the Ground* and Theodor Hertzka's *Freeland*. For the general reader this is the ideal approach to the best of the fiction that has been written in this field.

Nelson, William, ed. *Twentieth Century Interpretation of Utopia*. Engelwood Cliffs, N.J.: Prentice Hall, 1968.

This is a collection of eighteen critical essays and commentaries devoted to Thomas More's *Utopia*. The selections in this volume by such outstanding scholars as C. S. Lewis, J. Max Patrick, G. R. Negley, Ernst Cassirer, Karl Kautsky and others, present thought provoking views and interpretations of this master-piece. They range from discussions of More's own views of *Utopia* to David Bevington's claim that *Utopia* has been "invoked to support the radical socialist states . . . as well as in support of the anti-communist position of the Papacy." The essays in this anthology show how *Utopia* lends itself to diverse and often incompatible interpretations of its intent and meaning.

Parrington, Vernon Louis, ed. *American Dreams: A Study of American Utopias*. New York: Russell & Russell, 1964.

This is a well researched, in-depth study of American utopian literature, beginning with John Eliot's *Christian Commonwealth*, written in 1659, and ending with Trang Werfel's *Star of the Unborn*, published in 1946. Many of the writers discussed "have in common only their interest in outlining a different government, or a better way of life," not necessarily the "perfect" society. Two chapters are devoted to Edward Bellamy, one dealing with his precursors and the other dealing with his critics. A postscript discusses a few of the famous utopian and dystopian novels written after 1946. The emphasis is on literary utopias. An eleven-page bibliography of general sources and works cited in the study, arranged in chronological order, enhances the value of this highly readable and outstanding contribution to the scholarship on utopias. It is possibly the most comprehensive account of less known American utopian fiction up to the mid-forties.

Plath, David. ed. *Aware of Utopia*. Urbana, Ill.: University of Illinois Press, 1971.

Seven scholars examine cross-cultural utopian thought, providing insights into past and present utopian movements in various parts of the world. The editor maintains that utopianism might provide the moral foundation for the practice of the social sciences and improve social planning through the scrutiny of the social world in which men might come to live. The essays include a comparison of Western and Japanese traditional utopias; a discussion of how computers might facilitate the design and study of alternative futures; consideration of utopian thought in Latin American culture, and a study of the utopian features of the Indian uprising against the British East India Company in 1857. The essays included originated in a conference on Utopia in Comparative Focus held at the University of Illinois in 1968.

Popper, Karl R. *The Open Society and Its Enemies*. 2 vols. Princeton, N.J.: Princeton University Press, 1966.

The dual purpose of these two volumes, I. *The Spell of Plato* and II. *The High Tide of Prophecy: Hegel, Marx and the Aftermath*, is to attack historicism, by which the author means the doctrines that there are inexorable laws of historical development which govern the course of history, and that "utopian social engineering," those "tribal" or holistic conceptions of society which reject reform and "piecemeal engineering" as the means to bring about social reconstruction, is both possible and desirable. Among proponents of utopianism, Plato, Hegel and Marx come under considerable criticism.

Popper, Karl "Utopia and Violence." *Hibbert Journal* 46 (January 1948), 109-116.

Richter, Peyton E., ed. *Utopia/Dystopia*. Cambridge, Mass.: Schenkman Publishing Co., 1975.

Roemer, Kenneth M. "The Heavenly City of the Late 19th-Century Utopians." *Journal of the American Studies Association of Texas* 4 (1973), 5-13.

Roemer, Kenneth M. *The Obsolete Necessity: America in Utopian Writings, 1888-1900*. Kent, Ohio: Kent State University Press, 1976.

This work, based on a Ph.D. dissertation written in 1971, seeks to demonstrate what utopian literature reveals about the stormy late nineteenth century. The author argues that the popularity of such works as Bellamy's *Looking Backward* and William Dean Howells's *A Traveler From Altruria* suggests an intense interest in both re-evaluating and perpetuating the American social and political ideals of the time. The author's thesis is that the desire for order and stability, mixed with pleas for radical and sudden changes found in the utopian literature, suggest parallels with colonial attitudes and contemporary anxiety about "future shock." It helps us understand our earliest attempts to define the "American Mission" as well as contemporary hopes and fears about the twentieth and twenty-first centuries. It contains a short, annotated, chronological bibliography, mostly of primary sources.

Roemer, Kenneth M. "Sex Roles, Utopia and Change: The Family in Late Nineteenth Century Utopian Literature." *American Studies* 13 (Fall 1972), 33-47.

Reynolds, E.E. "Three Views of Utopia." *Moreana*, nos. 31-32 (November 1971), 209-214.

Russell, Frances Theresa. *Touring Utopia: the realm of constructive humanism*. New York: Dial Press, 1932.

This meandering study outlines how various utopias view the realms of government, education, occupation, recreation, beauty and art, religion and morality, and domesticity. Utopias from the point of view of the satirist, of the socialistically oriented Bellamy, and of H. G. Wells are also incorporated. The author has devoted ten pages to classified lists of utopias, which will prove useful to those wishing a chronological sequence of the major and minor works discussed in this volume.

Sargent, Lyman Tower "Women in Utopia." *Comparative Literature Studies* 10 (December 1973), 302-316.

Shklar, Judith. *After Utopia: The Decline of Political Faith*. Princeton, N.J.: Princeton University Press 1957.

This book deals with the end of optimism about the possibility of social reconstruction along utopian lines. The author traces the decline of political philosophy from the Enlightenment to the pessimism of our age. Based on the author's doctoral dissertation, it bears the marks of its origin—unexciting prose and considerable documentation. This is a scholarly piece of research which diagnosis not only utopian, but radical thought as dead visions.

Sibley, Mulford Q. *Technology and Utopian Thought*. Minneapolis: Burgess, 1973.

First published in 1971, this study is devoted to the attitudes to technology which have influenced utopian views on it. The central theme of this work is to determine how these general attitudes have been reflected in utopian thought. The author also summarizes, evaluates and relates to contemporary questions, the treatment by utopists of both the advantages and problems brought about by technology.

Strauss, Sylvia, "Women in 'Utopia.'" *South Atlantic Quarterly* 75 (Winter 1976), 115-131.

Tod, Ian and Michael Wheeler. *Utopia: An Illustrated History*. New York: Harmony Books, 1978.

The authors provide a bird's eye, historical overview of the many visions of utopia in Western thought, extending from the epic of Gilgamesh, written circa 2000 B.C.E. to Buckminster Fuller of this century. All major utopian works are discussed, although one may wonder why Le Corbussier and other architects are included. What the authors have to say about the topic is not novel, but the 130 beautiful illustrations they have gathered, many of which are in color, makes this introduction to utopian thought unique. Several spelling mistakes and errors were noted, e.g. Josiah Warren appears as Joseph Warren and Burrhus F. Skinner as Bernard Skinner.

Tuveson, Ernest Lee. *Millennium and Utopia*. New York: Harper-Row, 1964.

This learned study argues that the concept of the "stages of advancement of mankind" have come to hold for the modern man very much the same significance that "grace" and "millennial" redemption held for Anglican thinkers of the XVII century. The heavenly city of the eighteenth century philosophers and nineteenth century utopian visionaries, he maintains, retains many features of the bygone, religious vision of the New Jerusalem. This fascinatingly stated thesis is a serious attempt to persuade the reader that the utopia of the mechanistic philosophers is a transformation of what was, essentially, a religious idea.

Walsh, Chad. *From Utopia to Nightmare*. New York: Harper, 1962.

The author argues that utopias may have provided the foil for the dystopian thought of such writers as Orwell and Huxley. Anti-utopian thought is said to be rooted in the discovery that the visions of utopian thought are either distasteful, boring, or straight-jacketing. Nonetheless, Walsh invites us not to give up the utopian impulse, but to envision ideal societies more intelligently, with a full awareness of how the corruption of power can stifle the creation of better social conditions.

Weber, Eugene. "The Anti-Utopian of the Twentieth Century." *South Atlantic Quarterly*, 58 (Summer 1959), 440-447.

Weinkauf, Mary S. "Five Spokemen for Dystopia." *Midwest Quarterly* 16 (January 1975), 175-186.

White, Howard B. "Political Faith and Francis Bacon." *Social Research* 23 (Fall 1976), 635-678.

Wiener, Philip, ed. "Utopia." In *Dictionary of the History of Ideas: Studies of Selected Pivotal Ideas*. New York: Scribner's, 1973.

This work presents a comprehensive, bird's eye view of utopian literature from its earliest expressions in Greek culture to Skinner's *Walden Two*. The emphasis is on conceptual analysis rather than in detailed accounts of individual works. One of the major assets of this well written essay is its bibliography. It lists works containing lengthy bibliographies. Those interested in gaining a general understanding of the concept of utopia and in securing a good list of bibliographic sources on utopian literature would do well to read this article. The articles on utopias and utopianism by George Kateb and Karl Mannheim published in the *International Encyclopedia of the Social Sciences* and the *Encyclopedia of the Social Sciences* aptly supplement and enrich Wiener's treatment of the subject.

Woodcock, George "Utopias in Negative." *Sewanee Review* 64 (Winter 1956), 81-97.

General Works on Utopian Communities

Armytage, W. H. G. *Heavens Below: Utopian Experiments in England, 1560-1960*. London: Routledge and Kegan Paul, 1961.

Despite the title, the bulk of this scholarly book is devoted to the history of British "ideal settlements" between 1560 and 1900. This piecemeal, historical account of utopian experiments in Britain attempts to show that, while temporary and shortlived, these experiments have had a considerable impact on the social development of that country. Some of the best known utopian thought and experiments, i.e. the early sectarian proto-socialism of the Diggers, Levellers, Quakers, Moravians and the Owenite Movement, are given a detailed historical scrutiny. The author sympathetically argues that these "duodecimo editions of New Jerusalem," as Marx called them, are among the most important and universal ways in which societies maintain their vitality and advance in type.

Bestor, Arthur Eugene, Jr. *Backwoods Utopias: The Sectarian and Owenite Phases of Communitarian Socialism in America*: 1663-1829. Philadelphia: University of Pennsylvania Press, 1850.

The bulk of this thoroughly documented and concise historical account of the development of "communitarian socialism" in the New World up to 1829, is devoted to Robert Owen, his views on society, New Harmony, his utopian settlement in Indiana, and Owen's legacy to America. Chapter II. Holy Commonwealth: The Communitive Sects traces the earliest history of communitarian religious movements in the United States. Its lengthy bibliographical essay will be extremely valuable to those wishing to find sources on the principal sectarian communities before 1830 and on Owenism and the New Harmony experiment.

Communal Societies in America: A Reprint Archive of Secular and Religious Experiments in Communal Living. 160 vols. New York: Ames, 1975.

Included in this collection are over one hundred hitherto out of print writings on such variegated communitarian groups as the Associationists (Fourierists, Brook Farm, etc.), Brotherhood of New Life, Dunkers, Ephrata, Icarians, Moravians, Mormons, New Harmony, Oneida, Owenites, Rappites, Schwenkfelder, Shakers and Sweden-borgians. A substantial number of these titles bear a XIX century, or turn of the century imprint. Many books were written by individuals who had firsthand knowledge of life in these settlements. This is a timely and useful collection, which provides rich sources of information on the followers of Robert Owen, Etienne Cabet, Charles Fourier, George Rapp, as well as on the many religious utopian communities which thrived in XIX century America.

Calvert, Victor Frances. *Where Angels Dared to Tread*. New York: Arno, 1941.

Calvert presents a sympathetic history of utopian colonies in the United States, from the Rappites, Shakers, and Mormons to Father Divine, and from Brook Farm and Fruitlands to the Oneida Community. The author argues that most of these utopian experiments were an inspiring example of man's effort to improve his social and spiritual condition. This is a carefully researched account of utopian colonies in the U.S. which the serious student of American millenarianism will want to consult.

Fellman, Michael. *The Unbounded Frame: Freedom and Community in Nineteenth Century American Utopianism*. Westport, Ct.: Greenwood, 1973.

The author's controversial thesis is that the same intellectual discomfort, passion for reform and ideological stirrings which inspired the utopian founders of Brook Farm and Oneida, also prompted the views of many XIX century social reformers, ten of which are considered—Horace Mann, Margaret Fuller and William Curtis being among the most notable. Primary sources are extensively used and a lengthy bibliographical essay is appended.

Fogarty, Robert S. *Dictionary of American Communal and Utopian History*. Westport, Ct.: Greenwood, 1980.

Preceded by a critical introduction to the history of utopian and communal settlements, this ambitious and well-researched reference work provides short biographies of nearly 150 utopian thinkers and charismatic leaders, from Bronson Alcott and John Humphrey Noyes to Father Divine and Jim Jones. Also surveyed are fifty-eight important utopian communities such as Brook Farm, New Harmony and the Shakers. Each biographical entry is completed with a list of important works written by the biographee and at least one secondary source on him or her. The entries on communities usually list several important primary and secondary sources at the end. Two appendices complete the dictionary. One provides essential facts on 270 utopian communities founded between 1787 and 1919. The second is an update of Fogarty's 1973 *Choice* bibliographic essay on communal history in America. The emphasis is on biographical facts and social history, not the intellectual output of the individuals or communities considered.

Graus, F. "Social Utopias in the Middle Ages." *Past and Present* No. 38 (December 1967), 3-19.

Graus attempts to prove, contrary to general opinion, that utopianism existed during the Middle Ages.

Hayden, Dolores. *Seven American Utopias: The Architecture of Communitarian Socialism, 1970-1975*. Cambridge, Mass.: MIT, 1976.

This book focuses on the architecture and physical design of seven communitarian settlements: the Shakers at Hancock, Massachusetts; the Mormons at Nauvoo, Illinois; the Fourierists at Phalanx, New Jersey; the Inspirationists at Amana, Iowa; the Union Colonists at Greeley, Colorado; and the Cooperative Colonists at Llano del Rio, California. The author attempts to show how these utopian communities dealt with participatory processes and the communal and private needs of its members through community planning, physical arrangement of living quarters and even furniture arrangement. Over 250 photographs and illustrations enhance the value of this skillfully done study.

Hine, Robert V. *California's Utopian Colonies*. New York: Norton, 1973.

This interesting and well documented account of the utopian communities (Fountain Grove, Point Loma, Icaria, Speranza, Kaweah, Altruria, Llano del Rio, and ten other of less importance), which flourished in California between 1850 and 1950, traces with great skill the birth, growth and death of countless experiments in the Golden State and provides insights into the causes of their ineluctable failures. An indispensable tool for the study of California's utopian communities. Additional sources can be found in chapter 10, which consists of a sixteen page bibliographic essay.

Hinds, William A. *American Communities and Cooperative Colonies*. 3rd ed. 1908. Reprint. Philadelphia: Porcupine, 1975.

This work, first published in 1908 and written by an Oneida resident who visited other utopian communities, is a collection of primary sources on the Shakers, the Owenites, Brook Farm, Fourierist phalanxes, the Oneida Community, Icaria, Point Loma, Helicon and countless other utopian settlements in the United States. It should satisfy the needs of those wishing to read firsthand accounts of the communitarian movement during the XIX century. For those interested in seriously studying American utopian settlements, it is indispensable.

Holloway, Mark. *Heavens on Earth: Utopian Communities in America, 1680-1880.* Rev. ed. New York: Dover, 1966.

Although without pretentions of scholarship, this broad, popular introduction to two centuries of utopianism will appeal to those interested in getting an overall summary account of the growth of the utopian ideal in America and of the deeds of its proponents.

Infield, Henrik F. *Utopia and Experiment: Essays in the Sociology of Cooperation.* New York: Praeger, 1955.

The first part of this work describes and compares different modern cooperatives, mostly farming settlements, including the Kibbutzim of Israel, co-operative farms in Saskatchewan, the pre-Communist Chinese industrial cooperatives and others. The second part describes the use of various tests designed to measure the degree of success in a given cooperative community and indicates the lines along which an improvement in the community might take place. It is only peripherally "utopian" in the usual sense of this term.

Kateb, George. *Utopia and Its Enemies.* Rev. ed. New York: Schocken, 1972.

In this essay, various anti-utopian positions are described and evaluated in the name of "modern utopianism." The avowed bias of the work is utopian. It attempts to enable utopianism to survive anti-utopian critiques against perpetual peace, guaranteed abundance and conditioned virtue, by suggesting revisions and improvements in the utopian arguments advanced in their support. This is an eminently readable and engagingly written work which is also presented with a remarkable degree of philosophical flair.

Kanter, Rosabeth Moss. *Commitment and Community: Communes and Utopias in Sociological Perspective.* Cambridge, Mass.: Harvard University Press, 1972.

In this work the ideas and values underlying utopian communities and communal living are explored. The varieties of organization and structure that built commitment in the long-lived communes of the 19th century and the dilemmas faced by communities in the past are carefully considered. A comparison is made between the utopian communities of the past and "similar" 20th century communities, such as Synanon, Cumbraes, and Koinonia. It concludes by examining issues raised by the commune movement.

Lewis, Arthur Orcutt, ed. *Utopian Literature.* New York: Arno, 1971.

This is a series consisting of forty-one American utopian books, mostly "fin de siècle," all of which were out of print and had faded into obscurity. Some works should be read for historical reasons, for instance, Arthur Bird's *Looking Forward: A Dream of the United States of the Americas in 1999,* a dull, jingoistic, racially-biased paen for manifest destiny. Others, like the editor's compilation of selected utopian short fiction, air, with literary flair in some cases, concerns of the present generation, i.e. women's liberation and thought control. The editor provides no criteria for inclusion. The reader will be pleasantly surprised by the quality of some of these works and appalled by that of others, but it will prove to be indispensable to those wishing to get acquainted with the less important utopian writings in America.

Manuel, Frank E. *The Prophets of Paris.* Cambridge, Mass.: Harvard University Press, 1962.

An authoritative historical and biographical discussion of five French social thinkers, who lived roughly between 1750 and 1850. Since five of the prophets considered—Saint Simon, Fourier, Condorcet, Fourier and Comte—are known for their utopian schemes, this well-structured, compendious and scholarly book will be useful to those readers who wish to have a composite picture of these men, both as human beings and as utopian thinkers.

Muncy, Raymond Lee. *Sex and Marriage in Utopian Communities: Nineteenth Century America*. Bloomington, Indiana: Indiana University Press, 1973.

This is a readable and knowledgeable study of the nineteenth century colonies' attitudes toward marriage, sexual customs, proselytizing, child rearing, housing, the status of women, family life and the external pressures brought to bear on these attitudes and practices. The author argues that, although in many cases free love was an imposition based on a contrived ideological formula rather than based on spontaneity, it helped emancipate women from some of the subservient roles played by their counterparts in traditional society of that time, and brought a measure of equality to the sexes, even though males were predominant in the leadership of the communities. Included are firsthand accounts by Nordhoff, Noyes and Hinds.

Noyes, John Humphrey. *History of American Socialism*. 1870. Reprint. New York: Hillary House, 1961.

An historical account of the numerous utopian communities which were formed by various sects and groups in America from the middle of the XVIII century to roughly the late 1860's. Such communities as New Harmony, Brook Farm, the Oneida Community, as well as some minor ones, like Nashoba and Yellow Springs, are sympathetically considered by John Humphrey Noyes, who appears as the author although he only wrote one sixth of the book. Noyes, who was the founder of the Oneida Community, was the first to provide a fairly detailed description of the daily lives of the inhabitants of these communities and of the various events that took place.

Webber, Everett. *Escape to Utopia: The Communal Movement in America*. New York: Hastings, 1959.

A fictionalized, popular historical account of the major XIX century utopian leaders and settlements, such as the Shakers, George Rapp and his acolytes, Owen and his followers, Josiah Warren and Brook Farm, James J. Strang's "saints," John Humphrey Noyes and Oneida, and many other American utopian experimenters and colonies. This work borders on historical fiction, but reads well. It is not for those seeking serious scholarship on the subject. Its fourteen page bibliography is a good source of hard to find information on these groups.

Rexroth, Kenneth. *Communalism: From its Origins to the 20th Century*. New York: Seabury, 1974.

The outstanding American poet and critic turns his attention in this well written book, to a broad range of utopian ventures from the dawn of history to the present. He attempts to bring out similarities between psychological and literary movements and the practices and views of the various utopian movements, i.e. dance and sexual prescription. It is marred by its lack of a bibliography and footnotes.

Sherman, Ray Wesley. *How To Win An Argument With a Communist*. New York: Dutton, 1950.

The author examines classic utopias and utopian-communistic societies in America—the Plymouth Colony, Fourierism, the Icarian communism of Cabet, Shakers, Oneida Community, Harmonists, etc. He concludes that they inevitably lead to dictatorship. Communism is then studied; after which he attempts to show that the *Communist Manifesto* is one more unworkable utopia with its concomitant dictatorship. It is highly partisan, controversial, and low-brow, but thought provoking.

Veysey, Laurence. *The Communal Experience: Anarchist and Mystical Communities in Twentieth-Century America*. Chicago: University of Chicago Press, 1978.

Most of this sympathetic work consists of comprehensive studies of four little-known communities: two structured in an Eastern religious vein and two inspired by anarchism. Veysey compares the history of secular communities, such as the early Ferrer Colony and Modern School of Shelton, New Jersey, with contemporary anarchist communes in New York, Vermont and New Mexico. Although the members of these communities did not identify themselves as "utopian," many of their goals show that these settlements shared many of the characteristics of XIX century utopian settlements—the perfectionist impulse to create a gratifying and alternate way of life.

Works Devoted to Individual Utopian Communities

Amana

Perkins, William Rufus and Barthinius Wick. *History of the Amana Society or Community of True Inspiration*. Iowa City: University of Iowa, 1891.

This volume is a reprint in the Hyperion Press series, *The Radical Tradition in America*. The authors intended with this work to present a historical sketch of the origins and development of the Amana Society. The account is purely historical. The first part deals with the history of mysticism and pietism, followed by a history of the Society from its earliest beginnings to the year 1817, illustrated by account of the lives of its most important members. A sketch of the revival of 1817 and a history of the emigration to Ebenezer, New York, and finally to Iowa, concludes the monograph.

Although the emphasis is historical, brief consideration is given to the communistic principles, the mode of life and the final success of the society. The appendixes provide its constitution, an estimate of their property and a list of sources consulted. This unpretentious and factual work will be of value to those interested in this particular brand of religious communism.

Shambaugh, Bertha Maud (Horack). *Amana That Was and Amana That Is*. 1932. Reprint. New York: Arno, 1969.

This is a lengthy and well documented descriptive account of the Amana Society, a Lutheran communal settlement which flourished in Amana, Iowa between 1855 and 1932. It gives its history since 1835, and its social conventions, means of livelihood and ideals.

Yambura, Barbara with Eunice W. Bodine. *A Change and A Parting: My Story of Amana*. Ames: Iowa State University Press, 1960.

A somewhat fictionalized account of growing up in the society of True Inspirationists in Amana, Iowa, a religious communist organization which was administered by church elders. The author writes engagingly about her happy childhood, in spite of an austere and pious upbringing.

Brook Farm

Dwight, Marianne Orvis. *Letters From Brook Farm 1844-1847.* Poughkeepsie, N.Y.: Vassar College, 1928.

These letters from "Mary Ann," or Marianne Dwight, were considered at the time of publication the only considerable body of letters which was written on the spot, by a member of the Brook Farm Community, with the intention of describing the daily life of the settlement. Nothing of importance was omitted regarding not only day to day activities, but also the hopes and dreams of the participants in this social experiment. It provides fascinating insights into the psychological climate of the community as reflected by a literate and sensitive member.

Codman, John Thomas. *Brook Farm: Historic and Personal Memoirs.* 1894. Reprint. New York: AMS, 1971.

As a narrative of daily life at Brook Farm, the Fourierian communal experiment, by a member who lived there for fifty years, this book provides many vignettes of average dwellers, their activities, hopes and problems.

Curtis, Edith Roekler. *A Season in Utopia: The Story of Brook Farm.* 1961. Reprint. New York: Russell, 1971.

This book recounts how a group of idealistic social reformers led by George Ripley, a unitarian minister and scholar, banded together to found Brook Farm in West Roxbury, Massachusetts, in 1841. Included among the "farmers" were such men of letters as Nathaniel Hawthorne and Charles Dana. A readable description is given of Brook Farm, its experimentation with Charles Fourier's ideas, the adoption of the Fourieristic phalanx in 1845, and, finally, of its dispersion in 1847. It reflects years of research, incorporating materials from published as well as unpublished sources.

Myerson, Joel. *Brook Farm: An Annotated Bibliography and Resources Guide.* New York: Garland, 1978.

This is a selective annotated compilation of writings about, and a guide to manuscript collections, containing information on the Brook Farm settlement and its members. The book is arranged in seven topical sections: Members, Visitors, Contemporaries, Histories, *The Harbinger*, Ana: (creative works on Brook Farm and those incorrectly assumed to be about the settlement) and finally, manuscripts. Major literary figures that were involved with the project, such as Hawthorne, are covered adequately. In addition to books, this bibliography also provides scholarly journal citations, masters' theses and doctoral dissertations.

The reader interested in Brook Farm has, for the first time, a sizeable bibliography which brings under one cover obscure materials and updates what hitherto had to be culled from many sources.

Swift, Lindsay. *Brook Farm: Its Members, Scholars and Visitors.* Secaucus, N.J.: Citadel, 1973.

Having first been published in 1900, this is a personal and informal narrative of events and personalities who lived or visited Brook Farm, not a history of the Fourierian settlement.

Bruderhof

Zablocki, Benjamin. *The Joyful Community.* Baltimore: Penguin, 1971.

This is a study of The Bruderhof, one of the older and most successful utopian communal experiments. A description is given of each of the three settlements, comprised of approximately 250 persons who shared, beside their Anabaptist faith, all things in common. The author also describes the evolution of the social structure based on the ultimate goal of utilization of "collective behavior energy" and "routinized joy." An interesting, intimate and analytical picture is also presented of how a neophyte became a brother or sister through resocialization and "ego loss," and of their life style in general.

The Harmonists

Ardnt, Karl J. R. *George Rapp's Harmony Society, 1785-1847*. Rutherford, N.J.: Fairleigh Dickinson University Press, 1972.

This detailed study of the Harmonites (Rappists) deals with one of the most prosperous and well known of the German religious millenial groups of the XIX century. It covers the history of the movement from its beginning in Europe through its growth in Indiana, ending with the death of its founder, George Rapp, in 1847. Thorough coverage is given to the theology and to the agricultural and manufacturing activities of the settlers. The author has amassed a wealth of maps, drawing and photographs, and an adequate listing of sources. He has followed this book with another entitled *George Rapp's Successors and Material Heirs*, which covers the second and final phase of the settlement between 1847 and 1916.

Arndt, Karl J. R. *George Rapp's Successors and Material Heirs, 1847-1916*. Cranbury, N.J.: Fairleigh Dickinson University Press, 1972.

A sequel to *George Rapp's Harmony Society (1785-1847)*, the present volume begins with the demise of Rapp and concludes with the dissolution of the Harmony colony in 1916. This is a standard reference work for those interested in the rise and fall of this communal endeavor.

Kring, Hilda Adam. *The Harmonists; A Folk-Cultural Approach* Metuchen, N.J.: The Scarecrow Press, 1973.

This is a sympathetic study of the Harmony Community founded in 1805 by George Rapp, a Separatist from Wurttemberg, Germany, which lasted until 1905. Although it makes a contribution to the literature of this famous XIX century religious utopian "commune," it is not engagingly written. A thirteen-page bibliography of primary and secondary sources is appended. It also contains several photographs of the buildings and interiors of the communal settlement in New Harmony, Indiana.

New Harmony

Lockwood, George B. *The New Harmony Movement*. New York: August M. Kelley, 1970.

This timely reprint of the 1905 edition is perhaps the most detailed of the earliest accounts of New Harmony. It traces the vicissitudes of the community from its Rappite beginnings to its disintegration in 1847, and its later development under the guidance of Robert Owen. Owen's educational experiments receive extensive treatment. In spite of its lack of focus and turgid XIX century prose, the student of Owenism will want to examine this work. Two chapters are devoted to Josiah Warren, the libertarian thinker and one to Robert Owen's son.

Harrison, John F.C.

See Owen, Robert

Bestor, Arthur Eugene, Jr.

See *General Works on Utopian Communities*

Owen, Robert

See *Works by Utopian Authors*

Wilson, William Edward. *The Angel and the Serpent: The Story of New Harmony*. Bloomington, Indiana: Indiana University Press, 1964.

This volume provides a historical survey of the social experiments of George Rapp and Robert Owen at New Harmony, the utopian colony founded by the former. Both Rappites and Owenites shared the same goal, but not the same perspective—Rapp, a religious millenarian expected the millenium to come at some distant future, whereas Owen believed that he had ushered the millenium. Against this factual background, the author views the ideals of these men as a noble angelic impulse, and the "serpent" as the recalcitrant facts of human nature which doom such experiments to failure. A chapter is devoted to New Harmony after Owen returned to England and William MacClure took over. A selective bibliography and an appendix, containing two Rappite documents, enhance the value of the book.

Oneida

Carden, Maren Lockwood. *Oneida: Utopian Community to Modern Corporation*. Baltimore: John Hopkins University Press, 1969.

The result of a thorough field work and examination of primary sources, this book traces the history and philosophical principles of John Humphrey Noyes and the Oneida Community, from its foundation in 1848 to its subsequent development into the silverware company, known as Oneida Ltd. Organized according to the principles of religiously inspired self-perfection and communalism, Oneida was perhaps the most successful, and certainly one of the best known, of the XIX century American colonies. Rather than present a rigorously theoretical account of this experiment of communal living and marriage, the author chose to give a comprehensive view of the workings of the original community and its successor. It contains numerous photographs and illustrations, and a bibliography of firsthand sources.

Noyes, George Wallingford. *Religious Experience of John Humphrey Noyes Founder of the Oneida Community*. New York: Macmillan, 1923 Reprint. (Arno. no date.)

Relying on letters and journals published by Noyes, founder of Oneida, the utopian community in the city with the same name, the author provides a detailed account of the first 27 years of the leader's life.

Parker, Robert Allerton. *Yankee Saint: John Humphrey Noyes and the Oneida Community*. New York: Putnam, 1935.

This was the first lengthy biography of John Humphrey Noyes to have been published. The author reconstructs the life of Noyes, the founder of the Christian utopian community of Oneida, and its leader for about 30 years, and discusses his ideas on "complex marriage," communitarianism and selflessness. He sheds considerable light on the most important events of the community Noyes aptly led. However, it should be supplemented by the more intimate and authoritative accounts of Oneida written by Maren Carden Lockwood and Constance Noyes Robertson. (see)

Robertson, Constance Noyes. *Oneida Community: An Autobiography 1851-1876*. Syracuse, N.Y.: Syracuse University Press, 1970.

This collection of excerpts chosen out of the periodicals of the Oneida community by the granddaughter of its founder, comes mainly from the *Circular*, the *Daily Journal* and the *American Socialist*. According to the author, they were chosen for their power to reveal and evoke the lives and experiments of the members of the community. They are arranged in twelve topical sections: Where They Lived, How They Lived and Worked, What They Played, Business, Complex Marriage, Women, Children, Stirpiculture (their word for eugenics and family planning). The introduction traces the history of the community and the epilogue discusses the stresses that led to the breakup of the community in 1880. This is a useful and sympathetic collection of primary sources, with excellent illustrations.

Point Loma

Greenwalt, Emmett A. *California Utopia, Point Loma: 1897-1942*. San Diego: Point Loma Publications, 1978.

First published in 1955 with the title *The Point Loma Community in California, 1897-1942: A Theosophical Experiment*, this revised and enlarged edition provides a documentary overview of one of California's most colorful religious utopias. Begun under the guidance of Katherine Tingley, this community adopted the theology and ethics of Theosophy.

Puget Sound

Le Warne, Charles Pierce. *Utopias on Puget Sound, 1885-1915*. Seattle: University of Washington Press, 1978.

This work deals with the history of five communitarian settlements in the state of Washington. The author delves into the strengths and weaknesses of each, and attributes the failure of each experiment to their being out of step with the rampant push toward urbanization and capitalistic industrialization. It shows how they contributed to the nurturing of ideas of reform in that state.

Quakers

Wisbey, Herbert A., Jr. *Pioneer Prophetess: Jemima Wilkinson, the Publick Universal Friend*. Ithaca, N.Y.: Cornell University Press, 1964.

This is a biographical study of Jemima Wilkinson, the daughter of a Quaker farmer in Rhode Island, who underwent an intense religious awakening in 1776 to become a traveling preacher, proclaiming herself the Publick Universal Friend. She gradually built up a band of devoted followers and in the 1790's founded the community of New Jerusalem on the west side of Seneca Lake on the New York frontier, where she spent the rest of her life. A separate chapter is devoted to the extensive folklore created by her career. Wisbey attempts to put to rest, claims that she engaged in sexual and financial irregularities.

Shakers

Andrews, Edward Deming. *The People Called Shakers: A Search for the Perfect Society*. New York: Oxford University Press, 1953.

This documented history of the United Society of Believers in Christ's Second Coming, known sometimes as the Believers, but better known as the Shakers, is the culmination of twenty-five years of research. The text begins with the foundation of the society in England in the eighteenth century and continues with its immigration to America, its progress, and finally its decline. One of the most successful experiments in communal living, it differed from other communities in that celibacy was one of its basic principles. The Shakers also incorporated the principles of community of goods and the conscientious objection to the bearing of arms. This carefully documented work includes a copy of the Millennial Laws of the Shakers which implement the doctrines of the order. A statistical survey of Shaker communities is also included.

Desroche, Henri. *The American Shakers: From Neo-Christianity to Pre-Socialism*. University of Massachussetts Press, 1971, 357.

This is an analysis of the Shaker sect from the XVIII century to its disappearance in our century. The author skillfully examined scholarly sources available in Europe. He gives a thorough account of the Shakers' communitarianism, but fails to sufficiently cover the socio-historical background of the movement in America. Its main merit lies in the detailed comparison it draws between the Shakers' views on utopianism, education and relations between the sexes and those of other millenarian sects.

Twin Oaks

Kinkade, Kathleen. *A Walden Two Experiment: The First Five Years of Twin Oaks Community*. New York: William Morris, 1973.

This is a well-written, firsthand account of communal life, by a participant of Twin Oaks, an agricultural settlement in Virginia modelled after the fictional utopian community described by B. F. Skinner in *Walden Two*. The book describes not only how the community began, operates, and deals with its problems, but also the behaviorist group policies that shape communal equality among its members. B. F. Skinner has penned an approving foreword to the book.

Works by Utopian Authors

Andrea, Johann Valentin

Andrea, Johann Valentin. *Christianapolis: An Ideal State of the Seventeenth Century*. New York: Oxford University Press, 1916.

This typical XVII century city-state utopia, with geometric layout and emphasis on religion anticipates some of the views of XIX century utopian thought. Andrea's emphasis on science and its application to industry as the way to bring untold wealth, singles this work as a remarkable forerunner of later utopias which emphasized scientific discoveries. Guilds, ideals of brotherhood and respect for craftsmanship are made an integral part of the commonwealth. It is one of the few utopias which holds that people are innately wicked and must be made to observe moral rules.

It exhibits the tensions between remnants of the dying feudal order and an ambivalence towards the technology of capitalism, with suspicion of its social values.

Anonymous

"The Civil and Religious Constitution of Antangil." In *French Utopias: An Anthology of Ideal Societies*, edited by Frank E. and Fritzie P. Manuel. New York: Free Press, 1966.

This work first appeared in 1617 and is considered the first complete French utopia. Considered by some to be the dullest French utopia of the 17th century, the anonymous author borrowed almost all of his ideas from More, with the exception of its militarism. Fifteen chapters are devoted to the organization of the police force. Because of this, it has been speculated that the author must have been a professional soldier.

Bacon, Francis Sir

Bacon, Francis Sir. *New Atlantis*. Oxford: Clarendon Press, 1915.

Set in the island of New Atlantis, this unfinished fable portrays life in Bensalem, a state ruled by an absolute monarch, and the activities of an autonomous scientific college, Salomon House. Unlike other utopias which came into existence through social reform or upheaval, the author describes a society which has given scientists power to improve man's welfare through technology and scientific research. They form a caste endowed with autonomous powers and even the right to withhold secrets from the monarch. Nonetheless, Bensalem preserves the wealth and class distinctions of Jacobean England. It may be regarded as the most famous expression of the belief that social renovation can be brought about by scientific progress.

Bierman, Judah. "Science and Society in the *New Atlantis* and Other Renaissance Utopias." *Publications of the Modern Language Association of America* 78 (December, 1963), 492-500.

Blodgett, Eleanor Dickinson. "Bacon's *New Atlantis* and Campanella's *Civitas Solis*: A Study in Relationships." *PMLA* 46 (September 1931), 763-780.

Green, A. Wigfall. *Sir Francis Bacon*. New York: Twayne, 1966.

Most critical works of Bacon's thought are written with the scholar or the specialist in mind. They must be read slowly and patiently, if any understanding is to be derived from them. This study manages the almost impossible task of introducing the layperson to his complex thought in a manner that is unassuming, clear and appealing. Chaper 19 is devoted to a discussion of *New Atlantis*, Bacon's *soi-disant* utopia. Sources, similarities, setting, structure and influences of the work are briefly but pertinently discussed. It provides a good introduction to the essentials of the book.

Spitz, David. "Bacon's 'New Atlantis': A Reinterpretation." *Midwest Journal of Political Science* 4 (February 1960), 52-61.

Beaconsfield, Benjamin Disraeli

Beaconsfield, Benjamin Disraeli. *The Voyage of Captain Popanilla*. New York: Arno, 1934.

First published in 1828, this is a satire reminiscent of the writings of Swift or Voltaire. It describes a voyage from an utopian South Sea island to the England of the times, whose utilitarian philosophy and its social and political institutions are attacked.

Bellamy, Edward

Bellamy, Edward. *Looking Backward, 2000-1887*. Cambridge, Mass, Harvard University Press, 1967.

A future social and economic order is described by Julian West, a young wealthy Bostonian who falls asleep in 1887 and awakens in the year 2000 to find the United States converted into a regimented Utopia. By means of dialogues between Dr. Leete, a retired XX century physician and West, Bellamy's describe the Nationalist society, a planned, moneyless society in which the state provides full employment and free education all and assigns citizens to the jobs that will best suit their needs and those of the state. Although the author believed that his collective reorganization of wealth and industry would result in a nobler future, contemporary readers would find many features in this fictional scheme wholly anti-utopian. The popularity of this work led to the formation of Bellamy clubs which promoted his social ideals and the foundation of the Nationalist Party which did not survive Bellamy's death. In 1897, Bellamy published *Equality*, a reply to attacks made on *Looking Backward*. In it, he details how to carry out the plans described in *Looking Backward*.

Bellamy, Edward. *Equality*. 1897; rpt. Boston, Mass.: Gregg, 1969.

Published shortly before the death of the author in 1898, as an answer to his critics, this is Bellamy's vision of the classless society, written in the form of a utopian romance. Like *Looking Backward*, it is written from the point of view of a man projected into an utopian society, commenting on the conditions of exploitation and degradation prevalent in late nineteenth-century Boston. The author states that he has utilized the framework of *Looking Backward* as the starting point for this work, since in the former, he "was not able to get into it all I wished to say on the subject." More argumentative in form and more scathing in its attack on Capitalism, the vision of the Cooperative Commonwealth presented here goes farther than *Looking Backward* in showing the theoretical underpinnings of Bellamy's utopian fiction.

Bellamy, Edward. "How I Came to Write *Looking Backward*." *The Nationalist* 1 (May, 1899), 1-4.

Bowman, Silvia E. et. al., eds. *Edward Bellamy Abroad: An American Prophet's Influence*. New Haven, Ct.: College and University Press, 1962.

The major thrust of this sweeping and carefully researched work is to delineate Bellamy's popularity, or reactions to it, in both major and minor geographical and ideological areas of the world. Chapters are devoted to major European and English-speaking countries of the world where Bellamy's influence was strongly felt. In the next to the last chapter, his impact on Japan, India, Hungary and other small slavic countries is assessed. In the final chapter the patterns of Bellamy's influence are related, where possible, to those of his own country. This volume ends with an international bibliography, which lists by country translations of Bellamy's work, as well as books and articles written about him. It is highly recommended for the Bellamy enthusiast and scholar.

Dudden, Arthur P. "Looking Backward: 2000-1887." In *Landmarks of American Writing*, edited by Hennig Cohen. New York: Basic Books, 1969.

Franklin, John Hope. "Edward Bellamy and the Nationalist Movement." *New England Quarterly* 11 (December 1939), 739-772

Gilman, Nicholas P. "Bellamy's Equality." *Quarterly Journal of Economics* 4 (October, 1889), 50-76.

Gutek, Gerald. "An Analysis of Formal Education in Edward Bellamy's '*Looking Backward*.'" *History of Education Quarterly* 4 (December 1964), 251-263.

Levi, Albert William. "Edward Bellamy: Utopian." *Ethics* 55 (January 1945), 131-144.

Madison, Charles A. "Edward Bellamy, Social Dreamer." *New England Quarterly* 15 (September 1942), 444-466.

Michaels, Richard. *Looking Further Forward: An Answer to Looking Backward*. 1890. Reprint. New York: Arno, 1971.

> A spirited but pedestrian attack on Edward Bellamy's work, this work, published in 1890, argues that Bellamy's scheme would lead to loss of personal liberty and sloth. The author maintains that any ideal society must be based on the prevention of undeserved poverty and competition.

Roberts, J. W. *Looking Within: The Misleading Tendencies of Looking Backward Made Manifest*. 1893. Reprint. New York: Arno and New York Times, 1971.

> The object of this dystopian novel is to present an opposite picture of the Boston described in Edward Bellamy's *Looking Backward 2000-1887*. The protagonist wakes up, after a prolonged loss of consciousness, in a society of "willing slaves, selling their royal birthright for a mess of pottage," and in which the government has become a "wholesale robber." Production has fallen, citizens lack the interest, enthusiasm and motivation to be productive, and drink and gambling prevail.

Roemer, Kenneth M. "Edward Bellamy." *American Literary Realism* 8 (Summer 1975), 191-198.

Borges, Jorge Luis

Borges, Jorge Luis. "Tlon, Uqbar, Orbis Tertius." *Fictions*. trans. Antony Kerrigan. London: Calder, 1962.

> This is the story of a group of scholars who invent a planet and lay out its cultural life, its languages, system of ethics, customs and philosophy. Upon completion, they disseminate information about it to the peoples of the earth, who "submit to the minute and vast evidence of an ordered planet." The invented planet becomes a reality and its way of life overcomes Dialectical Materialism, anti-Semitism, Nazism and "other systems of thought which human beings in the past devised to regulate existence on our planet."

Irby, James E. "Borges and the Idea of Utopia." *Books Abroad* 45 (Summer 1971), 411-420.

Zaniello, Thomas. "Outopia in Jorge Luis Borges' Fiction." *Extrapolation*, 9 (December 1967), 3-17.

Lytton, Edward George Bulwer-Lytton

See Bulwer-Lytton, Edward

Buber, Martin

Buber, Martin. *Paths in Utopia*. Boston: Beacon, 1958.

> From a vantage point highly sympathetic to the libertarian socialist ideals of Proudhon, Kropotkin, and the Jewish anarchist, Gustav Landauer, Buber attempts to give a developmental account of utopian socialism. He contrasts what he takes to be the humanistic search for an eudaemonic and free society with the statist "systems," particularly that of Marx. The emphasis is on the philosophical merits of utopian socialism rather than on its historical roots and growth.

Bulwer-Lytton, Edward

Bulwer-Lytton, Edward. *The Coming Race*. 1871 ed. Reprint. Santa Barbara, California: Woodbridge Press, 1979.

> As a result of a mine accident, an unnamed young American, who is also the narrator of the events in this novel, falls into Vrilya, a subterranean society peopled by comely and blissful beings. Unlike the citizens of Western societies, they enjoy full equality and Epicurean living conditions. They are also possessed, in equal amounts, of Vril, a power capable of destroying an enemy or promoting his welfare. Yet, in spite of these tantalizing advantages, the narrator longs, in the end, to escape from this paradisiacal society. The main objective of this anti-utopian novel is to show that an equal, passionless and perfect existence would lead to ennui, mediocrity and the extinction of individual achievement.

Burgess, Anthony

Burgess, Anthony. *The Wanting Seed*. New York: Norton, 1976.

> Set in the reign of King Charles VI of Great Britain, this fast-paced novel is concerned with the vicissitudes of Tristram Foxe and his wife Beatrice-Joanna, who live in a dystopian society which stages wars, glorifies homosexuality and condones cannibalistic dining clubs in order to control population growth. The novel conveys the frightening idea that today's free choices may become the grounds for tomorrow's dystopian horrors.

Butler, Samuel

Butler, Samuel. *Erewhon*. New York: Dutton, 1959.

> In this satirical romance, the narrator, a young man on a sheep farm, finds a pass through the mountains which leads him to the country of Erewhon (an anagram for "nowhere"). Butler uses the description of the institutions of Erewhon as a vehicle to satirize contemporary English attitudes toward religion, criminals, science and social values. In Erewhon, disease is considered a crime and robbers are hospitalized. Machines have been scrapped out of fear that human beings would become their slaves. This satire is considered by many to be one of the most brilliant examples of how the concept of utopia was used as a means to castigate the social evils of the XIX century. A sequel, *Erewhon Revisited*, was published in 1901. In it, the author provides an acerbic satire of religion.

Holt, Lee E. *Samuel Butler*. New York: Twayne, 1964.

> This book is directed to the reader who desires to know what Butler thought and why he challenged his age in the way he did. The second chapter summarizes the plot of *Erewhon*, discusses the main ideas it puts forth, and briefly attempts to elucidate its meaning.

Popper, Karl "The Erewhonians and the Open Society." *Etc.*, 20 (May 1963), 5-22.

Samaan, Angele Botros. "Butler Erewhon: A Centenary Tribute." *Moreana* No. 36 (December 1972), 97-102.

Cabet, Etienne

Cabet, Etienne. *Voyage to Icaria*. Clifton, N.J.: Kelley, A. M., 1973.

> Having originally been published in Paris in 1848, the first part of this work of the imagination describes the discovery of the egalitarian, utopian island of Icaria by Cabet, in the company of an English aristocrat, Lord Carisdall. This communist state is divided into 100 provinces, which in turn are divided into six communes

each, with a town, eight villages and various farms. Decisions above the commune level are made by elected delegates to a national assembly. At the commune level, everyone is part of the assembly, which collectively decides the minutest details of daily life, i.e. how its members are to dress, what they will eat, how food will be distributed, etc. Individualism has completely disappeared under the weight of a regimented social life and daily timetables. As in Campanella's and More's utopias, cities and towns in Icaria have been built with precise geometrical symmetry by the leader and lawgiver of the state, Icarus, who not only has given his name to the capital, Icara, but to the country as well. One critic has written that the love of uniformity, centralization and state control is carried to such extremes in this fantasy as to make it resemble, in many parts, the satirical anti-utopia of our century. This work, the most important of Cabet's writings, remains untranslated. There is a translation of his *History and Constitution of Community*, published by the Ames Press in 1975.

Johnson, Christopher H. *Utopian Communism in France: Cabet and the Icarians, 1839-1851.* Ithaca, N.Y.: Cornell University Press, 1974.

This thoroughly researched study of Etienne Cabet's French utopian communist movement is perhaps the most scholarly account of his movement published in the last three decades. It relies on archival materials and numerous primary sources. The author succeeds in presenting a first rate social history of one of the most important utopian movements of the XIX century.

Piotroswski, Sylvester A. *Etienne Cabet and the Voyage en Icarie: A Study in the History of Social Thought.* Washington, D.C.: Catholic University of America, 1935.

Shaw, A. *Icaria.* Philadelphia: Porcupine Press, 1972.

This study of Cabet's *magnum opus* was originally published in 1884, under the title *Icaria, A Chapter in the History of Communism*, and continues to be one of the few good sources in English on Cabet's utopian scheme.

Batkin, Leonid M. "The Paradox of Campanella." *Diogenes*, no. 83 (Fall, 1973), 77-102.

Blodgett, Eleanor

See Bacon, Francis Sir

Campanella, Tommaso

Grillo, Francesco. *Tommaso Campanella in America: A Critical Bibliography and a Profile.* New York: S.F. Vanni, 1964.

Leo, Robert Joseph. "Tomasso Campanella: Rhetorician and Utopia." Ph.D. dissertation, University of Washington, 1968.

Capek, Karel

Capek, Karel. *R.U.R.* Nw York: Washington Square, 1969.

In this well known play, *R.U.R.* (Rossum's Universal Robots) scientists have learned to build robots capable of doing all the manual and intellectual activities performed by human beings. The robots, whose manufacture resulted from a new way of organizing material components, look and act very much like human beings, except that they lack feelings, which were purposefully omitted to improve their performance. A scientist at Rossum's Robot factory, aware that the robots' insensitivity to pain often lead to accidents, changes the manufacturing blueprint to give them emotions. The experiments succeed, but the new robots, now possessed of love and hate, consider themselves man's equals, and frustrated by their lowly status, rebel and destroy human beings. This is a fascinating and perhaps a prophetic vision of our cybernetic world and its potential dangers.

Matuska, Alexander. *Karel Capek: An Essay.* Brno, Czechoslovakia: Tisk, 1964.

The author maintains that he is concerned with Capek as a writer who deals with some of our current problems having to do with the impact of technology on science fiction, and the facts and realities of our time. R.U.R. (see) is lengthily treated as a visionary allegory of a machine civilization which is already a social reality.

Cyrano de Bergerac

Cyrano de Bergerac, Savinien. *Voyages to the Moon and the Sun* Trans. by Richard Aldington. New York: Orion Press, 1962.

This whimsical utopian fantasy locates the good life on the moon and the sun. On these planetary bodies all worldly sorrow disappears, poetry is enshrined, and the author, with Campanella for a guide, is free to philosophize with the greatest thinkers of the world. Monarchs are chosen among the weakest and most peaceful of human beings and are changed every six months. Even the brutes have veto rights on what the ruler decides. There is no political or social message in these tales, but the thoughts expressed reflect a yearning for a pleasurable reality and a new social order.

Harth, Erica. *Cyrano de Bergerac and the Polemics of Modernity.* New York: Columbia University Press, 1970.

The author argues that Cyrano de Bergerac's work reveals what was in the intellectual atmosphere of the mid-seventeenth century in France and exemplifies his "modernism," that is, intellectual libertinism, a satirical treatment of man and society as well as scientific precocity. She claims that although Cyrano's social and political ideas contain not a few utopian elements, his purpose was not to depict a political utopia or even advocate any particular kind of government at all.

Normano, J.F. "A Neglected Utopian: Cyrano de Bergerac, 1619-55." *American Journal of Sociology* 32 (November 1931), 454-457.

The author writes that although almost forgotten, Cyrano de Bergerac remains one of the most important precursors of Rousseau and the Natural Order movement, and that as an utopian thinker, he forms a connecting link between Campanella and the French movement of the eighteenth century.

Disraeli, Benjamin

See Beaconsfield, Benjamin Disraeli under individual authors.

Douglas, Norman

Douglas, Norman. *South Wind.* Baltimore, Md.: Penguin, 1976.

To a mediterranean island, Nephente, perceived by the author to be utopian and peopled by cosmopolitan natives of mostly English background, comes Mr. Heard, Bishop of Bampopo, Africa, to escort his cousin back to England. There he encounters a society of people who lead casual, hedonistic, leisurely, irreverent lives and do what suits their fancy. Caught up in the magic of this pleasure-bound atmosphere, the bishop becomes freed from his stodgy, moralistic upbringing to the point of even approving of the murder of an obnoxious blackmailer. The author's main purpose in writing this satirical novel was to place in opposition the carefree pursuit of civilized pleasures to outmoded and false concepts believed to be embodied in respectable and traditional European societies.

Lindeman, Ralph D. *Norman Douglas*. New York: Twayne Publishers, 1965.

> This readable and comprehensive study of all of Douglas' works briefly discusses the intent and import of *South Wind*, the highly idiosyncratic utopia envisioned by Douglas merely as a "jeu d'esprit."

Engels, Friedrich

Engels, Friedrich. *Socialism: Utopian and Scientific in Karl Marx and Friedrich Engels: Selected Works*. 2 vols. Moscow: Foreign Languages Publishing House, 1951.

> Engels argues that as the modern class struggle develops, the utopian critique of society loses all practical and theoretical justification. While the originators of utopian schemes—Saint Simon, Fourier, Owen and others—were in many respects revolutionary, their disciples' dreams of founding experimental settlements yield reactionary results by standing apart from the contest between the bourgeoisie and the proletariat.

Suvin, Darko. " 'Utopian' and 'Scientific': Two Attributes for Socialism from Engels." *Minnesota Review* (New Series) 6 (Spring 1976), 59-70.

Ernst, Morris Leopold

Fenelon, François de Salignac de la Mothe

Fenelon, François de Salignac de la Mothe. *Adventures of Telemachus with a Life of Fenelon by Lamartine*. Boston, Mass.: Houghton, Mifflin, 1899.

> The adventures of Telemachus in search of his father Ulysses are told in the form of a novel, to convey the fundamental philosophical ideas of the author on government and society. The overarching ideas of this book are characterized by a horror of despotism, the preference for a constitutional monarchy tempered by law, and a belief in the future brotherhood of the inhabitants of the earth in accordance with the Christian Gospel. Although included in most utopian bibliographies, this work is utopian only in the mildest of senses.

Forster, E.M.

Forster, E.M. "The Machine Stops." In *The Eternal Moment and Other Stories*. New York: Harcourt, Brace and World, 1928.

> In this scientific Utopia not only the unseen mysticism of Nature, but all the values derived from it have been ruthlessly erradicated. Living underground in a controlled and artificial environment, persons are fed by the Machine—a foil for "ideas," intellectualism and advanced rationality. Kuno, a heretic makes his escape to nature, soon to be dragged back into the bowels of the earth by the Machine's surrogates. All the horrors of dystopian works are anticipated by Forster: a society "perfected" by technology, totalitarianism in the name of reason, and the denial of the body and its instincts. This is one of the first contemporary works in which barren rationality expressed as social control is identified as a destroyer of the human soul.

Fourier, Charles

Fourier, Charles. *Harmonian Man: Selected Writings of Charles Fourier*, edited by Mark Poster. Garden City, N.Y.: Doubleday, 1971.

Charles Fourier's bizarre conceptions of a harmonic universe, his theory of attraction by which the passions gravitate to their natural ends, and his scathing criticism of monogamous marriage, educational theory, sex repression and the dehumanization of labor are well represented in this selective anthology of his writings. There are also excerpts of Fourier's writings on communal socialism, built in phalansteries—autarchic communities of less than 2000 persons, in which each member would do the labor best suited to his personality. Poster argues in the introduction that Fourier raised the possibility of a non-repressive society and foreshadowed some of the ideas of Reich, Brown and Marcuse about the effects of capitalist society on the human psyche. This is without doubt the most suitable anthology of Fourier's writings for the beginner.

Fourier, Charles. *The Utopian Vision of Charles Fourier: Selected Texts on Work, Love and Passionate Attraction*. Trans. and Ed. with Introduction by Jonathan Beecher and Richard Bienvenu. Boston, Mass.: Beacon, 1971.

The timely selections of this book concentrate on those aspects of Fourier's thought that are relevant to contemporary social and political theory. The reader is introduced to, among other things, his scathing criticism of bourgeois sexual practices and mercantile hypocrisy, his notions of the ideal community, the phalanstery, his general account of the necessary conditions for attractive work and his proposed sexual ethics for "the New Amorous World." The editors' selections show how carefully Fourier built up the case against the society of his day as a form of dystopianism flawed by poverty, sexual psychopathology, usury, and cheating of every kind. Chapter V, the Ideal Community, is one of the best primary source introductions to Fourier's detailed blueprint for the ideal community: an egalitarian and self-sustaining utopia of calm felicity, having less than 2,000 members, following his law of "passionated attraction," which was destined to "conduct the human race to opulence, sensual pleasure, and global unity." This is an excellent introduction to the writings of one of the most provocative of the XIX century utopian thinkers. It also contains a short bibliography and a glossary.

Brisbane, Albert. *Social Destiny of Man: Or, Association and Reorganization of Industry*. New York: Burt Franklin, 1968.

First published in 1840, this expository work attempts to "lay before the American public, the profound and original conceptions of Charles Fourier on 'Reform in Labor or a Reorganization of Industry.'" With this goal in mind, this American disciple of Fourier proposes the replacement of the "present monotonous and repugnant system" by "attractive industry." The main value of this book is historical. However, it provides an adequate summary of Fourier's doctrine in somewhat dull prose.

Godwin, Parke. *A Popular View of the Doctrine of Charles Fourier*. New York: AMS Press, 1974.

First published in 1844, it attempts to furnish the public "with a brief synthetic view of all the doctrines of Fourier. It limits itself, however, to "give results only and not discussions." The author urges the reader to consult the works of Fourier to see any subject fully developed. It is written in the stodgy style typical of XIX century tracts. However, if the reader bears with it and with the small print of the book, he will acquire an overview of the Fourieran system.

Riasanovsky, Nicholas V. *The Teaching of Charles Fourier*. Berkeley: University of California Press, 1969.

The avowed purpose of this book is to state Fourier's system in its own terms, not in terms of its possible contribution to other ideological systems, and to place the totality of his thought in the "intellectual map of the modern world." Even though it is not a detailed biographical or psychological investigation of the thinker, many of these topics can be gleaned by reading it. All the important ideas of Fourier, i.e. the "calculus of destinies," the "laws of passionate attraction" and his utopian state of harmony are sufficiently covered. While engagingly written, it unfortunately fails to compare Fourier's thought to that of the New Left. Nevertheless it is still one of the best introductions to this important utopian figure.

Roberts, Alfred Dominic

See Zola, Emile

France, Anatole

France, Anatole. *The Penguin Island*. New York: Modern Library, 1933.

An old Breton monk, Saint Mael, lands on an island in the Arctic and fails to perceive that the inhabitants he baptizes are penguins and not human beings. The penguins are miracuously transmogrified into human beings by God and their island towed to the coast of Brittany. After many centuries, the former penguins evolve into a "civilized" people, who accept revolutions, war, poverty, racial and industrial hatred and inequitable taxation. In the final chapter of this burlesque of the human race, the author prophesizes an endless succession of wars, antagonisms and exploitation for the penguins. While it is not, strictly speaking an anti-utopian novel, it reaches the same negative conclusions.

France, Anatole. *White Stone*. London, 1910.

The hero of the novel recounts a dream in which he traveled to the year 2270 in an airplane and engaged in discussion with the citizens of a futuristic communist utopia. Although it reveals an attitude toward socialism that is quite sympathetic, the novel is not entirely without critical ambivalence. For example, the author considers the White Peril to the Asiatic races, and regards the movement towards socialism as a fatalistic tendency of history about which, individuals have little to say.

Virtanen, Reino. *Anatole France*. New York: Twayne, 1968.

The avowed purpose of the author is not to provide a detailed treatment of everything Anatole France wrote or did, but to inform the reader of his contribution to world literature. With this end in mind, little attention is paid to the minutiae of the author's life, or his political activities. Several pages are devoted to *The Penguin Island*, which is seen by the critic as an expression of historical pessimism.

Gilman, Charlotte Perkins

Gilman, Charlotte Perkins. *Herland: A Lost Feminist Utopian Novel*. New York: Pantheon, 1979.

Written in 1915 by a talented socialist feminist, this novel describes how three men, Terry, wealthy and sexist; Jeff, chivalric and conventional; and Van, a sociologist, enter a cooperative utopia inhabited only by women. The world of Herland lacks sex roles, "romance," jealousy, possessiveness and all the expectations of femininity and domesticity that thwart women in contemporary society. Through miraculous virgin births, the women beget only daughters, insuring perpetuation of their sex. The novel ends abruptly. Terry, convinced that women want to be dominated, attempts rape, while Van wants to take a "wife" to America. The result of these actions is the expulsion of the men from Herland. This is a biting and clever attack on our conception of femininity and an imaginative vision of a new sexual ethics.

Goodman, Paul

Goodman, Paul and Percival Goodman. *Communitas: Means of Livelihood and Ways of Life*. University of Chicago Press, 1947.

The authors present to the reader three paradigms of possible community life. There is the city of efficient consumption; the city with a community plan aimed at the elimination of the separation between the productive and consumptive activities which characterize modern American cities; and finally, a mildly socialistic scheme, completely separated from the market economy, which provides all citizens with a minimum standard of living without obligation. Often included in utopian bibliographies, *Communitas* is more a plea for efficient social planning than a truly utopian work.

Graves, Robert

Graves, Robert. *Watch the North Wind Rise*. New York: Creative Age, 1949.

A bewitched post-war poet, Edward Venn-Thomas, visits New Crete, an utopian land placed in a distant future, where the White Goddess is worshipped and wars last one day. In attempting to explain to the New Cretans life in the Late Christian era (our own), the author satirizes through the mouth of the poet our shortcomings, and revels in a paradisiac fantasy about a well-ordered, but not explicitly described utopia.

Harrington, Alan

Harrington, Alan. *Paradise I*. Waltham, Mass.: Little Brown, 1978.

Set in the year 20007, A.D., this utopian fantasy envisions a society in possession of an "immortality serum" capable of arresting the aging process. However, its scarcity gives rise to black markets, riots and corrupt political leadership, until Arthur Franklin restores social order by bringing to trial Dr. Paul Peacock, the ruler of the world. Only those who regard deathlessness as eminently desirable would regard the society depicted in this work as being in any sense of the term "utopian."

Harrington, James

Harrington, James. *The Common-Wealth of Oceana*. London: 1656.

Published four years after Winstanley's *Law of Freedom*, it depicts a small-scale, property-owning democracy which the author identifies as England. Its ruler, a prince or Archon, is elected like all other magistrates by the people. Popular representatives must be males, at least 30 years of age, have undergone military service, be married and own land, goods and money to a minimum value of 100 pounds. Because Harrington believed that property, especially landed property, was the prime basis of power, property in Oceana was limited, "so that no one man or number of men . . . can come to overpower the whole people." Strictly speaking, Harrington's blueprint lacks some of the essential features of utopian writings, i.e. it is not a prescription for the good life or the moral life. However, insofar as it attempts to prevent tyranny and abuse of power, it could be regarded as a mildly utopian tract.

Blitzer, Charles. *An Immortal Commonwealth: The Political Thought of James Harrington*. New Haven, Conn.: Yale University Press, 1960.

This book has been written "in the conviction that the political theories of past ages can profitably . . . be treated as constituting moments in a continuing intellectual and institutional development." It contends that Harrington's political thought was concerned with the issues of sovereignty and constitutionalism — *Oceana* being his conception of the governmental structure which he believed would be suited for XVII century England. Chapter 5 deals with Harrington's utopian work, *The Commonwealth of Oceana*. It provides a good analytical account of the philosophical reasons why Harrington believed an agricultural society of small proprietors and gentry would constitute the answer to Britain's social and political ills of the time.

Clarke, I. F. "Harrington's *Oceana*: Or the Long Arms of Utopia." *Futures*, 5 (June 1973), 317-322.

Hauptmann, Gerhard Johann Robert

Hauptmann, Gerhard Johann Robert. *Island of the Great Mother; or, the Miracle of the Iles de Dames; a Story from the Utopian Archipelago*. New York: Viking Press, 1925

A number of shipwrecked women and a boy, Phaon, found a colony in the Island of the Great Mother in the Utopian archipelago. Thanks to the active love life of the lad, the population increases by leaps and bounds. The development of this orderly society and the erotic affairs of Phaon provide the substance of this farcical fable.

Steinhauer, H. "Hauptmann's Utopian Fantasy, *Die insel der grossen mutter*." *Modern Language Notes* 53 (November, 1938), 516-521.

Hawthorne, Nathaniel

Hawthorne, Nathaniel. *The Blithdale Romance*. New York: Dell, 1964.

Miles Coverdale visits Blithdale Farm (modelled after Brook Farm), located near Boston. There he meets Silas Foster, a farmer and his wife Zenobia, Priscilla, a former seamstress, and Hollingsworth, an idealistic blacksmith. Both women fall in love with Hollingsworth who is more concerned with his altruistic dreams than with romantic love. Coverdale returns to the city and meets the members of the settlement as they lead their traditional lives. Zenobia, he finds out, is a wealthy woman and in reality, Priscilla's half sister, a fact that is not known. Priscilla falls in love with the mesmerist Westervelt, from whom she is rescued by Hollingsworth. Upon their return to Blithdale Farm, Hollingsworth marries Priscilla, driving Zenobia into suicide, unable to endure an unrequited love. After marriage, Hollingsworth loses his mental stability and peace of mind, while Priscilla becomes disillusioned and broken. At the end of the romance, Coverdale remains unpersuaded that happiness can be secured through utopian experimentation. Since Hawthorne lived in Brook Farm for a short period of time, and it is believed that the character Zenobia, was inspired by the life of Margaret Fuller, this work is, to some extent, historical fiction, and to a very limited extent utopian.

Hertzka, Theodor

Hertzka, Theodor. *Freeland: A Social Anticipation*. New York: Appleton, 1891.

The author, an Austrian economist of the Liberal Manchester school who did not consider himself an utopist, attempts to conciliate Individualism and socialism in this detailed plan for a better society. Hertzka proposes that the land, capital and means of production should belong to the State but that every association of producers be accorded the right to lease from the State the common land and the means of production on demand. In this social blueprint only personal objects, houses and gardens would be regarded as exclusively personal property and the inequality of wages, based on the value of the work done, was maintained. This vision of the "free social order" is hardly known today, even though it was received with great enthusiasm shortly after its publication in Europe, where nearly a thousand Freeland societies were organized with the intention of putting Hertzka's plan into immediate effect.

Ransom, Arthur. *Dr. Hertzka's Freeland*. Bedford: Times Office, 1892.

Hess, Moses

Weiss, John. *Moses Hess, Utopian Socialist*. Detroit: Wayne State University, 1960.

This intellectual biography of the "the first German Socialist," best remembered for his influence on the early views of Marx and Engels, clearly describes Hess's youthful utopian socialism based on moral principles, his conversion to Marxist socialism, and finally his rejection of both the uncompromising radicalism of Utopian and of Marxist socialism in favor of a people's state in which all classes (expect finance capitalists) would benefit from state ownership and management of production. It has a selective bibliography of Hess's works in German.

Howells, William Dean

Howells, William Dean. *Through the Eye of the Needle*. 1907; rpt. New York: AMS.

This sequel to *A Traveler From Altruria*, deals with the visit Mr. Homos, an inhabitant of the utopia Altruria, pays to Mr. Makeley, a well-known middle class intellectual, while the latter courts Mrs. Eveleth Strange. Homos is puzzled by the ways of capitalist America, where businessmen ruin their lives in order to acquire money, which they then proceed to squander. Homos takes Mrs. Strange to Altruria, a society which has eliminated money, competition and crime, and uses its national wealth to improve the well-being of its citizens.

Howells, William Dean. *Traveler From Altruria*. New York: Sagamore Press, 1957.

Mr. Homos, a visitor from the altruistic utopia of Altruria comes to spend his summer vacation at a fashionable summer resort, where he engages Mr. Twelvemough, a well-known novelist, and other wealthy residents, in a discussion of the merits of the Christian communism practiced in Altruria. They turn a deaf ear to his arguments. But the local minister and the farmers of the area listen to Mr. Homos with considerable sympathy, as he describes the economy of his utopia. Altruria, he tells them, requires all citizens to work three hours a day at manual labor in return for their food and other goods. It has outlawed private property and machines, civic needs take precedence over family life, and fashions and styles, be it in dress or art, are overseen by an "aesthetic commission."

Howells, William Dean. "Edward Bellamy." *Atlantic Monthly* 82 (August 1898), 253-256.

Hough, Robert Lee. *The Quiet Rebel; William Dean Howells As A Social Commentator*. Lincoln: University of Nebraska Press, 1959.

The author painstakingly focuses on Howells's writings between 1900 and 1920, the year of his death, to show that, contrary to some prevalent views, he did not lose interest in social and economic issues after publishing *Traveler from Altruria*. This work will be of value to those interested in deepening their knowledge of Howells's social philosophy.

Kirk, Clara Marburg. *W. D. Howells, Traveler from Altruria*. 1889-1894. New Brunswick, N.J.: Rutgers University Press, 1962.

The author states that this book is, in a sense, an interpretation of Howells's view of the American scene between 1889 and 1894 seen through what Howells was experiencing at the time. Howells, she maintains, identified with both the traveler from Altruria, Mr. Homos, the visitor from the utopian island where the Christian and Classical worlds had mingled under the aegis of socialism and with Mr. Twelvemough, the fictional and apolitical novelist who challenges Mr. Homos' ideas. She argues each character revealed a side of Howells's personality. This study also provides a detailed account of the social and psychological factors in Howells's life that played a crucial role in utopian fiction.

Hudson, W. H.

Hudson, W. H. *A Crystal Age*. New York, E. P. Dutton, 1906.

In this well written utopian romance, one Smith of Great Britain falls through a hole and wakes up in a land where money has no value, domestic animals have developed new forms of usefulness, cities have been abolished and passionate love is unknown. The latter attitude is the cause of embarrassment and even danger for Smith, and provides some amusing moments to the plot. A catastrophe, vaguely described, ends the narrative.

Hume, David

Hume, David. "Idea of a Perfect Commonwealth." In *Essays: Moral, Political, and Literary*. Fair Lawn, N.J.: Oxford University Press, 1963.

Hume's rather elaborate idea of a "perfect" commonwealth turns out to be a representative form of government in which the right to vote is based on a high property qualification: only freeholders worth 20 pounds a year and householders worth 500 pounds are to vote. The author's aim in designing this "ideal" system was apparently twofold: to avoid including among the politically powerful any person who by reason of his legal or economic standing might be thought incapable of clear reasoning, and to permit the wealthy politicians to govern without concern for selfish benefits. Unfortunately, though often included in utopian bibliographies, this work is not utopian. Hume entertained no dreams about the perfectibility of man or about abolishing selfishness from society.

Gauthier, David. "David Hume, Contractarian." *Philosophical Review* 88 (1979), 3-38.

The author contends that Hume's moral and political inquiries comprise three theories: a theory of moral sentiment, a theory of property and justice, and a theory of government and obedience. The concern of this article is with the latter two theories. He perspicuously shows that these two theories are contractarian.

Huxley, Aldous

Huxley, Aldous. *Brave New World*. New York: Harper & Row, 1978.

This dystopian fable describes life in the 7th Century A.F. (After Ford). A world state has divided the world into castes, the highest being the Alpha-Plus and the lowest the Deltas, who are made up of manual workers. In this society, human beings are hatched in incubators and brought up in accordance with the strictest methods of conditioning. The plot unfolds around Bernard Marx, an unhappy Alpha-Plus who after visiting a New Mexican reservation, peopled by Savages who cannot be conditioned, brings one back to London. The Savage is at first enchanted by the scientifically ordered society he encounters; but after sustained arguments with the World Controller, comes to the conclusion that a scientifically planned society with manipulated wants and needs is incompatible with human freedom and man's yearning for spirituality. After going beserk, the Savage kills himself. The ironic title of this book is taken from Shakespeare's *The Tempest*.

Huxley, Aldous. *Brave New World Revisited*. New York: Harper, 1958.

The author reconsiders the prophecies and fears he expressed in his 27 year old novel, *Brave New World*. He concludes that they may be fulfilled sooner than he thought. He points to China, Russia and the United States of America as places where brain-washing is practiced on entire populations by "organization men," either by means of political slogans or television commercials and subliminal advertising.

Huxley, Aldous. *Island*. New York: Harper and Row: 1972.

Pala, a hypothetical island between Ceylon and Sumatra, is the setting for this fictionalized prescription of an utopian society in our age. The island is beautiful and inhabited by a gentle and handsome race of people who were taught by Dr. McPhail, a Scottish surgeon of formidable intellect, to adopt the most desirable features of both Eastern and Western cultures. The islanders derive their knowledge of the good life from bio-chemistry, Mahayana Buddhism, Taoism, Tantra, Zen, psychodelics, E-therapy and countless other philosophical and psychotherapeutic insights. Although not well received by some critics, *Island* presents a fascinating and readable documentation of Huxley's views on man, politics and religion.

Brown, Edward James

See Zamyatin, Eugene

Calder, Jenni. *Huxley and Orwell: Brave New World and Nineteen Eighty-Four*. London: Edward Arnold, 1976.

This expositions aims at clarifying and evaluating Huxley's and Orwell's dystopian novels. Biographical facts are only considered if they throw light on the works themselves. The questions that the critic attempts to answer are: What kind of works are they? What are they trying to tell us? How good are they and why? Each novel is discussed according to the following headings: Origins and Objects, Plots and People, and Human Nature and Politics. This is an eminently readable aid to the understanding of these works.

Hillegas, Mark R.

See Wells, H.G.

Kessler, Martin

See Orwell, George

Meckier, Jerome. "Utopian Counterpoint and the Compensatory Dream," in his *Aldous Huxley; Satire and Structure*. London: Chatto and Windus, 1969.

This chapter deals with Huxley's three utopian novels: *Brave New World, Ape and Essence* and *Island*. Its thesis is that *Island* is the counterpoint to the earlier dystopian novels, that is, that it provides the right answers to the problems posed by the technocratic horrors of the future. The author also argues that Huxley's anti-utopian novels, as well as *Island*, his utopia, developed, almost inevitably from ideas put forth in his prose essays.

Walsh, Chad

See *General Works on the History and Concept of Utopia*

Woodcock, George. *Dawn and the Darkest Hour*. New York: Viking, 1972.

Although Huxley is best known to the average reader as one of the best fiction writers who attempted to portray the darker side of human nature in the context of social manipulation and control, this chronological survey tries to show Huxley's entire spectrum of literary concerns. It advances the thesis that his work is "the movement out of darkness towards light." According to the author, Huxley intended *Brave New World*, one of the novels discussed by him, as a "didactic work," as a warning of what the future has in store for us unless the advocates of political and social control are vigorously resisted.

Westlake, J.H.H. "Aldous Huxley's *Brave New World* and George Orwell's *1984*: A Comparative Study." *Neueren Spracher* 71 (N.S. 21), No. 2 (Feb. 1972), 94-102.

Kipling, Rudyard

Kipling, Rudyard. "As Easy as ABC." In *A Diversity of Creatures*. London: 1917.

In this novel, Kipling depicts the world in the year 2065 when, under the small benevolent and technological rule of the Aerial Board of Control, war, over-population, democracy and ill health have been eliminated. The story revolves around the successful suppression, with the use of a dreadful ray gun, of democratic dissenters and their "crowd" ideology. Although Kipling seems to endorse his elitist paradise, he puts in the mouths of some of his benevolent world rulers remarks which suggest their disillusionment with the perfect, unheroic world they have created. This work is reflective of Kipling's generally pessimistic views about the human race.

Faber, Richard. *The Vision and the Need; Late Victorian Imperialist Aims*. London: Faber & Faber, 1966.

The object of this book is to "analyse, situate and compare the aims of important British Imperialists toward the end of the century." About 19 pages are devoted to Kipling's works, including "As Easy as ABC." The author thinks that in this story Kipling's intention were twofold: "to show first what might be the result of improved communications and techniques, and second what he expected to be the eventual reaction to Democracy . . . run riot." According to the author, with this story Kipling attempted to provide a reasonable solution to the world's increasingly complex problems—a solution that he saw infinitely preferable to democracy.

Kropotkin, Peter A.

Kropotkin, Peter Alexeivitch. *The Conquest of Bread*. London: Allen Lane/Penguin Press, 1972.

Although not intended by the author as an utopian tract, the exposition of communist anarchism espoused by the eminent XIX century anarchist theoretician, shares many of the goals of collectivist utopian thinkers. Kropotkin proposes the abolition of money and prices, the wage system, the division of labor and private property and defends his vision of the communist society, a society which would substitute the "ugly compulsions of the state and the economic machine" with autonomous, libertarian, propertyless communities.

Kropotkin, Peter Alexeyevich. *Fields, Factories and Workshops*. New York: Harper and Row, 1975.

Originally printed in 1898, this work asserts the author's conviction that we have come to a time when modern knowledge is capable of telling human beings that they can be materially well off without oppressing others, and that science will do away with the need for overwork. This noted anarchist thinker envisions communes which combine agriculture with industry, without private property or the circulation of money.

Osofsky, Stephen. *Peter Kropotkin*. Boston: Twayne, 1979.

The avowed purpose of this volume is to delve thoroughly and comprehensively into the essentials of Kropotkin's socio-economic and political views. The author advances the view that Kropotkin was, and remains, a very important social critic who helped define today's political and social issues. He succeeds in illuminating Kropotkin's hypotheses and critique without watering down or undermining whatever coherence his theory has. Even though he does not provide analyses of Kropotkin's individual works, his introduction to the thought of this eminent Russian anarchist, will prove to be quite enlightening to anyone wishing to gain a deep understanding of Kropotkin's ideas. A short but excellent selective bibliography of primary and secondary sources enhances the value of this study.

Landauer, Gustav

Landauer, Gustav. *For Socialism*. St. Louis: Telos Press, 1976.

This is a brilliant, albeit loose, plea for utopian anarchism by one of most sagacious of anarchist thinkers of the XX century. Utopia is conceived as a conglomerate of de-centralized, mutual help, voluntaristic communities in which neither private property nor collectivism hold sway.

Link-Salinger (Hyman), Ruth. *Gustav Landauer: Philosopher of Utopia*. Indianapolis: Hackett, 1977.

This is the first major study in English devoted to the theoretician of "free socialism," libertarianism and editor of *Der Sozialist*. Landauer's vision of a mutualistic, voluntaristic, "free" society, unfortunately, is not treated in detail, nor is the reader told what features of this vision make it "utopian." The author succeeds in providing an intellectual biography of the man, supported by a massive corpus of citations which rescues from oblivion an important figure in the history of German libertarian socialism. A lengthy bibliography of Landauer's work is provided.

Lenin, Vladimir Ilych

Lenin, Vladimir Ilych. *The State and the Revolution*. New York: International Publishing Co., 1932.

Picking up Marx's belief that communism will be the second and higher stage of socialism, the book describes the communist society of the future as one without external limitations of any kind for persons who have evolved into socialized beings and are committed to the ideal of communism. In this stage of social evolution, individuals are described by Lenin as freed from bourgeois selfishness and narrowmindedness. In these social conditions, the State will have withered away and very little social control will be needed to curb anti-social behavior.

Warth, Robert D. *Lenin*. New York: Twayne, 1973.

This highly readable short biography of Lenin briefly discusses what the author calls Lenin's "embarrassing strain of utopian anarchism" in *State and Revolution*.

Levin, Ira

Levin, Ira. *This Perfect Day: A Novel*. New York: Random House, 1970.

This dystopian novel describes a world populated by eight billion members of The Family, who regard hate and strife as psychopathological deviations. Living in cities known as EU55131 or USA60607, everyone is taught to worship Christ, Marx, Woo and Wei, and is programmed by UniComp to lead a redetermined life. Through the use of chemotherapy, any undesirable trait (anxiety, dissidence, worry, etc.) is removed. Chip, the protagonist, chooses to escape to an island of "incurables" rather than submit to the dullness and regimentation of life under UniComp. Though engagingly written, it lacks the subtlety and depth of the classics of dystopian thought.

Lin, Yu-T'ang

Lin, Yu-T'ang. *Looking Beyond*. New York: Prentice-Hall, 1955.

In the year 2004, a female anthropologist lands on an unknown Pacific island, (with a group of polyglot refugees) attempting to escape the Ten Year War which followed World War III. Her plane having been destroyed, the anthropologist, renamed Eurydice, and her companions join the utopia that they have found on this island. This utopia seems to combine the best features of Brook Farm with those of the island Eden, described in Norman Douglas' *South Wind*. Its philosopher king believes in moderate progress and technology, and cautions his followers that they should not strive for perfection given the weaknesses of human nature. The novel serves as a foil to advance the author's philosophy of leisure. Utopia for him is that society which can provide a comfortable life in the present, not one that constantly plans the future.

London, Jack

London, Jack. *The Iron Heel*. New York: Macmillan, 1908.

In this novel, a manuscript is discovered which, although penned seven centuries before, describes the political and economic events from 1912 to 1918 that led to the seizure of power by the Iron Heel, a totalitarian political organization. The protagonist, Ernest Everhard, fights the Iron Heel and the capitalist system until 1932, when the class-conscious working class deals a death blow to capitalism as a result of ever increasing economic crises and labor struggles. This is one of the few socialist novels which describes capitalist society in dystopian terms. It is also highly prophetic of the fascist political phenomenon that was to occur later in this century.

Madariaga, Salvador de

Madariaga, Salvador de. *The Sacred Giraffe. Being the Second Volume of the Posthumous Works of Julio Arceval*. New York: Harper & Bros, 1922.

Set in the year 6922 A.D., this mildly dystopian satire describes an imaginary society, the Ebonite Empire, in which males are assigned the subsidiary roles usually reserved for women in contemporary society. The affairs of state are managed by female ministers and doctors and the idea of justice is a "true regard for the majesty and power of the strongest party in the nation."

Marcuse, Herbert

Marcuse, Herbert. *Eros and Civilization: A Philosophical Inquiry into Freud*. Boston, Mass.: Beacon, 1974.

The author challenges Freud's belief that civilization is based on the repression of human instincts, especially sexuality. His speculation leads him to the view that the technology and economic wealth of modern industrial societies allow for the creation of a non-repressive society in which all libidinal impulses and socioeconomic needs of human beings could be satisfied.

Martin, Jay. "Marcuse's Utopia." *Radical America* 4 (April, 1970), 21-28.

Peretz, Martin. "Herbert Marcuse: Beyond Technological Reason." *Yale Review* 57 (June 1968), 518-527.

Steuernagel, Gertrude A. *Political Philosophy as Therapy—Marcuse Reconsidered*. Westport, Conn.: Greenwood Press, 1979.

This study focuses on the concept of political philosophy as therapy, and on Herbert Marcuse as the vehicle for the development of this approach to political philosophy. Chapter 3, "Marcuse in Depth: A More Detailed Examination of His Vision" deals with Marcuse's therapeutic vision and on the reasons why Marcuse believes that it is now possible to usher in an utopian society—a possibility stymied by certain subjective and objective factors, i.e., the present organization of the forces of production.

Marx, Karl

Marx, Karl. *Critique of the Gotha Program*. In *Selected Works of Karl Marx and Friedrich Engels*, vol. 2. New York: International, 1938.

In this work Marx subjects the program of Lasalle's German Workers Party to scathing criticism. In the course of the critique, he describes the Communist society as one governed by the principle, "from each according to his ability, to each according to his needs." The idea that each should be given what he or she needs is Fourierian in spirit, although the latter included sexual and psychological needs among the needs to be satisfied. He argues that in the socialist stage it may be necessary to allocate goods according to labor performed, but under communism this last remnant of the past will be transcended. This has been regarded as the most utopian of Marx's works.

Kalin, Martin G. *The Utopian Flight from Unhappiness: Freud Against Marx on Social Progress*. Chicago: Nelson-Hall, 1974.

This tersely written comparative study of Freud's and Marx's views on social progress, which the author believes represent the anti-utopian and utopian positions on the causes of human unhappiness, attempts to understand the problem rather than provide a solution to it. It attacks Marx's predictions about communism as utopian on the grounds that his theory about the proletariat's revolution suffers from unrealistic and romantic suppositions.

Kaufmann, Moritz

See *General Works on the History and Concept of Utopia.*

Olsen, Richard E. *Karl Marx*. Boston: Twayne 1978.

This clear and sympathetic exposition of Marx's complex thought is designed by the author in such a way that the reader should understand Marx's theories in greater and greater depth as he proceeds. Chapter 3, "Marx on Communist Society," discusses among other works, *The Critique of the Gotha Program* and the reasons why Marx thought that his vision of the egalitarian society was not like "the fantastic pictures of future society" produced by the utopian socialists.

Soloman, Maynard "Marx and Bloch: Reflections on Utopia and Art." *Telos* No. 13 (Fall 1972), 68-85.

More, Thomas

More, Thomas. *Utopia*. Vol. IV of the Yale Edition of *The Complete Works of St. Thomas More*. New Haven, Conn.: Yale University Press, 1965.

Written originally in Latin in 1516 and translated into English in 1551, this work is, without doubt, the most famous of the utopias. It describes a democratic and communistic commonwealth located in an imaginary island. More coined the name from the Greek words meaning "no place" in recognition of the fact that such a society had never existed. Divided into two parts, the first part introduces the main character, Raphael Hythloday, who gives an account of his conversation with a mariner whom he had met at the house of Peter Giles of Antwerp and who had just returned from Utopia. Through the mouth of Hythloday, More launches into an incisive and brilliant criticism of the British political institutions of his time and raises a number of moral and political questions which serve as foil for the justification of a more just and equitable social order. In the second part, Moore depicts a moneyless society where altruistic communitarian ideals are prevalent, such as the ownership in common of the means of production and dwellings. However, More's society expects hard work and conformity in exchange for equality. It deals harshly with idlers who are punished with forced labor, and it assigns jobs to people in accordance with the needs of the commonwealth, not personal need. Anyone seriously interested in utopian literature should place high on his list of readings this classic of utopian thought.

Abrash, Merritt. "Missing the Point in More's *Utopia*." *Extrapolation*, 19 (December 1977), 27-38.

Adams, Robert P. "The Philosophic Unity of More's *Utopia*," *Studies in Philology* 38 (January 1941), 45-65.

Ames, Russell. *Citizen Thomas More and His Utopia*. 1949. Reprint. New York: Russell, 1969.

This controversial study concerns itself with placing More in the middle class, and relates his thought to that of this class in England, in order to show that *Utopia* is not the vision of an individual genius, but a product of the rising capitalism's attack on feudalism, a decaying social order at the time the work was written. The author argues that though it is true that *Utopia* is somewhat anti-capitalist, the "core of the book is republican, bourgeois and democratic."

Avineri, Shlomo. "War and Slavery in More's Utopia." *International Review of Social History* (1962), 260-290.

Bogardus, Emory S. "More and Utopian Social Thought," in his *The Development of Social Thought* 4th ed. London: Longmans, Green, 1960.

Campbell, William Edward. *Moore's Utopia and His Social Teaching.* London: Eyre and Spottiswoode, 1930.

Carmichael, Montgomery. "Sir Thomas More's Utopia; Its Doctrine of the Common Life." *Dublin Review*, 191 (October 1932), 173-187.

Chambers, R. W. *Thomas More*. New York: Harcourt-Brace, 1935.

> Thomas More is presented as a benign bourgeois critical of the rise of capitalism, who envisioned a society capable of achieving medieval Christian ideals under the guidance of reason and who attempted to reconcile the best elements of feudal, capitalist and socialist ideas in his main work. *Utopia*, according to the author, was not a blueprint for subversion, but a condemnation of the abuses prevalent in the Europe of the times. By showing how far short of the utopian standards Europe fell, More attempted with *Utopia* to stimulate the exercise of the Christian virtues, especially charity.

Donner, H. W. *Introduction to Utopia*. Uppsala, Sweden: Sidgwick & Jackson, 1945.

> This essay is designed as an introduction to the study of Thomas More's *Utopia*. The author's thesis is that More's work is not, as the Socialists have believed, a plea for communism, nor as some German scholars have claimed, an incipient defense of British imperialism. Instead, he maintains, this work is a picture of the state society can attain without revelation; an appeal to mend our ways and ease the burden of our fellowmen. It does not describe an ultimate ideal, but one that is practicable enough to warrant serious consideration. Although this theological interpretation of *Utopia* is controvesial, the book succeeds in summarizing the most distinctive features of this classic. For a more scholarly defense of this interpretation see Chambers, R. W.

Kautsky, Karl. *Thomas More and His Utopia* New York: Russell & Russell, 1959.

> Originally issued in an English translation in 1890, this book conceives *Utopia* as a vision of the communist society of the future. It praises More as one of the earliest spokesmen of the embryonic working class of his time and as a tragic hero who stood alone at a time when it was impossible to bring communist ideals into fruition. More becomes, in Kautsky's hands, a Catholic social revolutionary thinker who was able to grasp the casual link between private property on the one hand and poverty, violence, and inequality on the other.

Gallagher, Ligeia, ed. *More's Utopia and Its Critics*. Chicago: Scott, Foresman, 1964.

Hamilton, Robert. "More's *Utopia*: Its Bearing on Present Conditions." *Hibbert Journal* 44 (1946), 242-247.

Hexter, J. H. *More's Utopia: The Biography of An Idea*. 1952. Reprint. Westport, Ct.: Greenwood, 1976.

Originally published in 1952, the aim of this scholarly study is to provide a biographical sketch of the idea for More's *Utopia*; that is, how it germinated in More's mind, remained there the duration of its life, and how it finally perished when the printed book, *Utopia*, became a "black and white" reality. For those who are interested in probing More's intentions, the meaning of curious paragraphs and terms, his alleged communism, the role of Christianity in the discourse of *Utopia*, and, in general, the relation between the structure of *Utopia* and the meaning and intent of its author, this study will prove to be of great value.

Johnson, Robbin S. *More's Utopia: Ideal and Illusion*. New Haven, Conn.: Yale University Press, 1969.

This provocative essay argues that More is more concerned with defining the proper position to take toward the "ideals and illusions of the utopian myth" than he is with presenting a perfected vision of the desirable society. According to the author, *Utopia* argues for an attitude of involvement within detachment. The pages of *Utopia*, reveal a man who struggles to present the human spirit's attempt to overcome overpowering realities, not a vision of the perfect commonwealth. The *List of Works Consulted* provides a considerable bibliography of periodical articles on utopianism and More.

Jones, Judith P. *Thomas More*. Boston: Twayne, 1979.

The purpose of this book is "to survey More's writing and show the extent to which it demonstrates his intellectual and spiritual development." In studying More's career as a humanist, polemicist and devotional writer, the author attempts to unfurl the qualities of character inherent in his personality. Section V of Chapter 2 provides a general discussion of the main ideas developed in *Utopia*, More's masterpiece, and tries to show that it is not just a book of social and political theory, but a literary product of Christian humanism as well. It also provides a summary, book by book, of *Utopia*.

Prince, J. F. T. "Nowhere Island: More's *Utopia*." *Blackfriars* 16 (1935), 422-424.

Skinner, Quentin. "More's Utopia." *Past and Present* No. 38 (December 1967), 153-168.

Steintrager, James "Plato and More's *Utopia*." *Social Research* 36 (Autumn 1969), 357-372.

Traugott, John. "A Voyage to Nowhere with Thomas More and Jonathan Swift: *Utopia* and *The Voyage to the Houyhnhnms*." *Sewanee Review* 69 (Autumn 1961), 543-565.

This lengthy comparison of *Utopia* and *Gulliver's Travels* argues that both works are discoveries of the moral and spiritual reality of utopia and that employ as a satirical device a traveler who is maddened by a glimpse of the good society in an imaginary land by the unreality of everyday life in England. According to the author, both satires abandon the voyagers to alienation and leave the reader with the burden of bridging the gap between an impossible truth that cannot be ignored and an unpleasant reality, the England of the times, that cannot be changed.

Morelly, Abbe

Morelly, Abbe. *Code of Nature*. Edited by Edouard Dolléans. Paris: Geuthner, 1910.

Having first been published in France in 1755, this work idealizes a system of private agricultural holdings owned by independent artisan enterprises ruled by an all powerful, but enlightened, philosopher-king. The spirit of communal equality and calm felicity is brought about through the curtailment of growth and monopoly.

Morris, William

Morris, William. *The Dream of John Ball*. In *Three Works by William Morris*. New York: International Publishers, 1968.

The narrator returns in a dream to XIV century England in the midst of the Peasant's Revolt of 1381. He hears an inspiring speech by John Ball, one of the leaders of the revolt who engages him in long discussions about the events that must occur before the ideals of socialism can come to pass, i.e. the growth of bourgeois relations, the transformation of guild artisans into wage laborers, the development of large-scale industry and finally the development of the pro-letariat as a revolutionary class capable of fulfilling Ball's ideal, a new kind of society in which all its members will enjoy a free and happy life.

Morris, William. *The Earthly Paradise*. 3 vols. London: 1868.

The prologue of this long collections of poems, modeled on Chaucer's, tells how certain "gentlemen and mariners of Norway" set sail to find the Earthly Paradise, as they flee from the Black Death. After many disappointments, they finally reach a "nameless city in a distant sea," peopled by descendants of the Early Ionians who dwell in pillared council houses surrounded by images of gold. This utopian fantasy reveals a serene yearning for a well-ordered society. Its main value is to show the literary wellsprings that nourished the thought of the author of *News From Nowhere*.

Morris, William. *News From Nowhere; or, An Epoch of Rest; Being Some Chapters from an Utopian Romance* (Classics of Radical Thought). New York: Monthly Review Press, 1966.

William Guest awakens, like the main character of Bellamy's *Looking Backward*, some two hundred years after a successful socialist revolution has destroyed "commercialism" in England and substituted it with a decentralized, compul-sion-free society, in which government and private property are a thing of the past; work has become one of the major sources of pleasure; the growth of craftsmanship has led to a rebirth of art; violence is practically nonexistent; the urban and rural cultures have mingled, and education is voluntary and unstruc-tured. Unlike Bellamy's character, Guest awakens from his dream with a message from the dwellers of this future: "Build up little by little, the new fellowship, rest and happiness." Written to counter Bellamy's centralized and bureaucratic vision of utopia, this work, first published in 1890, has deservedly become one of the classics of utopian fiction.

Bradley, Ian. *William Morris and His World*. New York: Scribner's, 1978.

One will find this volume to be an ably written biographical introduction to Morris, with detailed information on his social background and the social context in which he expounded his socialist ideas. It is useful primarily for those unacquainted with the details of his life and his main ideas, and offers one a broad understanding of the evolutionary development of Morris's utopian vision.

Bunge, Mario. "On William Morris' Socialism." *Science and Society* 20 (1956), 142-144.

Grey, Lloyd Eric. *William Morris; Prophet of England's New Order*. London: Cassell, 1949.

This highly readable biography provides a clear account of Morris's intellectual development and of the reasons why he thought labor, ethics, politics, art and economics were integral and inseparable factors in the struggle for the advancement of the human race. Chapter IX provides a short discussion of *News from Nowhere*. The biographer contends that Morris's utopian socialism aimed at the restoration of "native British idealism."

Helmholtz-Phelan, Anna A. Von. *The Social Philosophy of William Morris*. Durham, N.C.: Duke University Press, 1927.

This scholarly, readable and well developed study of William Morris's socialist philosophy gives the biographical and cultural background of the thinker needed to fully understand the medieval tone of *News From Nowhere*, as well as its concepts of humanized labor and social relations.

Meier, Paul. *William Morris, The Marxist Dreamer*. New York: Humanities, 1977.

This 600 page volume attempts to analyze Morris's conception of a well-ordered society described in *News from Nowhere*. But it offers more than that. The social and political thought of Morris is carefully dissected and an attempt is made to show that it is Marxist in nature. Meier contends that Morris's sketch of the ideal society was based on Marx, even though the latter had little to say on the communist society of the future. In spite of the fact that the argument is a bit far-fetched, those wishing to know more about the philosophical linchpins of Morris's important utopian novel will benefit by reading this lengthy scholarly work. It is written in an engaging and lucid style and should be enjoyed by the educated layman.

Thompson, E. P. *William Morris: Romantic to Revolutionary*. New York: Pantheon, 1977.

Approximately two-thirds of this study is devoted to Morris's left-wing political career and his place in the British socialist movement of the late XIX century. It argues that Morris integrated Marxism and literary romanticism and that they enabled him to embrace utopian visions and the Marxist views of social change simultaneously. It contains a valuable postscript, which is a bibliographic review of books and articles on Morris written between the early sixties and the mid-seventies.

Morrow, James

Morrow, James. *The Wine of Violence*. New York: Holt, Rinehart and Winston, 1981.

After a forced landing on an "invisible" planet, two "Nearthians," Francis Lostwax and Burne Newman, come face to face with the Quetzalians, a race of people who by means of psychosurgery, high technology and ancient Toltec myths, have managed to eradicate violence from their personalities and their society. In order to regain control of their space ship, the two Nearthians must initiate a train of events that turn the Quetzalians into violent beings. Because the narrative attempts to show that nonviolence is both desirable and unattainable, this novel is more than just another well written science fiction story. It is described by one of its reviewers as an "ambiguous utopia"—it suggests that the world can be immensely improved but not made perfect.

Nichols, Robert

Nichols, Robert. *Gahr City*. New York: New Dimensions, 1978.

In this anarchist fictional utopia, anarchosyndicalist workers have done away with all forms of government, substituting in their place local "anarchist bureaucracies," direct democracy, shamans, and group festivals. Politics technology, education and public and private affairs are based on ecological concerns and are wisely planned.

Nichols, Robert. *Arrival*. New York: New Dimensions, 1977.

Set in the year 3670 in an imaginary place in Central Asia, this novel describes the happenings in the lives of three visitors to Gahr City, William Blake, Jack Kerouac and Alvarez, a Cuban film maker. They have been summoned by the Shamans, who, amidst a festival atmosphere, discuss with them the principles of their society, which are permeated by both a sense of sacredness and a sense of playfulness. With *Gahr City, Arrival* is to become a part of a tetralogy, entitled "Daily Lives in Nghsi-Altai.

Noyes, George Wellington

See Oneida

Nozick, Robert

Nozick, Robert. *Anarchy, State and Utopia*. New York: Basic Books, 1977.

The central argument of this scholarly book is that the only morally justified state is what the author calls "the minimal state," a state concerned solely with the prevention of force, theft and fraud on the one hand and with the enforcement of contracts made by willing parties on the other. It views as ideal a society made up of voluntary groups of people each working out their own conception of the good life. It reflects, with brilliant argumentative strokes, a Lockean view of natural rights with a libertarian abhorrence of any unjustified governmental control.

Kateb, George. "The Night Watchman State." (Review of *Anarchy, State and Utopia* by Robert Nozick) *American Scholar* 45 (Winter 1975/76), 816-826.

This sympathetic review of Nozick's libertarian position argues that his conception of the person is mangled by an absolute right of property which would not permit or require the state to be anything more than a "night watchman" without any obligation to relieve the suffering of its citizens. The reviewer concludes that Nozick's contention that no one is obliged to relieve the misery of another vitiates his antiredistribution argument and his political philosophy.

Olerich, Henry

Olerich, Henry. *A Cityless and Countryless World: An Outline of Practical Cooperative Individualism*. New York: Arno, 1971.

This is a reprint of a libertarian communist novel, published in 1893. Set in Mars, it describes a bucolic aggregation of small communities in which all work is done according to ability. Each woman freely chooses her mate, and leaders are democratically selected to do specific jobs, and not to supervise or control the lives of other members of the community. Olerich's views are remarkably similar to those of Peter Kropotkin's in *Factories in the Field*.

Grant, H. Roger. "Henry Olerich and Utopia: The Iowa Years." *Annals of Iowa* 43 (1976), 349-361.

Orwell, George

Orwell, George. *Animal Farm*. New York: New American Library, 1974.

> The animals of Mr. Jones's farm successfully revolt against their human owner and the pigs become their leaders. Soon afterward, one of the pigs, Napoleon, usurps power and replaces human tyranny with a new kind of tyranny, under the pretense that "All animals are equal, but some are more equal than others." Some critics have regarded this satirical fable as a dystopian work, but others regard it simply as a satire against the Soviet Union and by implication against all totalitarian revolutions. Napoleon, the cynical and ruthless dictator represents Stalin; Snowball, the exiled idealist pig represents Trotsky, and Boxer, the noble and honest horse represents the common man. This fable is, without doubt, a literary masterpiece that illuminates some of the issues debated by utopians and anti-utopians, namely whether noble ideals can withstand the test of survival among their professed adherents.

Orwell, George. *Nineteen Eighty-Four*. New York: New American Library, 1971.

> This is a masterful and grim depiction of a totalitarian state set in the future, where the power of Big Brother is enshrined, privacy is abolished, history and language are made to serve the needs of the rulers and deviance from the party line means death. Winston Smith, the main character of the novel is caught by the Thought-Police, after having had a brief unapproved love affair. A long period of intense brain-washing, makes him a submissive, unquestioning servant of the State who upon being released mechanically parrots the party line. This classic of dystopian thought shows the extent to which unrestrained power could go to impose its will on an entire society.

Brown, E.J.

See Huxley, Aldous

Calder, Jenni

See Huxley, Aldous

Connors, James

See Zamyatin, Eugene

Edrich, Emanuel. "George Orwell and the Satire in Horror." *Texas Studies in Literature and Language* 4 (1962/63), 96-108.

Fromm, Eric. "Afterward." In *1984* by George Orwell. New York: New American Library, 1961, pp. 257-267.

> Fromm views Orwell's novel as a warning of the reality that human beings confront in modern times: a soulless society of acquiescing automatons—not as a veiled description of Stalinist barbarism.

Green, John. "The Tyranny of an Idea: George Orwell's *Nineteen Eighty-Four*," *Sixty-One* 5 (October 1964), 11-16.

Gross, Miriam, ed. *The World of George Orwell*. New York: Simon & Schuster, 1971.

> This collection of essays attempts to see George Orwell both in terms of what his literary work means today and as a man whose achievements need to be set in the context of his own times. The first group of essays are biographical in nature and reveal a great deal about Orwell's middle years. The second group of essays describes the social world—marked by the Depression of the thirties and fascism—which Orwell knew. The third group of essays is devoted to Orwell's

immediate political positions. One of the essays, Matthew Hodgart's "From Animal Farm to Nineteen Eighty Four" contends that these literary works are predictions of things to come rather than metaphors of the present state of society or of the permanent human condition. The editor has incorporated many illustrations of Orwell's life and times.

Hillegas, Mark R.

See Wells, H.G.

Hynes, Samuel, comp. *Twentieth Century Interpretations of 1984.* Englewood Cliffs, N.J.: Prentice-Hall, 1971.

The compiler and twelve contributors of this volume assess the events and times that caused Orwell to pen this novel. They evaluate its place in contemporary literature and provide an encompassing look at its theme, plot, style and literary devices which make it one of the most powerful and well written fictional indictments of political realities in our century. The participation of such notables as V.S. Pritchett, Lionel Trilling, Stephen Spender and George Kateb, to mention a few, makes this collection of essays required reading for anyone wishing to gain a deeper understanding of Orwell's classic. A two page bibliography of secondary source adds to the value of the book.

Howe, Irving. "Orwell: History As Nightmare." *American Scholar* 25 (Spring 1956), 193-207.

Kessler, Martin. "Power and the Perfect State: A Study in Disillusion- ment as Reflected in Orwell's *Nineteen Eighty-Four* and Hux- ley's *Brave New World*." *Political Science Quarterly* 72 (1957), 565-577.

Lief, Ruth Ann. *Homage to Oceania: The Prophetic Vision of George Orwell.* Columbus: Ohio State University Press, 1969.

This exposition on Orwell's prophetic political ideas reveals a quintessential understanding of the man and his ideas. The author draws comparisons between Orwell and writers such as Arnold, Milton, Blake, and Forster. She also extrapolates from his novels and essays to illustrate his ideological concerns. This careful documentation and synthesis of Orwell's political thought reveals Orwell's relevance to contemporary social issues.

Meyers, Jeffrey and Valerie Meyers. *George Orwell; An Annotated Bibliography* of Criticism. New York: Garland Publishing Co., 1977.

This annotated bibliography of critical writings summarizes 500 books, articles and major reviews devoted to Orwell's writings. It excludes newspaper articles, most book reviews and dissertations. Emphasis is placed on those publications which appeared between 1950 and 1977. Citations in the major foreign languages, and some minor ones, have been included. The authors distinguish the more significant works by means of an asterisk. The citations are arranged alphabetically. Unfortunately, this work is marred by the lack of index.

Smith, Marcus. "The Wall of Blackness: A Psychological Approach to *1984*." *Modern Fiction Studies* 14 (Winter 1968-1969), 423-433.

Steinhoff, William. *George Orwell and the Origins of 1984.* Ann Arbor: University of Michigan Press, 1975.

This critic argues that if we wish to enlarge our knowledge about Orwell's answers to such questions as, What is and ought to be the relation between the individual and other individuals when the power of others manifests itself in the form of the state? Why did people permit a society to develop which they knew might enslave them? What were the forms such a society might take? What were the motives of those who shaped the system and how did they obtain and keep power? etc., we must regard *1984* as a novel which almost epitomizes ideas, attitudes, events and readings which are embedded in Orwell's life and earlier works. Three chapters are devoted to a consideration of the important works which appear to have contributed to Orwell's last novel. A fifteen page bibliography of works by and about Orwell, as well as of works that might contribute to the understanding of this novel, enhances the value of this scholarly work.

Walsh, Chad

See *General Works on the History and Concept of Utopia.*

Williams, Raymond. *George Orwell*. New York: Viking, 1970.

The noted British literary critic defends the view that Orwell's fiction is indistinguishable from his nonfiction. Although this is a moot approach to Orwell's literary *opus*, this book succeeds in showing how Orwell's views permeated his aesthetic and literary work.

Woodcock, George. *The Crystal Spirit: A Study of George Orwell*. Boston, Little, Brown, 1966.

This study conbines literary criticism and biography. It perceptively delineates the complexity of George Orwell and the changes in the evolution of his ideas. Woodcock holds that an examination of Orwell's early writings reveals ideas and images found later in *Nineteen Eighty-Four*. This clear critical analysis of Orwell's writings provides a welcome introduction for the novice.

Woodehouse, C. M. "Introduction" to *Animal Farm: A Fairy Story*. New York: New American Library, 1964.

This well-known critic writes that *Animal Farm* is not a work of fiction at all, but rather a view of life that has been transcribed into highly simplified symbolic terms, leaving the reader with a feeling of rebelliousness against the totalitarian "truth" of our time.

Owen, Robert

Owen, Robert. *A New View of Society*. 1813. Reprint. Clifton, N.J.: Kelley, 1972.

Many critics regard this theoretical work as Owen's clearest and most ambitious formulation of his social philosophy. In it, he advances the argument that human character is moulded by the environment, and that to create a good person one must create a sound environment. He then argues that such an environment was achieved in New Lanark, the socialistic agricultural community of some 1,200 persons he founded in Scotland, of which he gives a detailed description. This treatise is the best exposition of the author's ideas and should be read by anyone interested in a full understanding of the intellectual foundation of his experiments.

Bestor, Arthur Eugene Jr.

See *General Works on Utopian Communities*

Butt, John, ed. *Robert Owen: Aspects of His Life and Work*. New York; Humanities, 1971.

Biography is essentially the purpose of the eight sympathetic essays gathered in this volume. The essays concentrate on Robert Owen and not on Owenism. The abilities of Owen as a businessman, educator, factory reformer and economic thinker are well documented. The book is also profusely illustrated.

Cole, G. D. H. *The Life of Robert Owen*. Hamden, Conn.: Archon Books, 1966.

Written by the eminent theoretician of guild socialism, this biography does not attempt to give a detailed account of Owen's life or of the Owenite movement. Its main concern is to give "the salient facts of Owen's life and influence" and connect them with "the various social and economic movements which his doctrines vitally affected." Lucidly written, this work provides an excellent introduction to the sage of New Lanark and to his ideas for social reform. Appendix F in the book is a list of books useful for the study of Owen and Owenism.

Cole, Margaret. *Robert Owen of New Lanark*. New York: Augustus M. Kelley, 1969.

According to the author, this work in no way supplements or supersedes the biographies of Owen written by Frank Podmore and G. D. H. Cole (see), but it provides a more detailed account of Owen's organizational abilities and activities in New Lanark, and gives more information about his ill-fated New Harmony settlement in the United States and the uprising of pre-chartist trade unionism. A short two page bibliography concludes the book.

Harrison, John F. C. *Quest for the New Moral World; Robert Owen and the Owenites in Britain and America*. New York: Scribner's, 1969.

This is not so much a study of Robert Owen as it is of Owenism, the transatlantic movement that prospered in Britain and the United States of America. It discusses the philanthropic origins and anatomy of the movement, its definition of socialism, its efforts to build a new moral world and the means it employed to transmit its ideas, i.e. education. The author explains why the movement became associated with working class agitation in England, but took on a millenarian and communitarian aspect in America. One third of the book is devoted to a bibliography of works by and about Owen and on Owenism.

Harrison, John F. C. ed. *Utopianism and Education: Robert Owen and the Owenites*. New York: Teachers College Press, 1968.

One of the most fascinating things about Owenism, as the editor of this collection tells us, was the importance that Owenism placed on education as a means of character formation and social improvement. The carefully chosen selections from the writings of Owen, as well as some of his followers, like Abram Combe, William Thompson and William MacClure, included in this book, attest to this claim.

Leopold, Richard William. *Robert Dale Owen: A Biography*. 1940. Reprint. Seattle, Wash.: Octagon, 1969.

This scholarly biography deals with the life of Robert Owen's eldest son, who, like his father, used his wealth to further social change. The period he spent as a young man in his father's utopian settlement, New Harmony, is well documented and sheds light on this important experiment. It has a helpful bibliography as well.

Pitzer, Donald E. *Robert Owen's American Legacy: Proceedings of the Robert Owen Bicentennial Conference*. Indianapolis: Indiana Historical Society, 1972.

Published in commemoration of Owen's two hundreth birthday, the five papers making up this volume deal with three phases of Owen's American legacy. First they focus on Owen's effort at New Harmony; secondly, on Owen's ideas and his impact upon America, and thirdly, on Owen's interest in music and dance as part of a person's enjoyment and physical exercise. This is required reading for those interested in Owen's efforts to bring the millenial dream to this side of the

Atlantic. It contains an introduction to the premiere of the documentary film "New Harmony: An Example and a Beacon."

Podmore, Frank. *Robert Owen: A Biography*. Two vols. in one. 1906. Reprint. New York: Augustus M. Kelley, 1968.

> For those seeking a massive amount of detail on Owen's life this work is a must. The main elements of Owen's social philosophy are also accurately reflected in the biographical narrative, i.e. the concept of labor exchange and paedagogy, etc. Unlike Cole's biography (see), the author approaches his subject almost reverently, regarding him as a dreamer "whose dreams have helped to reshape the world." Owen's involvement with spiritualism is highlighted. Excellent illustrations and a bibliography of Owen's writings enchance the usefulness of this work.

Pollard, Sidney and John Salt. *Robert Owen: Prophet of the Poor*. Lewisburg, PA.: Bucknell University, 1971.

> This is a collection of twelve scholarly essays devoted to various facets of Owen's thought and his millenarian activities written by an international roster of academics to commemorate his two hundredth birthday. The essays succeed in reflecting the many-sidedness of this utopian visionary. They deal among other things with Owen's revolutionary politics, his community experiments, his educational views, his cooperative experiment in New Lanark, his utopian ventures in the United States and the impact of Owenism on France and Germany. Although the style of some contributions is at times stodgy and dry-as-dust, this is a work that every serious student of Owen should consult.

Plato

Plato, *Plato's Republic*. Vol. 2. *Essays*. Edited by B. Jowett and Lewis Campbell. 1894. Reprint. New York: Arno.

> Unquestionably the richest and most extensive of Plato's dialogues, it not only presents the blueprint of the just society, but also timeless discussions on ethics, politics, metaphysics, education, the philosophy of history and even sociology. It is divided into three parts. The first part discusses the creation of the ideal city and the reasons why its citizens must be divided into three classes: the Guardians (philosophers), who rule and guide the population; the Auxiliaries, who protect the state from military threats; and the Workers, who are concerned with the production of the means of subsistence. The second part develops the concept of the philosopher as "the just man," a wise, rational and self-restrained political leader. The third part discusses the merits of various political constitutions. Plato's ideas of a propertyless state, in which wives and children are shared communally, of art as needing ruthless censorship, and of the need for all individual creative or productive activities to be subordinated to the needs of the state, have found very few outright sympathizers among utopian thinkers, but they have doubtlessly influenced the thought of those, like Campanella and Moore, who put forth a collectivist blueprint of utopia.

Martínez, Julio A. *A Bibliography of Writings on Plato, 1900-1967*. San Diego: San Diego State University Library, 1978.

> This is a selective, unannotated bibliography of monographic and periodical works published during the first 67 years of our century. It lists about 137 titles devoted exclusively to the *Republic*. The section on general works includes many books which discuss this dialogue at some length.

McKirahan, Richard D., Jr. *Plato and Socrates: A Comprehensive Bibliography*, 1958-1973. New York: Garland, 1977.

> The intent of this unannotated bibliography is to provide information on any scholarly work published on Plato and Socrates during the years 1958 through 1973. It is arranged topically. The works placed under each category are

arranged chronologically by author within each year. There are about 199 titles of books and periodical articles on *The Republic* listed. It also includes many general works that discuss at length this dialogue.

Nettleship, Richard Lewis. *Lectures on the Republic of Plato*. London: Macmillan, 1963.

This most scholarly and detailed discussion of the *Republic* was originally published in 1897, but continues to preserve its relevance and importance. The author argues that instead of being a book of political philosophy, the *Republic* is rather a book of moral philosophy. His thesis is that to Plato, one of the leading facts about human existence is that it can only be lived well in some form of organized community, of which the Greek considered the civic community to be the ideal form. The *Republic*, then, in his eyes, is not so much a blueprint for an eudaemonic utopia as it is a blueprint for the achievement of the morally good life.

Steintraeger, James

See Moore, Thomas

White, Nicholas P. *A Companion to Plato's Republic*. Indianapolis: Hackett, 1979.

This highly readable book attempts to lead the reader, step by step, into what the author believes is the main argument of the *Republic*: the discovery of what justice is, and why it is more beneficial, in some sense of the word, than injustice. The second part of the book consists of summaries of each of the ten books that comprise the *Republic*. Key sections of each book are summarized with explanatory and interpretive notes.

Rabelais, François

Rabelais, François. *Gargantua and Pantagruel*. 3 vols. 1900. Reprint. New York: AMS.

The second part of this five part satirical work recounts Pantagruel's trip to the Kingdom of Utopia (after passing several imaginary cities whose names mean "nothing" and "laughable") to defend its inhabitants, the Amaurotes (Greek for "the obscure ones"), against the Dipsodes (Greek for "thirsty ones"). After having defeated the Dipsodes, Pantagruel becomes the leader of the Amaurotes and leaves the over-populated utopia with many of the Amaurotes to settle in the realm of the Dipsodes. Although this novel lacks the political system of the usual utopian romance, and fails to recommend a blueprint of the good society, it provides a highly readable satire of the existing institutions, humbug and prejudices of the times.

Rand, Ayn

Rand, Ayn. *Anthem*. Caldwell, Id.: Caxton, 1966.

Like Zamyatin's *We*, this novel is a condemnation of collectivism and enforced conformism. It depicts an imaginary society in which citizens have numbers and their lives are planned and regimented. Equality 7-2521 and Liberty 5-3000 play the roles of transgressors. When Equality 7-2521 rediscovers electricity, his discovery is rejected by the World Council of Scholars and he is condemned to death for his intransigence. He escapes to the forest where later he is found by Liberty 5-3000. Together they discover in a mountain retreat, a relic of the "unmentionable times": the written record of the past, with the symbol of personhood—the first person singular. Like Zamytian's *We*, this is a paen for individualism, although it is unable to match the brilliance and literary beauty of *We*, and confuses individualism with elitist selfishness.

Saint-Simon, Henri

Saint-Simon, Henri. *Henri Saint-Simon (1760-1825): Selected Writings on Science, Industry and Social Organization.* Trans. and Ed. Keith Taylor. London: Croom Helm, 1975.

The editor's avowed aim is to provide a comprehensive and representative selection of texts. Extracts from less known works are also included. Most of the texts used have been translated from the six-volume *Oeuvres de Claude Henri de Saint-Simon* (Paris, 1966). The selected writings fall under the following categories: Part I. Science and the Progress of the Human Mind; II. Proposal for Post-War Reconstruction; III. From the Government of Men to the Administration of Things (1817-20); and Part IV. The True Christianity (1821-5). Part III will be by far the most appealing to those interested in Saint-Simon's utopian thought; but Ionescu's anthology (see) is preferable.

Dondo, M. M. *French Faust: Henri de Saint Simon.* New York: Philosophical Library, 1955.

The purpose of this study is to discuss in detail the life of Saint Simon, not his writings or the social theories derived from them. This is one of the first full-length biographical studies of the French thinker to be published in English. The biographer claims that like the German fictional prototype Faust, Saint Simon's most noticeable characteristic was a craving for knowledge. Although no biography of a thinker is expected to discuss in detail his ideas, attention should have been paid to them; hence Dondo's book is flawed. Nevertheless it should be required reading for those who would like to know the sort of person Saint Simon was.

Ionescu, Ghita, ed. *The Political Thought of Saint-Simon.* London: Oxford University Press, 1976.

This collection of Saint Simon's writings, emphasizing his political thought, focuses on those contributions that are bound to appeal to the educated layman. According to this editor, they show that Saint Simon's work is a theory of the system of the industrial-technological society, with special regard for its political organization. An excellent introductory essay makes this volume one of the most suited for beginning students of Saint Simon's works.

Manuel, Frank Edward. *New World of Henri Saint Simon.* Cambridge, Mass.: Harvard University Press, 1956.

One of the best biographical and critical surveys written on Saint Simon. It encompasses all the aspects of the man and his ideas. Saint Simon's place in the history of utopian thought, as well as his economic, political, ethical and religious views are adroitly covered in the expository part.

Simon, Walter, "History for Utopia: Saint-Simon and the Idea of Progress." *Journal of the History of Ideas* 17 (1956), 311-331.

Skinner, B. F.

Skinner, B. F. *Walden Two.* New York: Macmillan, 1948.

Walden Two is a non-competitive, collectivist community in the Mid-West. It is run on behaviorist lines by a psychological genius, Frazier, and controlled by social engineers—"Managers" and "Planners"—versed in the science of human behavior. The thousand participants live in phalanstery-like dwellings and are rewarded by a system of "labor credits" and "industrialized housewifery." Into this elysium come two G.I.'s, Steve and Rodge; Mary and Barbara, their sweethearts, Professor Burris, the narrator and Augustine Castle, a professor of philosophy suspected of "intuitionism, rationalism, or . . . Thomism." In the end, Steve and Mary are won by Walden and Burris struggles back to the Behaviorist

Shangri-La, persuaded that this experiment in personality-design is the best hope for establishing the good and harmonious society.

Skinner, Burrhus Frederick. "Utopianism. II The Design of Experimental Communities." In *International Encyclopedia of the Social Sciences*, David L. Stills, ed. New York: Macmillan, 1968, 271-275.

The famous behaviorist theoretician argues that any community design having as its goals the highest level of happiness, and the security and personal fulfillment of the potential members of the community, must consider what sort of behavior is most likely to contribute to these goals and how such a behavior can be generated. Not surprisingly, Skinner argues that positive reinforcement must play a crucial role in the mechanics of inter-personal relations within the community.

Freedman, Anne E. *The Planned Society: An Analysis of Skinner's Proposals*. Kalamazoo, Mich.: Behaviordelia, 1972.

Unit III of this work is devoted to a discussion of *Walden Two*. In it, the author presents a critique of the novel and the "absence of democracy" in Walden II, followed by a spirited defense of the role of democracy in society. The contents of the book are described in a straightforward and summary fashion, and the principles and government of the settlement are well analyzed.

Krutch, Joseph Wood. *The Measure of Man: On Freedom, Human Values, Survival and the Modern Temper*. Indianapolis: Bobbs-Merrill, 1954.

The author argues against all attempts to shape social values and conditions on the assumption that man's behavior is both predictable and controllable. He levels much of his attack against Skinner's account of society reflected in *Walden Two*. He contends that even if a society like *Walden Two* were possible, it would be morally undesirable because such a community would result in a dictatorship capable of molding a person in any way the rulers desired. He advocates that before any manipulative techniques are tried, there should first be some general agreement of the goals sought.

Swift, Jonathan

Swift, Jonathan, *Gulliver's Travels*. New York: Oxford University Press, 1977.

This is not, properly speaking, an utopian novel. It is rather a caustic social satire of the political life and values of Swift's England. However, one of the adventures described in the book—the discovery by Lemuel Gulliver of Houyhnhnmland, a nation of rational horses who lord over Yahoos, irrational human creatures—suggests that Swift looked with a jaundiced eye at the idea of human perfectibility. The Houyhnhnms have done away with wars and legal systems; friendship, benevolence and equality prevail in their midst, but they are deprived of pain, pleasure, lust and life-long attachments to members of the opposite sex. By endowing horses, and not human beings, with the capacity to create such a society and by suggesting that it can be achieved by passionless beings, Swift puts into question the possibility of a human utopia.

Brady, Frank, ed. *Twentieth Century Interpretations of Gulliver's Travels: A Collection of Critical Essays*. Englewood Cliffs, N.J.: Prentice-Hall, 1968.

Two contributions to this scholarly collection of essays on *Gulliver's Travels* deal specifically with the Houyhnhnms and the Yahoos, the creatures Gulliver discovers in his Fourth Voyage, which serve as foils for Swift's views on the nature of man and his ability to lead the sort of lives which would make possible the good society on the planet.

Crane, R. S. "The Houyhnhnms, the Yahoos, and the History of Ideas in *Reason and Imagination: Studies in the History of Ideas 1600-1800.* J. A. Mazee, ed. New York: Columbia University Press, 1962, 231-253.

The major consideration in this important study is Swift's reduction to absurdity of man's pretensions to being a rational creature, which had been taken for granted by the logicians of the time. This work is also reprinted in Brady'a anthology (see).

Eddy, William A. *Gulliver's Travels: A Critical Study.* Princeton, New Jersey: Princeton University Press, 1923.

This study, originally published as a dissertation, provides a detailed examination of each of the voyages of Gulliver.

Suits, Conrad "The Role of the Horses in 'A Voyage to the Houyhnhnms.' " *University of Toronto Quarterly* 34 (1965), 118-132.

Williams, Kathleen M. "Gulliver's Voyage to the Houyhnhnms." *Journal of English Literary History*, 18 (1951), 275-286.

Vonnegut, Kurt

Vonnegut, Kurt. *Player Piano*. Totowa, N.J. Scribner, 1952.

This is a novel about a future United States of America in which technocrats control human beings on the basis of the computer "Achievement and Aptitude Profiles." Satirical and often humorous, the story revolves around George Proteus, a brilliant thirty five year old administrator, his progressive disillusionment with the technocratic system and his revolt against it. Proteus and like-minded persons succeed and machinery in some cities is destroyed. But history repeats itself when the rebels, tinkering with the remnants of the machines manage to put them back together. The loss of human value is shown through a series of subplots linked to Proteus. By setting this novel in Ilium, New York, the author seems to contrast the faceless and regimented roles human beings will be asked to play in the America of the future with the heroic and unstratified Troy depicted by Homer. Although often regarded as science fiction, the anti-utopian message is unmistakable.

Mayo, Clark. *Kurt Vonnegut: The Gospel from Outer Space: Or, Yes We Have No Nirvanas*. San Bernardino, Ca.: Borgo Press, 1977.

This introductory and readable analysis of Vonnegut's best known works devotes several of its pages to *Player Piano*, Vonnegut's first novel. The author asserts that the plot is stolen from *Brave New World* and Zamyatin's *We*. Like these works, *Player Piano* is alleged to be a negative technological utopia concerned with the nature and destiny of man.

Schatt, Stanley. *Kurt Vonnegut, Jr.* Boston: Twayne, 1976.

In this highly readable study of Vonnegut's fiction, the author's avowed purpose has been to trace both the development of the writer's style and of his philosophy. Schatt believes that Vonnegut's medium is often closely related to his message. He traces Vonnegut's develoment from his earliest novels, including his anti-utopic *Player Piano*, to *Slapstick*. The reasons why Vonnegut chose in *Player Piano* to warn his readers about the possibilities of a nightmarish future will be better understood through the examination of Vonnegut's social vision. This work provides the means to achieve this understanding.

Wells, H. G.

Wells, H. G. *Men Like Gods*. New York: Macmillan, 1923.

This work expresses Wells' mature optimistic views about humanity's potentiality for perfecting itself and society. In his first work, *A Modern Utopia*, he did not regard as possible the immediate achievement of a perfect society and he asserted that there must always be a certain amount of tension, conflict, and waste in his World State. However, in the World State described in this book, nearly all of the moral constraints, coercion, and bureaucracy which dominated his first utopia have been eliminated. Set in another, more developed planet, this society is without an ultimate seat of sovereignty, laws as we know them, or private wealth. Decisions on any matter are made by a caste of knowledgeable and highly intelligent individuals called "samurais." Wells also contends that although man is an animal he is also the product of a long evolutive process as a result of which he has developed a need to gratify his natural impulses to love, play and learn.

Wells, H. G. *A Modern Utopia*. Lincoln, Neb.: Universtiy of Nebraska Press, 1967

This is the first utopian work to present a worldwide blueprint for society. Unlike other utopian writers, Wells denies in this work the possibility of achieving a perfect state, except perhaps after many generations of experimentation. He claims that "in Utopia there must also be friction, conflicts, and waste, but the waste will be enormously less than in our world." In this fascinating scheme, Wells has the World-State as the sole owner of the earth, with local governments working under it with delegated powers. He does not abolish private property or money for "a man without some negotiable property is a man without freedom." Unemployment is nonexistent, and all of the benefits of the contemporary welfare state are instituted. The World-State keeps a check on all the citizens of the planet by means of an elaborate indexing system in which all aspects of an individual's life are recorded. Undesirable genetic traits are controlled by means of eugenic measures. As in Plato's *Republic*, a governing class of guardians, the Samurai, govern but owe their positions neither to elections nor to a line of succession. The introduction by Mark R. Hillegas sheds considerable light on the aims of this work first published in 1905.

Wells, Herbert G. *New Worlds for Old*. London: Constable, 1908.

For those who would like to read most of Wells's utopian works, such as *Anticipations of the Reaction of Mechanical and Scientific Progress Upon Human Life and Thought* (1902), *The Discovery of the Future* (1913), *Tales of Space and Time* (1899), *When the Sleeper Wakes* (1899) and others, this collection will constitute quite a treat.

Bergonzi, Bernard. *The Early H. G. Wells: A Study of the Scientific Romances*. Manchester: Manchester University Press, 1961.

Several of Wells's minor utopian works are discussed in this study, e.g. *The Time Machine* and *When the Sleeper Wakes*. However, this study is primarily devoted to the "fin de siecle" literary features in Wells's romances.

Collins, Christopher

See Zamyatin, Eugene

Connelly, Wayne. H. G. Wells' 'The Time Machine': Its Neglected Mythos." *Riverside Quarterly*, 5 (1972), 178-191.

H. G. Wells Society. *H. G. Wells: A Comprehensive Bibliography*. London: H. G. Wells Society, 1966.

Hillegas, Mark R. *The Future as Nightmare: H. G. Wells and the Anti-Utopians*. Carbondale: Southern Illinois University Press, 1974.

This work is divided into two parts, with the first being devoted to a discussion of the futuristic works of H. G. Wells: *The Time Machine, The Island of Dr. Moreau,* "When the Sleeper Wakes" and "The First Men in the Moon," and others. The second part argues that the great anti-utopias of other contemporary writers are "both continuations of the imagination" of H. G. Wells and reactions against that imagination. The conclusion focuses on Huxley's *Brave New World*, Orwell's *Nineteen Eighty-Four* and Evgenii Zamyatin's *We*, and other anti-utopian works, in order to bring out the literary debt that these writers owe to Wells's fictional utopianism.

Hyde, William J. "The Socialism of H. G. Wells in the Early Twentieth Century." *Journal of the History of Ideas* 17 (April 1956), 217-234.

Raknem, Ingvald. *H. G. Wells and His Critics*. Oslo: Universitiesforlaget, 1962.

Wilde, Oscar

Wilde, Oscar. "The Soul of Man Under Socialism." In *Complete Works of Oscar Wilde*, edited by Vyvyan Holland, London: Collins, 1948.

Wilde's concern in this essay is with a type of socialism based on individualism, voluntary associations, and the development of human beings through art. In this society, work would be done by machines. He seems to have derived this idea from William Morris' *News From Nowhere*. Wilde also addresses himself to what he regards as the evils of capitalism and government: the thwarting of individual potential for aesthetic self-realization.

Ericksen, Donald H. *Oscar Wilde*. Boston: Twayne, 1977.

This study devotes five pages to the analysis of the "The Soul of Man Under Socialism." The author argues that Wilde's essay is neither about the soul nor about socialism. Rather it is concerned with individualism and art. If the world depicted in this essay seems utopian, the critic points out, is because a world that does not include utopias is not worth our concern. This analysis proposes that Wilde's utopian vision has more in common with anarchism than with Marxian socialism.

Nicholas, Brian. "Two Nineteenth-Century Utopias: The Influence of Renan's 'L'Avenir de la science' on Wilde's 'The Soul of Man Under Socialism.'" *Modern Language Review*, 59 (1964), 361-370.

Winstanley, Gerrard

Winstanley, Gerrard. *The Law of Freedom in a Platform: or True Magistracy Restored*. New York: Schocken Books, 1973.

By no means a literary utopia in the tradition of Thomas Moore or Tommaso Campanella, this work was designed as a blueprint for immediate and practical reform. The author argues for a commonwealth without lawyers, magistrates, or private ownership of the means of production. He would place government in the hands of popular representatives elected on a yearly basis and allow no person to own more land than he can labor himself. The blueprint had some disquieting features, however. Capital punishment, retributive justice ("an eye for an eye . . .") and even slavery are prescribed as punishment for criminals. A 46 page scholarly introduction to the work is provided by Robert W. Kenny.

Petegorsky, David W. *Left-Wing Democracy in the English Civil War: A Study of the Social Philosophy of Gerrard Winstanley*. New York: Haskell House, 1972.

This book, originally presented as a doctoral dissertation, supports the thesis that one of the most arresting chapters in the early history of socialism was that written by Winstanley and the Diggers Movement during the Civil War in the XVII century. The author succinctly shows that "Winstanley's Utopia" was a constitutional and institutional organization of a new social order in which private ownership of the means of production was to be abolished, commerce rigidly restricted and money rendered obsolete, for the socialized product was to be freely distributed. The comparison of Winstanley's ideas with those of other utopian thinkers does much to deepen the understanding of this English precursor of communism.

Wolfe, Bernard

Wolfe, Bernard. *Limbo*. New York: Random House, 1952.

This work has been hailed by some critics as the only American dystopian novel worthy of comparison with Zamyatin's *We* and Huxley's *Brave New World*. Dr. Martine, a neurosurgeon exiled to the tropical island of the Mandunji since 1972, returns to civilization where his isolation is disturbed by unwanted visitors. On his return to the Inland Strip (the remnant of the United States remaining after World War III), he finds that the humorous notes he once took about the way to achieve a pacifist society have been taken seriously by Martine's colleague, Helder, and by Theo, his confederate, the present rulers of the society. In this futurist setting, social peace is achieved by means of brain surgery, repression of "potential" killers, and a transposition of sexuality.

Geduld, Carolyn. *Bernard Wolfe*. New York: Twayne, 1972.

This is an elegantly written study of Wolfe's "archetypal" novels: *Really the Blues, Limbo*, and *The Great Prince Died*. Chapter three is devoted to an extensive analysis of *Limbo*, which the author labels utopian science fiction. The themes of ambivalence, masochism and humor are carefully probed. The author concludes that psychic masochism is the most crucial element in Wolfe's dystopia and that an understanding of this neurosis remains a point of reference for unraveling the meaning of the novel.

Zamyatin, Eugene

Zamyatin, Eugene. *We*. Gregory Zilboorg, tr. Boston, Mass.: Gregg, 1975.

In this dystopian novel about a futurist United We, the citizens no longer have names, only numbers. Sealed off from nature in a transparent, glass-enclosed city, they function as anonymous parts of an impersonal social mechanism. The action evolves around D-503's fall from the state of perfection and his apostasy from the worship of the Well-Doer, brought about by I-330, a female leader of Mephi (a subversive group named after Mephisto), whose goal is to demolish the glass wall, so that numbers may be reunited with nature. Although successful in demolishing part of the glass wall, our hero is captured, lobotomized and turned into a meek number who in the end watches approvingly as I-330 is tortured to death by the Well-Doer. *We* is the quintessential example of the best in this literary genre.

Brown, Edward James. *Brave New World, 1984, and We; An Essay on Anti-Utopia*. (Zamyatin and English Literature). Ann Arbor, Mich.: Ardis, 1976.

> This short study attempts to deal with Zamyatin and his work as an important figure of contemporary literature, to "indicate the nature of his thematic interest and stylistic behavior, and to trace certain key terms through his own work and that of the English writers who have an affinity with him." The relationship of his work to that of H.G. Wells is briefly indicated. A three page bibliography of works by and about Zamyatin enhances the value of this handy introduction to his work.

Collins, Christopher. "Zamyatin, Wells and the Utopian Literary Tradition." *Slavonic and East European Review* 44 (1966), 351-360

Connors, James. "Zamyatin's *We* and the Genesis of *1984*." *Modern Fiction Studies* 21 (1975), 107-124

Fischer, Peter Alfred. "A Tentative New Critique of E. I. Zamjatin." Ph.D. dissertation, Harvard University, 1967.

Shane, Alex M. *The Life and Work of Evenij Zamyatinj*. Berkeley: University of California, 1968.

> This study examines Zamyatin's role in Soviet literary circles from 1917 to 1931 and his contribution to Soviet literature. The major themes of his literary creations, including that of *We*, are elucidated. A lengthy bibliography includes his published works, translations, critical reviews, as well as other items.

Zola, Emile

Zola, Emile. *Work. Travail*: A Novel. New York: Harper, 1901.

> The main character of the novel, Luke, comes to La Crêcherie to give advice to the owner of the blast furnace, Monsieur Jordan, concerning the sale of the property to a competitor. In the process he manages to persuade Monsieur Jordan to establish a Fourierian cooperative, which fluorishes and eventually controls all the industry and business in its district, and ultimately in all of France. The novel, in addition to trying to show the nobility of work and the advantages that cooperative labor reaps on individuals and society as a whole, is the clearest and most notable exposition in fiction of Fourier's scheme of social reorganization. The objective of *Work* is to point to the need to reorganize modern industrial society along the lines proposed by Fourier. In such a society, Zola believed, there would be social equality combined with individual freedom to develop as human beings and as members of the social group.

Case, Frederick Ivor. *La cité ideale dans Travail d'Emile Zola*. Toronto: University of Toronto Press, 1974.

> The author attempts to apply sociological analysis to Zola's novel: to study the social conditions that led to its creation in order to show that the Crêcherie of the novel is the product of the imagination of a writer living at the turn of the century. He argues that *Travail/Work* is profoundly rooted in the French reality of the times and can be fully understood in the context of a historical assessment of the French proletariat and Zola's determinism and social conscience. At the same time, the author avoids any hypothesis concerning the origin of the novel that depends entirely on a subjective reading of Zola's biographies. This is, without doubt, the most recent and important study devoted to Zola's novel. It is hoped that an English translation will soon appear of this important work.

Roberts, Alfred Dominic. *Zola and Fourier*. Ph.D. dissertation, university of Pennsylvania, 1959.

The concern of this dissertation is with the question of when in his career, and in what manner, Zola became acquainted with Fourier's utopian doctrine, as well as the extent to which this doctrine entered into his literary work. The author maintains that with *Travail/Work*, Fourierism is worked into the fabric of the novel to such an extent, that it becomes almost a fictional transposition of Fourier's philosophy. As a consequence of this transposition, he concludes, the novel is artistically inferior to Zola's earlier works.

Notes

1 Paradise and Golden Age

1 This unattested but plausible scene is set in Mesopotamia during the early Babylonian era, about the reign of Hammurabi. A simplified chronology of Mesopotamian civilization runs thus: Ubaidians 4500 B.C., Sumerians 3500, Akkadians 2300, Babylonians 2000, Assyrians 1000, Chaldeans 600; in 539 Cyrus the Persian took Babylon, and in 330 it fell to Alexander. General reference: Samuel Noah Kramer, *The Sumerians: Their History, Culture, and Character* (Chicago: University of Chicago Press, 1963); A. Leo Oppenheim, *Ancient Mesopotamia* (Chicago: University of Chicago Press, 1964).

2 I.e., the Euphrates; Buranun was the name borrowed from the Ubaidians by the Sumerians.

3 The tablet was excavated from the ancient site of Nippur; it was copied and published by Stephen Langdon as "Sumerian Epic of Paradise," *Publications of the Babylonian Section*, 10.1 (Philadelphia: University of Pennsylvania, 1915). This excerpt is based on lines 5-24 of Samuel Noah Kramer's translation in *Ancient Near Eastern Texts Relating to the Old Testament*, ed. James Pritchard, 3rd ed. (Princeton: Princeton University Press, 1969), p. 38.

4 The bibliography of mythology is extensive and the various competing theories are tempting. I would suggest, therefore, that one turn first to the reasonably objective and cautious approach of G.S. Kirk, *Myth: Its Meaning in Ancient and Other Cultures* (Cambridge: Cambridge University Press, 1970) and *The Nature of Greek Myths* (Baltimore: Penguin Books, 1974), esp. Chap. 1, "Problems of Definition," and Chap. 3, "Five Monolithic Theories," whence one may proceed to appropriate works by Lang, Jung, Lévi-Strauss, Cassirer, Malinowski, Eliade, et al.

5 Mircea Eliade, *Cosmos and History: The Myth of the Eternal Return,* trans. W.R. Trask (1954; reprinted., Princeton: Princeton University Press, 1971), esp. Chap. 3.

6 Father Abraham came from Ur of the Chaldees c. 1800 B.C.; the Babylonian Captivity extended from 586-538. For a survey of the Mesopotamian relationship to the *Genesis* creation see S.H. Hooke, *Middle Eastern Mythology* (Baltimore: Penguin Books, 1963), pp. 105-117; cf. Louis F. Hartman and J. Henschen, "Paradise," *Encyclopedic Dictionary of the Bible* (New York: McGraw-Hill, 1962) and Alexander Heidel, *The Babylonian Genesis*, 2nd ed. (Chicago: University of Chicago Press), Chaps. 2-3, *passim*. One must bear in mind that the *Genesis* account is an amalgam of two traditions, Canaanite as well as Mesopotamian. Paradise as the source of rivers does not fit well with a Mesopotamian Dilmun, but it does match the mountainous picture in Ugaritic texts which place the god El at a distant northern source of rivers; cf. "God's holy hill" (Ezekiel 28:14, 16).

7 E.g., Ashtoreth/Astarte of the Phoenicians, Asherah of the Canaanites, and Cybele of the Phrygians; see Joseph Campbell, *The Masks of God: Occidental Mythology*

(1964; reprint ed., New York: Penguin Books, 1976), pp. 9-17; also John H. Armstrong, *The Paradise Myth* (London: Oxford University Press, 1969), pp. 15-36.

8   Mythical Eden and mythical Dilmun are not to be confused or identified with places by the same names known to the ancients; see, e.g., Geoffrey Bibby, *Looking for Dilmun* (New York: Alfred A. Knopf, 1969).

9   The *Vidēvdāt (Vendīdād)* is the last book of the *Avesta* ("Text"?), the bible of Persian Zoroastrianism; the *Avesta* was written between 600 B.C. and A.D. 400, the *Zend* ("Interpretation") was added A.D. 200-900; included are the *Yashts*, or "Hymns" to angels and heroes; all of which see below.

10   Literal translation from Hebrew Massoritic text; cf. *New English Bible* (Oxford and Cambridge, 1970).

11   For an analysis of the most respected presentation of the Indo-European theory see G. Scott Littleton, *The New Comparative Mythology: An Anthropological Assessment of the Theories of Georges Dumézil* (Berkeley: University of California Press, 1966).

12   Pausanias, fl. A.D. 150, wrote a ten-book *Description of Greece*. The name Elysium is of unknown origin; see below, n. 14. For a general discussion of paradises as rewards for the dead, see "Blest, Abode of the," *Encyclopaedia of Religion and Ethics*, ed. James Hastings (New York: Charles Scribner's Sons, 1924).

13   The composition of the Homeric poems is now assigned to the latter seventh century B.C. This and other literal translations from the Greek, including the New Testament, are mine.

14   Robert Graves, *The Greek Myths* (Baltimore: Penguin Books, 1960), I, 123-124, holds that Avalon and Elysium derive from the same root and would have them mean "Apple Land." Graves's interpretations have met with due criticism; still, one can't help but recall Heracles' adventure to fetch the golden apples from the garden of the Hesperides, the "Daughters of the West"—where a dragon guards the apple tree (Euripides *Heracles Mad* 394-399).

15   Hesiod's moralistic farmer's almanac, the *Works and Days*, is less important to mythologists than his *Theogony*.

16   Written c. 900 B.C., one of the four *Vedas* ("Wisdoms") which have served as a bible for the Brahmanic and Hindu religions; by tradition, the priest Atharvan instituted fire worship.

17   Eliade, pp. 112-115.

18   Hesiod's Roman counterpart Ovid respects the symmetry of the original myth of four ages (*Metamorphoses* 1.89-150).

19   Mercury, Venus, Moon, Sun, Mars, Jupiter, Saturn.

20   See n. 9.

21   *Precession*, because the constellations turn in a direction against the zodiacal *pro-cession*. See Giorgio de Santillana and Hertha von Dechend, *Hamlet's Mill: An Essay on Myth and the Frame of Time* (Boston: Gambit, 1969), esp. pp. 58-68; also Campbell, *The Masks of God: Oriental Mythology* (1962; New York: Penguin Books, 1976), pp. 117-121. It so happened that the Age of Pisces was introduced in 6 B.C. (a more likely date for the birth of Jesus) by a conjunction of Saturn and Jupiter; recall the celestial phenomena in Kubrick's *Space Odyssey: 2001.*

22   Publis Vergilius Maro (70-19 B.C.), greatest of the Roman poets, best known for his *Aeneid;* the *Eclogues* ("Selections") were published in 37 B.C., a few years before Octavian's acquisition of supreme power.

23   See Gilbert Highet, *The Classical Tradition* (New York: Oxford University Press, 1957), pp. 72-74.

24   Hesperia, "Evening Land," was the name given it by Greeks *(Aeneid* 1.530); Italy's remoteness and untried fruitfulness were stuff that exotic fantasies were made of; see n. 14 above.

25   For the legend see Livy 1.7.

26   One of two poems called the *Einsiedeln Eclogues,* from a tenth-century MS published in 1869.

27   For those with Italian, I recommend Arturo Grof, *Miti, legende e superstizioni del Medio Evo,* Vol. 1 (1892; reprint ed., New York: Burt Franklin, 1971), "Il Mito de paradiso terrestre."

2   Place in No Place

1   William Morris, ed., *American Heritage Dictionary* (New York: American Heritage Publishing Company, 1969), p. 1411.

2   Myron P. Gilmore, *The World of Humanism, 1453-1517* The Rise of Modern Europe (New York: Harper Torchbook, 1962), p. 137.

3   Sir Thomas More, *Utopia,* trans. and ed. Robert M. Adams (New York: W.W. Norton, 1975), p. 51.

4   Edward Surtz, S.J., *The Praise of Pleasure* (Cambridge: Harvard University Press, 1957), pp. 151-152.

5   Ibid., p. 182.

6   More, p. 41.

7   Ibid., p. 49.

8   Ibid., p. 40.

9   Ibid., p. 64.

10   B.F. Skinner, *Walden Two* (New York: Macmillan, 1948; reprint ed., 1976), p. 54.

11   More, p. 50.

12   Surtz, p. 5.

13   Ibid., p. 193.

14   C.S. Lewis, *English Literature in the Sixteenth Century Excluding Drama* The Oxford History of English Literature, Vol. III (Oxford: The Clarendon Press, 1954), p. 168.

15   More, p. 65.

16   Ibid., p. 73.

17   Ibid., p. 91.

18   Skinner, p. 162.

19   Ibid., pp. v-xvi.

20   Nathaniel Hawthorne, *The Blithedale Romance* (New York: W.W. Norton, 1958), pp. 87-88.

21   Richard Chase, *The American Novel and Its Tradition* (Garden City, New York: Anchor-Doubleday, 1957), p. 84.

22   Lewis, p. 168.

3   Illusions of Endless Affluence

1   Richard Leakey and Roger Lewin, *Origins* (New York: E.P. Dutton, 1977), p. 248.

2   Adam Smith, *An Inquiry into the Wealth of Nations*, Vol. I (Homewood, Illinois: Richard D. Irwin, 1963), p. 65.

3   Karl Marx, "Economic and Philosophical Manuscripts," in *Marx-Engels Collected Works*, Vol. III (New York: International Publishers, 1975), p. 275.

4   Karl Marx, *Grundrisse*, trans. Martin Nicolaus (Baltimore: Penguin Books, 1973), p. 492.

5   Karl Marx, *Capital*, Vol. I (New York: International Publishers, 1967), p. 179.

6   Maurice Dobb, *Theories of Value and Distribution Since Adam Smith* (Cambridge: Cambridge University Press, 1973), p. 143. Note the apparent contradiction in Marx's treatment of nature. On the one hand humanity is a part of nature—so that there can be no irreconcilable conflict—and on the other, the development of human forces of production raises *homo sapiens* above nature, annexing passive nature to human purposes.

7   Marx, *Grundrisse*, p. 705.

8   Thomas Robert Malthus, *An Essay on the Principle of Population* (Baltimore: Penguin Books, 1970), pp. 23-24.

9   Ibid., p. 75.

10 Ibid. The 25-year doubling period is accounted for by Malthus's assumption of a 3 percent annual growth rate in population.

11 Ibid., p. 106. This is the type of concept that forms the bulwark of stationary-state reasoning, although Malthus seemed ignorant of such implications. For a general discussion of the stock-flow distinction and the stationary state, see Kenneth Boulding, "The Economics of the Coming Spaceship Earth," in *Economic Growth Versus the Environment*, Warren Johnson and John Hardesty, eds. (Belmont, CA: Wadsworth Publishing Co., 1971). Many examples of the use of this reasoning are possible. Just as the number of fish in an oceanic reservoir is stable or varies in relationship to the reproduction rate versus the annual fish catch, so too can the carrying capacity of the ecosphere be thought of as a finite reservoir. If effluents pour in faster than the natural ability to detoxify wastes, the carrying capacity will eventually be overwhelmed and collapse. This concept is applicable even to our stock of fossil fuels which comprise a great reservoir which is being augmented through an infinitely slow process. When it is drawn down to zero, only the flow of energy from the sun, the tides, and the radioactivity of the earth will remain.

12 John Stuart Mill, *Principles of Political Economy* (New York: Green and Company, 1929), pp. 750-751.

13 Ernest Mandel, *Marxist Economic Theory*, Vol. II (New York: Monthly Review Press, 1970), p. 618.

14 J.M. Keynes, "Economic Possibilities for Our Grandchildren," in *Essays in Persuasion*, excerpted in Johnson and Hardesty, eds. (Belmont, California: Wadsworth Publishing, 1971), p. 192.

15 Ibid., pp. 192-193.

16   Geophysicist M. King Hubbert estimates that 50 percent of all the oil the coterminous United States will ever produce was already out of the ground by 1966. Hubbert, "Energy Resources," in *Environment: Resources, Pollution, and Society*, William W. Murdoch, ed. (Sunderland, Maryland: Sinauer Associates, 1971), pp. 102-103.

17   Paul R. Ehrlich, Anne H. Ehrlich, and John P. Holdren, *Human Ecology* (San Francisco: W.H. Freeman, 1973), p. 10.

18   Herbert Marcuse, "The End of Utopia," in *Five Lectures* (Boston: Beacon Press, 1970), p. 63.

4   The Russian Utopia

1   Revelation 21:4. Both Christ's millennium and God's post-millennial abode on earth were considered periods of beatitude. For the sake of convenience and because of standard usage, the term millennium will be employed for the entire post-historic era.

2   Revelation 19:20-21.

3   Hugh Seton-Watson, *The Russian Empire, 1801-1917* (London: Oxford University Press, 1967), p. 363.

4   Vladimir Weidle, *Russia: Absent and Present*, trans. by A. Gordon Smith (New York: Vintage Books, 1961), p. 86.

5   See Sergei Zenkovsky, *Russkoe starobriadchestvo* (Munchen: Vilhelm Fink Verlag, 1970), pp. 28-40. Sergei Bulgakov, *Pravoslavie* (Paris: Y.M.C.A. Press, 1965), pp. 70-79. James H. Billington, *The Icon and the Axe: An Interpretive History of Russian Culture* (New York, Alfred A. Knopf, 1966), pp. 54-77. Paul Miliukov, *Outlines of Russian Culture*, Part I: *Religion and the Church*, trans. by Valentine Ughet and Eleanor Davis (New York: A.S. Barnes and Company, Inc., 1960), pp. 42-46. V.V. Zenkovsky, *A History of Russian Philosophy*, trans. by George L. Kline (London: Routledge & Kegan Paul Ltd, 1953), pp. 26-27, 37, 41-42.

6   Norman Cohn, *The Pursuit of the Millennium: Revolutionary Millenarians and Mystical Anarchists of the Middle Ages* (New York: Oxford University Press, 1974), p. 29. Billington, *Icon and Axe*, pp. 55-56.

7   Billington, *Icon and Axe*, pp. 49-52. Miliukov, *Religion*, pp. 9-14.

8   G.P. Fedotov, *The Russian Religious Mind* (New York: Harper & Brothers, 1960), pp. 3-20, 385-86. B.D. Grekov, *The Culture of Kiev Rus*, trans. by Pauline Rose (Moscow: The Foreign Languages Publishing House, 1947), pp. 35-42.

9   Michael Cherniavsky, *Tsar & People: Studies in Russian Myths* (New York: Random House, 1969), pp. 30-39.

10 Cherniavsky, *Tsar & People*, pp. 36-43.

11 V.V. Zenkovsky, *Russian Philosophy*, I, pp. 47-48.

12 Miliukov, *Religion*, p.117.

13 Ibid., pp. 77-121.

14 Paul Avrich, *Russian Rebels, 1600-1800* (New York: Schocken Books, 1972), p. 86.

15 K.V. Chistov, *Russkie narodnye sotsial'no-utopicheskie legendy* (Moskva: Izdatel'stvo "Nauka," 1967), pp. 78-91, 327-40.

16 I. Shchipanov, ed., *Izbrannye sotsial'no-politicheskie i filosofskie proizvediia Dekabristov*, 3 vols. (Moscow: State Publisher of Political Literature, 1951), I, pp. 296-329.

17 Shchipanov, *Proizvedeniia Dekabristov*, II, pp. 75-162.

18 The most succinct treatment in English is still probably N.V. Riasanovsky, *Russia and the West in the Teaching of the Slavophiles: A Study of Romantic Ideology* (Gloucester, Mass.: Peter Smith, 1965).

19 The definitive study of Populism remains Franco Venturi, *Roots of Revolution: A History of the Populist and Socialist Movements in Nineteenth Century Russia* (New York: Alfred A. Knopf, 1960).

20 See V.A. Desnitskii, ed., *Dela petrashevtsev* (3 vols; Moscow-Leningrad: Academy of Sciences, 1937), I, pp. 5-196.

21 Riasanovsky, *Russia and the West*, p. 85.

22 A.I. Gertsen, *Sobranie sochinenii* (30 vols.; Moscow: Academy of Sciences, 1955), VI, pp. 58-59.

23 Quoted from E.H. Carr, *Michael Bakunin* (New York: Vintage Books, 1961), pp. 116-117.

24 V.E. Egrafov, ed., *Filosofskie i obshchestvenn-politicheskie proizvedeniia petrashevtsev* (Moskva: Gospolitizdat, 1953), pp. 330-331.

25 Desnitskii, *Delo*, II, p. 89.

26 Ibid., II, p. 89.

27 V. Burtsev, *Za sto let, 1800-1896: Sbornik po istorii politicheskikh i obshchvennykh dvizhenii v Rossii* (The Hague, Europe Printing, 1965), p. 45.

28   E. Lampert, *Sons against Fathers: Studies in Russian Radicalism and Revolution* (Oxford: Clarendon Press, 1965), 238-39. Seton-Watson, *Russian Empire*, p. 364.

29   Seton-Watson, *Russian Empire*, p. 364.

30   Lampert, *Sons against Fathers*, pp. 184-85. See also B.P. Kozmin (ed.), *N.G. Chernyshevskii: Polnoe sobranie sochinenii* (15 vols.; Moscow: State Publisher of Fine Literature, 1939), I, p. 357.

31   Lampert, *Sons against Fathers*, p. 182.

32   Burtsev, *Za sto let*, pp. 94-95.

33   Ibid., p. 175.

34   N.F. Belchikov, *Dostoevskii v protsesse petrashevtsev* (Moscow-Leningrad: Academy of Sciences, 1936), p. 79.

35   F.M. Dostoevskii, *Dnevnik pisatelia za 1877 god* (Paris: Y.M.C.A. Press, n.d.), p. 337.

36   Avrich, *Russian Rebels*, p. 269.

37   Oliver Radkey, *Agrarian Foes of Bolshevism* (New York: Columbia University Press, 1962), pp. 3-46.

38   Riasanovsky, *History of Russia*, p. 528.

39   The Bolshevik (meaning "majority") faction of the Russian Social Democratic Labor Party was formed in 1903. On March 8, 1918, the Bolsheviks assumed the name of Communist Party. Both designations have been popularly used since that time.

40   A good summary is found in Nicholas S. Timasheff, *The Great Retreat: The Growth and Decline of Communism in Russia* (New York: E.P. Dutton & Company, Inc., 1946). Also see Alex Inkeles and Kent Geiger, *Soviet Society: A Book of Readings* (Boston: Houghton Mifflin Company, 1961).

41   Karl Marx, "Communist Manifesto," *Contemporary Civilization in the West*, 2 vols. (New York and London: Columbia University Press, 1961), II, p. 687.

42   See Alex Nove, "Is the Soviet Union a Welfare State?" in Inkeles and Geiger, *Soviet Society*, pp. 500-10.

43   Riasanovsky, *History of Russia*, p. 551.

44   *United Nations Statistical Yearbook, 1977* (New York: United Nations, 1978).

45   A joke that the present writer heard when doing graduate study at Leningrad University in 1966-67.

46   Eugene Zamiatin, *We*, trans. and foreword by Gregory Zilboorg (New York: E.P. Dutton & Co., Inc., 1952), pp. 12-13.

47   Ibid., p. 215.

48   Andrei Amalrik, *Will the Soviet Union Survive Until 1984* (New York and Evanston: Harper & Row, Publishers, 1970), p. 46.

49   Ibid., p. 64.

50   Ibid., p. 65.

51   Alexander Solzhenitsyn, "The Exhausted West," *Harvard Magazine* (July-August, 1978), p. 24.

5   Auguste Comte and the Positivist Utopia

* The writing of this essay was partially underwritten by a fellowship from the Institute of American Culture at the University of California, Los Angeles. The support of the Institute is gratefully acknowledged.

1   For a good biography of Comte, see Henri Gouhier, *La vie d'Auguste Comte*, 2nd revised edition (Paris: Librarie Philosophique J. Vrin, 1965). For a briefer account, see W.M. Simon, *European Positivism in the Nineteenth Century* (Ithaca, New York: Cornell University Press, 1963), pp 3-18; and Frank Manuel, *The Prophets of Paris* (Cambridge, Massachusetts: Harvard University Press, 1962), pp. 251-296.

2   Auguste Comte, *Cours de philosophie positive*, 5th edition, 6 volumes (Paris: Schleicher Frères, Éditeurs, 1907); *Système de politique positive*, 4 volumes (Paris: Librarie Scientifique Industrielle de L. Mathias, 1851. Reprinted in Paris by Éditions Anthropos, 1969). For the English translations of the relevant passages of the *Cours* and the *Système*, see *Auguste Comte and Positivism*, edited with an introduction by Gertrude Lenzer (New York: Harper Torchbooks, 1975). Unfortunately, she uses Harriet Martineau's abridged and *freely* interpreted translation of the *Cours*. For a more accurate translation of some of the more important passages of the *Cours*, see *The Essential Comte*, edited with an introduction by Stanislav Andreski, translated by Margaret Clarke (London: Croom Helm, 1974). An excellent introduction to Comte is his *Discours sur l'esprit positif*, Introduction and notes by Paul Arbousse-Bastide, Colection 10/18 (Paris: Union Générale d'Editions, 1963). For the earliest exposition of these ideas we have to go back to the 1822 pamphlet, "Plan des travaux scientifiques nécessaires pour réorganiser la société," which was reprinted in an appendix to vol IV of the *Système*. See Lenzer, *Auguste Comte and Positivism*, pp. 9-67.

3   Comte, *Cours*, 1:11-14 (76-77), 4:167ff. (223ff.). Numbers in parenthesis refer to the Lenzer edition. See also H.B. Acton, "Comte's Positivism and the Science of Society," *Philosophy* 26 (1951): 291-310, and Harry Elmer Barnes, "The Social and Political Philosophy of Auguste Comte: Positivist Utopia and the Religion of Humanity," in *An Introduction to the History of Sociology*, edited by H.E. Barnes (Chicago: University of Chicago Press, 1948), pp. 81-109. For Comte as a sociologist, as seen by a disciple, see F.S. Marvin, *Comte, the Founder of Sociology* (New York: Russell & Russell, 1965).

4   Comte, *Cours*, 1:1-63, passim (71-101).

5   In this respect, see Manual, *Prophets of Paris*, where he discusses the views of Saint-Simon, Condorcet, Fourier, Turgot and other predecessors and contemporaries of Comte.

6   Comte, *Discours*, 55-91. For the laws of structure and the methods of statics, *Cours* 1:323-355 (123-125); for the laws of change and the methods of dynamics, *Cours* 1:356-380 (125-127). For their extension to "the social science" *Cours* 4:167-68 (223-24). An extended discussion of social statics can be found in *Cours* 4:283-327 (263-278). For social dynamics, *Cours* 4:328-87 (279-97).

7   Comte, "Plan des travaux," in Lenzer, *Auguste Comte and Positivism*, p. 29. In the *Cours*, the law is introduced in 1:2 (72), and in the *Système* at 1:33 (328). For the historical antecedents to the law of the three stages, see George Boas, *French Philosophies of the Romantic Period* (New York: Russell & Russell, 1964), pp. 264-76. See Acton, "Comte's Positivism," pp. 292-93; M. Mandelbaum, *History, Man and Reason: A Study of Nineteenth Century Thought* (Baltimore: Johns Hopkins Press, 1971), pp. 63-65; T. Whittaker, *Comte and Mill* (New York: Dodge Publishing Co., n.d.), pp. 21-28.

8   *Cours*, 4:330-33 (280-81).

9   *Cours*, 1:4 (73); also 4:331 (280-81).

10   *Cours*, 1:8-9 (75).

11   *Cours*, 1:30-1 (85-6); *Discours*, pp. 74-75.

12   *Cours*, 1:35 (88); *Discours*, p. 82.

13   *Système*, 1:2 (317).

14   "Plan des travaux," in Lenzer, *Auguste Comte and Positivism*, p. 47; *Discours*, pp. 178, 187; *Système*, 4:17-18 (453). Also Lenzer, Introduction to *Auguste Comte and Positivism*, p. lvii.

15   Barnes, "Social and Political Philosophy of Comte," pp. 97-103.

16   *Système*, 1:164-66, 1:194-97. For Comte's views on education, 1:171-78.

17   *Système*, 1:375 (387-88).

18   *Système*, 2:412. "Le travail ne peut jamais manquer," *Système*, 4:455.

19   *Système*, 1:204-274. For the function of animals, see *Système*, 1:612, 3:105, 4:142.

20   Coming from a man whose merits were never recognized, and who felt that a wall of silence had been built around his works, the psychological inferences are tempting.

21   *Système*, 1:167-68 (364).

22   *Système*, 1:124-25; 2:294, 320:415-16; 4:306.

23   *Système*, 4:20.

24   *Système*, 1:92-97 (337-339). Quote on p. 92 (337).

25   *Système*, 1:164-65 (362-63).

26   In this respect, see the Comte-Henry Edger correspondence, R.L. Hawkins, *Positivism in the United States 1853-1861* (Cambridge, Mass.: Harvard University Press, 1938), passim. Edger was the first full convert in the United States.

27   Classics such as the *Iliad* and the *Odyssey* (in one volume, without any notes), Virgil, Dante, Cervantes, select plays of Shakespeare, Molière, *Tom Jones*, select works of Byron (Don Juan is to be suppressed), Goethe, *The Arabian Nights*, Descartes' *Geometry* followed by Auguste Comte's *Analytical Geometry*, *The Theory of Functions* by Lagrange, the *Chemistry* of Lavoisier, Duméril's *Natural History*, Hume's histories of England and his philosophical essays, Tacitus, Leonardo's *Treatise on Painting*, *The Koran*, Bacon's *Novum Organon*, Diderot's "Essay on the Beautiful," followed by Barthez's *Theory of the Beautiful*, Cabanis's *The Relation Between Man's Physical and Moral Natures*, and *The Positive Philosophy of Auguste Comte*, condensed by H. Martineau, to give a few examples. Altogether, there are about 150 entries that, while dated, are, nonetheless, fascinating. Lenzer, *Auguste Comte and Positivism*, pp. 477-480.

28   Among these we have Moses, Homer, Aristotle, Archimedes, Caesar, St. Paul, Charlemagne, Dante, Gutenberg, Shakespeare, Descartes, Frederic II, Bichat, representing the thirteen months of the calendar. Less prominently, Buddha, Mohammed, Aristophanes, Virgil, Socrates, Plato, Galen, Alexander, St. Augustine, St. Francis of Assisi, Milton, Columbus, Mozart, Kant, Hume, Cromwell, Galileo, Newton, Lamarck, Gall, etc. representing the days of the year. Adding alternative names for leap years, the list names over 560 "saints." Lenzer, *Auguste Comte and Positivism*, pp. 472-73.

29   *Système*, 4:88 (462).

30   Important means of positivist diffusion were the various journals published around the world. In Paris, *La revue occidentale, philosophique, sociale et politique*, (1878-1914) edited by Pierre Laffitte, Emile Littré and G. Wyrouboff's *La philosophie positive* (1867-1884); in Brazil, *O Positivismo*, edited by T. Braga and J. de Mattos (1879-1892); in Mexico *La revista positiva, científica, filosófica, so-*

cial y política, (1901-1914), edited by Horacio Barreda and Augustín Aragón; in England, *The Positivist Review*, (1893-1906) edited by E.S. Beesly, among the most important.

31   Compare John Edwin McGee, *A Crusade for Humanity: The History of Organized Positivism in England*, (London: Watts & Company, 1931), with Leopoldo Zea, *Positivism in Mexico*, translated by J. Schulte, (Austin, Texas: University of Texas Press, 1974). For the dimensions of the movement in Latin America see Leopoldo Zea, *The Latin American Mind*, translated by J. Abbott and L. Dunham, (Norman, Oklahoma: University of Oklahoma Press, 1963).

32   For a bibliography on European positivism, consult Simon, *European Positivism*, pp. 283-376. See also D.G. Charlton, *Positivist Thought in France During the Second Empire*, (Oxford: Clarendon Press, 1959); R.L. Hawkins, *Auguste Comte and the United States, 1816-1853*, (Cambridge, Mass. Harvard University Press, 1936); Leopoldo Zea, *The Latin American Mind*; C.D. Cashdollar, "European Positivism and the American Unitarians," *Church History* 45 (1976): 490-506, and "Auguste Comte and the American Reformed Theologians," *Journal of the History of Ideas*, 39 (1978): 61-79. Biographical references can be found in the above works; the following are of special interest: Carter Jefferson *Anatole France: The Politics of Skepticism*, (New Brunswick, N.J.: Rutgers University Press, 1965), pp. 160-61. For an intimate look at English positivists particularly Richard Congrave, H.E. Lewes, Frederic Harrison, Edith Simcox, see Gordon S. Haight, *George Eliot, A Biography*, (Oxford: Clarendon Press, 1968), pp. 298-302, 383, 389-90, 493-96. Cf. *George Eliot's Life as Related in her Letters and Journals*, edited and annotated by J.W. Cross, 3 vols. (New York: Harper & Brothers, 1903), 1:94, 1:200, 1:227-28 and the often quoted 2:224; 3:302. Samuel Gompers, *Seventy Years of Life and Labour*, 2 vols., (New York: Dutton & Co., 1925), 1:104.

33   Workers like Fabien Magnin, aristocrats like Eugene de Roberty, radicals like E.S. Beesly and Frederic Harrison, women like Harriet Martineau, American patricians like Horace Binney Wallace and John White Chadwick, immigrants like Henry Edger, anarchists like Michael Bakunin, Max Stirner and P. Proudhon. See Fabien Magnin, Speech on the 21st Anniversary of Comte's Death, in Comte, *Discours*, pp. 293-307. René Verrier, *Roberty: Le positivisme russe et la fondation de la sociologie*, (Paris: Felix Alcan, 1934). For Edward Spencer Beesly's political activities see R. Harrison, "Professor Beesly and the Working Class Movement," in *Essays in Labor History*, edited by A. Briggs and J. Saville, (London: Macmillan & Co., 1960), pp. 205-41. Harriet Martineau, *Autobiography*, 3 vols., with memorials by Maria Weston Chapman, (London: Smith, Elder & Co., 1877), 2:371-404. For Comte's relations with Wallace, Chadwick and Edger, see Hawkins, *Positivism 1853-61*, passim. For Comte's influence on the anarchist movement see J.J. Martin, *Men Against the State: The Expositors of Individual Anarchism in America, 1827-1908*, (Colorado Springs: Ralph Mylers Publishers, 1970), pp. 159, 161. Also E.V. Zenker, *Anarchism, A Criticism and History of the Anarchist Theory*, (London: Methuen & Co., 1898), p. 30; Zenker also notes Comte's influence on Max Stirner. S. Dolgoff indicates that *Statism and Anarchy* is Bakunin's answer to Comte's sociological ideas, in *Bakunin on Anarchy*, edited and translated with introduction and notes by S. Dolgoff, (New York: A Knopf, 1972), pp. 324-25. For Comte's influence on Proudhon, see Henri ae Luboc, *The Un-Marxian Socialists*,

R.E. Scantlebury, trans. (London: Sheed & Ward, 1948) pp. 236-41, and Aaron Noland's excellent "History and Humanity—The Proudhonian Vision," in *The Uses of History*, compiled and edited by H.V. White, with a foreword by A.H. Kelly (Detroit: Wayne State University Press, 1968), pp. 70-71 and footnote 44, pp. 94-95.

34   Attending the 1826 lectures were Alexander von Humboldt, H.M. Blainville, C. Dunoyer, and in 1829, Esquirol and Fourier. Manuel, *The Prophets of Paris*, p. 263.

35   Frederic Harrison, *On Society*, (London: Macmillan & Co., 1918), pp. viii, 368-70, 416-19. For Pierre Laffitte's lectures, see Simon, *European Positivism*, p. 76. For references and texts of positivist lectures in the United States, see David Crooley, [C.G. David], *Positivist Primer: Being a Series of Familiar Conversations on the Religion of Humanity*, (New York: D. Wesley & Co., 1871), pp. 117-37. For references to positivist lectures in Brazil see J. Cruz Costa, *A History of Ideas in Brazil*, S. Macedo, trans. (Berkeley: Univ. of California Press, 1964), pp. 112-14. For the ritual see *Positivist Prayers Used by the Society of Humanists*, (Positivist Proletariat of New York, 188?). The English lectures on positivism were hardly composed of an audience of distinguished intellectuals, as those of Comte, at least during the 1860's. Then, they were given at St. Martin's Hall, Bow Street, London. St. Martin's Hall was built in 1847 and used as a meeting and concert hall. It was rented to the public and "occupied by noisy and crowded meetings where political and social questions were agitated." After a fire on August 26, 1860, it closed, reopening in 1862, and again in 1867, now as "The Queen's Theatre." E. Walford, *Old and New London*, 7 vols., vol 3 by W. Thornbury (London: Cassell, Petter & Galpin, n.d.), 3:269-70. It was at St. Martin's Hall that the International Workingman's Association was founded on September 28, 1864. Karl Marx and Frederic Engels, *Selected Correspondence, 1846-1895*, vol. 29, The Marxist Library (Westport, Connecticut: Greenwood Press, 1942), pp. 306-07. That English positivists met at St. Martin's Hall is confirmed by the advertisement of several pamphlets in the above cited *Positivist Prayers*, among them *"Sunday Evenings for the People." Lectures at St. Martin's Hall in the 1860's*, and the very tantalizing *"Religious Persecution," being a verbatim Report of the Proceedings at Bow Street taken by Mr. Robert Baxter against the Lesees of St. Martin's Hall on the allegation that "the Sunday Evenings for the People" rendered the place "a disorderly house."*

36   Dr. Kaines compiled the London Positivist Library, and "everything is perfectly free." Harrison, *On Society*, p. 370. Also Simon, *European Positivism*, p. 77.

37   For a description of the services at the London church, at Chapel Street, directed by Congrave, see "The Church of Humanity," *Current Literature*, 28 (1900): 75-76. For a discussion of the French rituals, and a picture of the altar at the rue Payenne, see "A Romance of the Religion of Humanity," *Current Literature* 40 (1906): 54-56. For positivist influences in Russia, see James H. Billington, "The Intelligentsia and the Religion of Humanity," *American Historical Review*, 65 (1960): 807-21.

38   Until recently one could worship at the Brooklyn Church. The Maison Auguste Comte is now a shrine, in the same condition Comte left it in 1854, to which many distinguished visitors go. When we visited it in 1975, the Brazilian Ambassador to

France and Salvador Dali had recently been there. It also houses a fine research collection of documents on the history of the positivist movement. See George Sarton, "Auguste Comte, Historian of Science," *Osiris*, 10 (1952): 357; Simon, *European Positivism*, pp. 134-36.

39   For Henry Edger, see Hawkins, *Positivism (1853-61)*, p. 133ff; Martin, *Man Against the State*, p. 77. For Frey, David Hecht, *Russian Radicals Look to America, 1825-1894*, (Cambridge, Mass.: Harvard University Press, 1947), pp. 200-203.

40   Cashdollar, "European Positivism," pp. 501-02, and "Auguste Comte," pp. 61, 66. For the lack of influence on American sociology, see "A Comtean Centenary," *American Journal of Sociology* 27 (1922): 510-13. For the influence of Comte on American sociology, see L.L. and J. Bernard, *Origins of American Sociology*, (New York: Thomas Crowell, 1943), pp. 115-219.

41   Simon, *European Positivism*, pp. 63-70.

42   "The working classes are the chief sufferers from the selfish and domineering men of wealth and power. For this reason they are the likeliest to come forward in defense of public morality." Comte, *Système*, 1:138 (351). This view is standard to most positivists: "If an omnibus horse falls down in the street, do "gentlemen," or "gentlemen's sons," lend a helping hand? Rarely. But mechanics, carmen, street pavers, and even butchers, instinctively run to the rescue." Calvin Blanchard, *The Essence of Science: or the Catechism of Positive Sociology and Physical Mentality by a Student of Auguste Comte*, (New York: C. Blanchard, 1859), p. 37. See also A. Keüfer, "Le huitième congrès du parti ouvrier," *Revue occidentale*, 20 (1888): 106-115.

43   Harrison, "Professor Beesly," pp. 205-206. G.D.H. Cole, *A Short History of the British Working-Class Movement, 1789-1947*, Rev. Ed., (London: George Allen & Unwin Ltd., 1948), pp. 175, 202-204.

44   McGee, *A Crusade for Humanity*, pp. 44-48; Malcolm Quin, *Memoirs of a Positivist*, (London: George Allen & Unwin Ltd., 1924), passim.

45   Ibid., pp. 112-151.

46   Harrison, "Professor Beesly," pp. 212-214. See also E.S. Beesly, "Trade Unions," *Westminster Review* 76 (1861): 275-93, for his concessions to political economy, and Frederic Harrison, *Autobiographical Memoirs*, 2 vols., (London: Macmillan & Co., 1911), 1:250-60.

47   Crooley, *Positivist Primer*, p. 66.

48   As late as 1921, J. Schabert accuses positivists of being the cause of social unrest: "Having no conception of an accepted ultimate, spiritual and ideal object in life, they generally seek a reason for existence in some kind of social service or uplift of humanity." "The Philosophy of Social Unrest," *American Catholic Quarterly*, 46 (1921): 654. He concluded that Catholics should give public lectures in order to counteract their influence. Ibid., p. 656. For the position of women in the

movement (and the admission that they are few in number), see Elizabeth Dudley, "The New York Positivists," *Old and New*, [Boston] 7 (1873): 299.

49 There is some evidence. Among the members of the A.F.L. there were some positivists, e.g., Hugh McGregor, Secretary of the Committee on Labels and Boycott, and R.K. Foster, of the Waiters Union. Gompers, *Seventy Years*, 1:104. Both are identified with the Humanist Labor Group and the Positivist Proletaries of New York. From a photograph "Society of Humanists of New York," (Philadelphia: D.J. Gallagher, 1889), now at the Maison Auguste Comte, and shown through the courtesy of M. Paul Carneiro. Gallagher was a printer of positivist literature. The fact that he printed the 1888 program of the A.F.L. seems significant. Again, we must stress that there is little information on the American positivist apostleship from 1861 on.

50 The Brooklyn Positivist League published a bulletin, fragments of which can be seen at the New York Public Library. *Positivist League*, 1922, v. 1.

51 F. Harrison, *On Society*, p. 371; but see p. viii. Also R. Harrison, "Professor Beesly," p. 226.

52 The 1864 International brought Beesly in contact with Karl Marx. For Marx's attitude toward positivism, see Karl Marx to Frederic Engels, London, 7 July 1866; Karl Marx to Edward Spencer Beesly, London 12 June 1871, both in *Selected Correspondence*, pp. 209-10, 313-315. For Comte's influence on Marx, see George Lichtenheim, "On the Interpretation of Marx's Thought," in *Marxism*, edited by Michael Curtis, (New York: Atherton Press, 1970), pp. 21-31. Also R. Harrison, "Professor Beesly," p. 239. In France, the movement seems to have been unable to grow roots in the working classes, Simon, *European Positivism*, pp. 76-77.

53 R. Harrison, "Professor Beesly," p. 237.

54 See *"Positivism in Latin America, 1850-1900*, edited by R.L. Woodward, (Lexington, Mass.: D. Heath, 1971). For the historical background see H. Bernstein, *Modern and Contemporary Latin America*, (New York: Russell & Russell, 1965). For the philosophical background in Latin America, W.J. Kilgore, "The Development of Positivism in Latin America," *Inter-American Review of Bibliography* 19 (1969): 133-45. For positivism in Argentina and Uruguay, see O.R. Martí, "The Reaction Against Positivism in Latin America: A Study in the Philosophies of Carlos Vaz Fereirra and José Ingenieros," Ph.D. dissertation, City University of New York, 1978.

55 Bernstein, *Latin America*, pp. 365-71.

56 Ibid., p. 373. Also Cruz Costa, *Brazil*, p. 173.

57 Cruz Costa, *Brazil*, p. 179. Also, Arturo Ardao, "Assimilation and Transformation of Positivism in Latin America," in Woodward, *Positivism*, p. 14. For the constitution of Rio Grande do Sul, see *A Ditadura Republicana*, J. Lagarrigue et al. Commemorative Edition, (Porto Alegre, Rio Grande do Sul, 1957), pp. 103-26. For an account of the socio-economic background and political strength of positivists,

see R.G. Nachman, "Brazilian Positivism as a Source of Middle Sector Ideology," Ph.D. dissertation, University of California, Los Angeles, 1972.

58   Cruz Costa, *Brazil*, pp. 127-129. Cf. Harrison, "Beesly," pp. 220, 239.

59   Cruz Costa, *Brazil*, pp. 96-100. Zea, *Latin American Mind*, p. 148. For some of the sympathizers who introduced positivism in Chile, see T. Bader, "Early Positivist Thought and Ideological Conflict in Chile," *The Americas*, 26, (1970): 376-93. Also Harold E. Davis, *Latin American Thought: A Historical Introduction*, (New York: The Free Press, 1972), pp. 80-87.

60   Zea, *Latin American Mind*, pp. 149-56.

61   Ibid., pp. 156-58. See also Juan Enrique Lagarrigue, *Tacna y Arica ante el Patriotismo Chileno*, (Santiago de Chile: Imprenta Cervantes, 1907).

62   Juan Enrique Lagarrigue, *Propuesta de solución para la actual crisis política*, (Santiago de Chile: Imprenta Cervantes, 1890).

63   Valentin Letelier, "Political Science in Chile," in Woodward, *Positivism*, pp. 29-31. Also, W.R. Crawford, *A Century of Latin American Thought*, (Cambridge, Mass.: Harvard University Press, 1963), pp. 74-78 and Solomon Lipp, *Three Chilean Thinkers*, (Waterloo, Canada: Wilfrid Laurier University Press, 1975), pp. 53-55.

64   Zea, *Latin American Mind*, pp. 162-66. Davis, *Latin American Thought*, pp. 110, 126. Lipp, *Three Chilean Thinkers*, pp. 84-90. Juan Enrique Lagarrigue, *Dictamen positivista sobre el conflicto entre el Gobierno y el Congreso*, (Santiago de Chile: Imprenta Cervantes, 1890). For the historical background, see Bernstein, *Latin America*, pp. 511-15.

65   There were few, but well placed, disciples. Pedro Contreras Elizalde, who joined the Positivist Society in 1857, was President Juárez's brother-in-law. Another well-known disciple was the editor of the *Revista positiva*, Augustín Aragón—see Zea, *Positivism in Mexico*, pp. 40, 56, 140; see also Patrick Romanell, *Making of the Mexican Mind*, (University of Notre Dame Press: Notre Dame, Indiana, 1967), p. 47; and Karl M. Schmitt, "Mexican Positivists and the Church-State Question," in Woodward, *Positivism*, p. 79.

66   Zea, *Positivism in Mexico*, pp. 31-32. See also his briefer "Positivism in Mexico," in Woodward, *Positivism*, pp. 65-70. Bernstein, *Latin America*, pp. 86-87 and Davis, *Latin American Thought*, pp. 107-108.

67   It probably was Contreras Elizalde who introduced Barreda to Comte's philosophy, making Barreda attend Comte's 1849 lectures. Alfonso Noriega, *Vida y obra del doctor Gabino Barreda*, Biblioteca Mexicana 41, (México: Porrua, 1969), pp. 36-37. Also Zea *Positivism in Mexico*, p. 39; *Latin American Mind*, pp. 276-79.

68   Gabino Barreda, "Oración Civica," in *Estudios*, with a prologué by José Fuentes
      Mares, (México: D.F.: Ediciones de la Universidad Nacional Autónoma de México,
      1941), pp. xxxiii, pp. 75-76.

69   Ibid., pp. 76-86.

70   Ibid., p. 109. Romanell, *Mexican Mind*, pp. 46-47.

71   W.N. Breyman, "The 'cientificos': Critics of the Diáz Regime," in Woodward,
      Positivism, pp. 87-94.

72   This was a rather complicated plan which appeared as *Rapport de la Société
      positiviste par la Commission chargée d'examiner la nature et le plan du
      noveau Gouvernement révolutionnaire de la République Française*, (Paris,
      1848). Reprinted in *Revue Occidentale* 23 (1889): 91-120.

73   Manuel, *Prophets of Paris*, pp. 273, 286.

74   *Système*, 1:152-57 (357).

75   John Stuart Mill, *Auguste Comte and Positivism*, (Ann Arbor, Michigan: Ann
      Arbor Paperbacks, 1973), pp. 181-84. Also Manual, *Prophets of Paris*, pp. 267-71.
      Mill had been quite laudatory of Comte's work in *A System of Logic*. For Mill's
      changes from the first to the eight editions, see Simon, *European Positivism*,
      pp. 275-79.

76   John Stuart Mill, *Autobiography*, edited by Jack Stillinger, (Oxford: Oxford Uni-
      versity Press, 1969), p. 127. See also Mill, *Auguste Comte*, pp. 199-200.

77   Marx to Engels, London, 7 July, 1866, in *Selected Correspondence*, p. 210. Simon,
      European Positivism, pp. 59, 202.

78   Simon, *European Positivism*, pp. 46-49.

79   For the Congrave-Beesly rift, see McGee, *A Crusade for Humanity*, pp. 112-151.
      For the Lemus-Constant, see Cruz Costa, *Brazil*, p. 126. For Lagarrigue's attempt
      to convert Letelier, see Zea, *Latin American Mind*, p. 161.

80   Simon, *European Positivism*, pp. 60-61.

81   Cruz Costa, *Brazil*, pp. 126-32.

82   Simon, *European Positivism*, pp. 62-70.

83   Arturo Ardao, *Espiritualismo y positivismo en el Uruguay*, Colección Tierra
      Firme 49, (México, D.F.: Fondo de Cultura Económica, 1950), pp. 112-130.
      Schmitt, "Mexican Positivists," p. 81. Cruz Costa, *Brazil*, pp. 176-32.

84   Zea, *Latin American Mind*, pp. 160-61. Simon, *European Positivism*, pp. 202-07.
      But see Miguel Lemos and R. Teixeira Mendes, *O ideal republicano de Benjamin
      Constant*, (Rio de Janeiro, Tipografia do Jornal do Commercio, 1936).

85   A.J. Balfour, "The Religion of Humanity" In N. Foerster et al., *Essays for College Men*, 2nd Series, (New York: Henry Holt & Co., 1915), pp. 190-217. Originally an address to the Church Congress in Manchester, 1888, it warns that positivism is better suited to the "prosperous classes" than to the working man. See also footnote 48, above, for similar "warnings."

86   *Cours*, 6:517-9 (298-99) Cf. I. Berlin, "Historical Inevitability," in *Four Essays on Liberty*, (London: Oxford University Press, 1969) pp. 41-117, and Karl Popper, *The Poverty of Historicism*, 3d Ed., (London: Routledge & Kegan Paul, 1976).

87   Compare Auguste Comte, *Catéchisme Positiviste*, with a chronology, introduction and notes by Pierre Arnaud, (Paris: Garnier-Flamarion, 1966), with *Appel aux Conservateurs*, (Paris, 1355), translated as *Appeal to Conservatives* translated by T.C. Donkin and Richard Congrave, (London: Trübner & Co., 1889). See also, Crooley, *Positivist Primer*, and Blanchard, *The Essence of Science*.

88   For Herbert Spencer's position see his *Reasons for Dissenting From the Philosophy of H. Comte and Other Essays*, (Berkeley: The Glendessary Press, 1968), pp. 2-25.

89   Alvin F. Nelson, "Lester Ward's Conception of the Nature of Science," *Journal of the History of Ideas* 33 (1972):636. José Ortega y Gasset, "The Sunset of Revolutions," in *The Modern Theme*, J. Cleugh, translated with an introduction by José Ferrater Moa, (New York: Harper Torchbooks, 1961), pp. 102-103.

90   See for instance, *Cours*, 4:170.

91   Manuel, *Prophets of Paris*, p. 280; Acton, "Comte's Positivism," pp. 299-300.

92   Comte, "Plan des Travaux," in Lenzer, *Auguste Comte and Positivism*, pp. 42, 48.

93   Ibid, p. 31; *Cours*, 1:2.

94   Comte, "Plan des Travaux," in Lenzer, *Auguste Comte and Positivism*, pp. 26-7; *Cours*, 6:529-34 (301-2); *Discours*, p. 178 ff. Also Acton, "Comte's Positivism," pp. 302-10.

95   Herbert Spencer, for instance. For another interpretation of the moral law, see his *Social Statics*, (New York: Robert Schalkenbach Foundation, 1954), pp. 391, 395-96. For a defense of egoism, see Spencer, *Principles of Ethics* 2 vols. (New York: D. Appleton, 1903), 1:187-241.

96   Comte, "Plan des Travaux," in Lenzer, *Auguste Comte and Positivism*, p. 47; *Discours*, pp. 78, 96.

97   On this point see Mill, *System of Logic*, VI, vi, 2; VI, x, 1; VI, xii, 6.

6 Women in Utopias

1 My thanks to my colleagues in the Women's Studies Department at San Diego State University for their encouragement, support and criticism.

2 Mary Griffith, "Three Hundred Years Hence," in *Camperdown: or, News from our Neighborhood* (Philadelphia: Corey, Lea & Blanchard, 1836). See also, Mary E. Bradley Lane, *Mizora, A Prophecy* (New York: G.W. Dillingham, 1889).

3 Quoted in Vernon Louis Parrington, Jr., *American Dreams: A Study of American Utopias*, 2nd ed. (New York: Russell & Russell, 1964, p. 19.

4 Barbara Welter, "The Cult of True Womanhood: 1820-1860," *American Quarterly* (Summer, 1966): 151-174.

5 See Ann J. Lane's introduction to Charlotte Perkins Gilman, *Herland* (New York: Pantheon Books, 1979). The *Forerunner* was published monthly from 1909 to 1916. *Moving the Mountain* appeared in 1911; *Herland* in 1915, and its sequel, *With Her in Ourland*, in 1916. Note also similar themes in Edward Bellamy, *Looking Backward, 2000-1887* (Boston: Ticknor and Co., 1888), although roles for women continue traditional perspectives.

6 Gilman, *Herland*, p. 11.

7 Ibid., p. 92.

8 Ibid., p. 60.

9 Ibid., p. 68.

10 Raymond Lee Muncy, *Sex and Marriage in Utopian Communities* (Bloomington: Indiana University Press, 1973), p. 216. There is a voluminous literature exploring the implications of utopian communities for United States society. The communities mentioned here were considered major United States social experiments, either because they were tremendously successful, or had radical visions.

11 Dolores Hayden, *Seven American Utopias* (Cambridge: MIT Press, 1976).

12 Muncy, *Sex and Marriage*, pp. 219-222.

13 Ibid., p. 21.

14 William Alfred Hinds, *American Communities and Co-operative Colonies*, reprinted with additions 1975 (1878, 1902, 1908) (Philadelphia: Porcupine Press, 1975), p. 28.

15 Kathleen Edgerton Kendall and Jeanne Y. Fisher, "Frances Wright on Women's Rights: Eloquence versus Ethos," *Quarterly Journal of Speech* 60 (1974): 58-68.

16 Hinds, *American Communities*, p. 469.

17   My thanks to Judy Taylor, a former student, for her initial research on women's communities in the nineteenth century.

18   Rev. Alexander Kent, *Cooperative Communities in the United States*, Bulletin of the Department of Labor, No. 35 (Washington: U.S. Government Printing Office, 1901), pp. 563-646. See also, Hinds, *American Communities*, pp. 435-441.

19   Hayden, *Seven American Utopias*, Appendix A, pp. 360-361.

20   Muncy, *Sex and Marriage*, p. 14.

21   Judith Fryer, "American Eves in American Edens," *American Scholar* (Winter, 1974-75): 74-81.

22   V.F. Calverton, *Where Angels Dared to Tread* (New York: Bobbs-Merrill, 1941, p. 191.

23   *Communities* 7 (March-April 1974): 13.

24   *Communities* 8 (May-June 1974): 3.

25   Ibid., p. 5.

26   Ibid., p. 6.

27   Hugh Gardner, *The Children of Prosperity: Thirteen Modern American Communes* (New York: St. Martin's Press, 1978), p. 45.

28   Ibid., p. 57.

29   Gardner quotes from pp.. 24-25 of "Beads of Truth," (Los Angeles: 3HO Publications, 1973), p. 132.

30   Kathleen Kinkade, *A Walden Two Experiment: The First Five Years of Twin Oaks Community* (New York: William Morrow & Company, Inc. 1973), p. 171.

31   Eric Raimy, "How to Get the Dishes Washed," *Communities* 20 (January-February 1976):28.

32   Dianna McLeod and Rachel Bedard, "Women in Community," *Communities* 25 (March-April 1977): 8.

33   "Mayday: What Happened When All the Men Left," *Communities* 14 (May-June 1975): 22.

34   Sherry Thomas and Jeanne Tetrault, *Country Women: A Handbook for the New Farmer* (New York: Anchor Books, 1976), p. xv.

35   Joreen (Jo Freeman), "The Tyranny of Structurelessness," in *Radical Feminism*, ed. Anne Koedt, Ellen Levine and Anita Rapone (New York: Quadrangle, 1973).

36   Pamela Sargaent, *Women of Wonder* (1974), *More Women of Wonder* (1976), *New Women of Wonder* (1977), *Quest* 2 (Summer 1975); *Frontiers* 2 (Fall 1977).

37   Ursula Le Guin, *Left Hand of Darkness* (New York: Ace Books, 1976) and *The Dispossessed: An Ambiguous Utopia* (New York: Harper & Row, 1974); Sally Gearhart, *The Wanderground* (Watertown, Mass.: Persephone Press, 1978); Suzy Charnas, *Motherlines* (New York: G.P. Putnam's Sons, 1978); Dorothy Bryant, *The Kin of Ata Await You* (New York: Random House, 1976); Doris Lessing, *The Four-Gated City* (New York: Knopf, 1969) and *The Memoirs of a Survivor* (New York, Knopf, 1975) and *Shikasta* (New York: Knopf, 1979); Marian Zimmer Bradley, *The Shattered Chain* (New York: Daw Books, 1976) and *Ruins of Isis* (Virginia: The Donning Company, 1978).

38   Joanna Russ, *The Female Man* (New York: Bantam, 1975); Marge Piercy, *Woman on the Edge of Time* (New York: Knopf, 1976).

39   Shalamuth Fireston, *The Dialectic of Sex* (New York: Bantam, 1971).

40   See C. Bunche and N. Myron, *Lesbianism and the Women's Movement* (Baltimore: Diana Press, 1974).

41   Fireston, *Dialectic*, pp. 207-209.

42   Piercy, *Woman*, p. 105.

43   Russ, *Female Man*, p. 81.

44   Ibid., p. 140.

45   See, among others: Susan Brownmiller, *Against Our Will: Men, Women and Rape* (New York: Bantam, 1975); Diana E.H. Russell and Nicole Van de Ven, ed., *Crimes Against Women* (California: Les Femmes, 1976); and Mary Daly, *Gynecology* (Boston: Beacon Press, 1978).

7 Kurt Vonnegut's American Nightmares and Utopias

1   For a fuller discussion of this end-of-the-decade literary mood, see my "Writers of the Troubled Sixties," *Nation*, 17 Dec. 1973, pp. 661-65.

2   The 1973 *Playboy* interview is reprinted in *Wampeters, Foma & Granfalloons* (New York: Dell, 1974). The quotation here is on pp. 283-84.

3   Ibid., p. 261.

4   See the paperback edition of *Player Piano* (New York: Bard Books/published by Avon, 1967), p. 15. Future pages will be parenthetically noted in the text of this essay. Except for his recent novels in hardback, Vonnegut is most accessible to readers in the paperback editions I cite which have followed upon his popularity in the late sixties.

5   See the Delta Book edition of *The Sirens of Titan* (New York: Dell, 1971), p. 26. Future page numbers appear in my text.

6   See the Dell paperback edition of *Cat's Cradle* (New York, 1970), p. 24. Other pagination is in my text.

7   My text is the Dell Book paperback edition (New York, 1970). The quotation is on pp. 37-38. Further pagination appears in my text.

8   See the Dell paperback edition (New York, 1975), p. 9. Other page numbers appear in the text.

9   At the invitation of Professor Glen A. Love, I elaborated on this public-minded Vonnegut of the early '70s in a paper, "Communiity and the American Writer," for the Pacific Northwest American Studies Association in April, 1975. A summary appears in the Association *Newsletter*, No. 24 (1975), pp. 2-3.

10 The 1975 interview by Harry J. Cargas was published as "Are There Things a Novelist Shouldn't Joke About?" *Christian Century*, 24 Nov. 1976, pp. 1048-50. The quotation is on p. 1050.

11 *Slapstick* (New York: Delacorte Press/Seymour Lawrence, 1976). In the prologue, Vonnegut comments on Laurel and Hardy films of the thirties. He does not mention a later pertinent fact; their last comedy (1950), wherein they inherit a Pacific island rich in uranium, is *Utopia*.

12 *Jailbird* (New York: Delacorte Press/Seymour Lawrence, 1979), p. 14. Other pagination is in my text.

Index

Vergil, cited, 24, 25, 26

Videvdat, cited, 19

Vietnam, 137, 138, 154, 157

Violence: influence on of millenarian tradition, 70, 71; cult of, 114; in feminist utopian novels, 130, 131; in post-war II U.S., 154

Vonnegut, Kurt, 137-173; "New," 138; new communal sense, 138, 157, 161; comic spirit of, 139, 145, 150, 154; theme of self-destruction, 139; on realism in literature, 146; as social critic, 145; on American Dream, 151; humanitarian, 152; as meliorist, 157; optimism of, 158, 161; pessimism of, 158; socialism, 158; on religion, 160-161; environmentalist, 160; utopian activism of, 163; on duty of writer, 164; on free will, 170; on family, 166-68; on progress, 170

Walden Two (Skinner), 42; as literature, 29; influence on Twin Oaks Community, 125

Walden Two (community), 36-38; government in, 36; labor credits in, 37; work and order in, 36; compared to Utopia, 36; family in, 37-38; population control in, 37; structure of, 36

Walden Two Experiment, A (Kinkaide), quoted, 125

Wandergound, The (Gearhart), 129

War, as influence on *Nineteen-Eighty-Four* (Orwell), 44

War Dads of America, 159

Ward, Lester, 101, 110

Waste heat, 63

Watergate, 138

We (Zamiatin), 89, 139

Weidlé, Vladimir, quoted, 71

Whitman, Walt, 140, 155, 164

Whileaway (community in *Female Man*), 132

Will the Soviet Union Survive Until 1984, quoted, 90

Wilkinson, Jemima, 119

With Her in Ourland (Gilman), 117

Wright, Frances, 120

Wolfe, Tom, 137

Woman's Commonwealth (community), 132

Woman on the Edge of Time (Piercy), 130, 131, 132, 133, 134

Women: in utopian literature, 119-136; moral superiority of, 116, 118, 135; and education, 116; rights of, 117, 135; virtues of, 117; work of, 121; superiority of as mothers, 132; function in positive polity, 95, 98, 99; equality of, 116, 135; property rights of, 134; in utopias, 115-36

World War Two, 140, 155; effects of on American society, 155-158

Women of Wonder (Sargaent), 129

Workers, in Soviet Russia, 87

Work, women's, 121

Works and Days (Hesiod), cited, 20

Workers, industrial, exploitation of, 30

Yahweh, 14, 16

Yashts, cited, 23

Youth, and paradise, 17

Zamiatin, Eugene, 139; quoted, 89, 90

Zarathushtra (Zoroaster), 19

Zend-Avesta, cited, 23

Zenobia (*The Blithedale Romance*), 47

Ziusudra (king of Sumeria), 14

This book was set in Garamond by Central Graphics, San Diego, California, on the Harris Fototron 4000 (CCI). It was printed and bound by Thomson-Shore, Inc. of Dexter, Michigan. Interior paper is Warren's Olde Style wove, 60 lb. The book was designed by Rachael Bernier.